THE NEGLECTED NORTHAMPTON TEXTS OF JONATHAN EDWARDS

Edwards on Society and Politics

Richard A. S. Hall

Studies in American Religion
Volume 52

The Edwin Mellen Press
Lewiston/Queenston/Lampeter

Library of Congress Cataloging in Publication Data

This volume has been registered with The Library of Congress.

This is volume 52 in the continuing series
Studies in American Religion
Volume 52 ISBN 0-88946-593-2
SAR Series ISBN 0-88946-992-X

A CIP catalog record for this book
is available from the British Library.

The Edwin Mellen Press
Box 450
Lewiston, N.Y.
USA 14092

The Edwin Mellen Press
Box 67
Queenston, Ontario
CANADA L0S 1L0

The Edwin Mellen Press, Ltd.
Lampeter, Dyfed, Wales
UNITED KINGDOM SA48 7DY

Printed in the United States of America

THE NEGLECTED NORTHAMPTON TEXTS OF JONATHAN EDWARDS

Edwards on Society and Politics

TABLE OF CONTENTS

ACKNOWLEDGEMENTS

I wish to thank a veritable "community" of
helpers, advisors, and edifiers to whom I am indebted
for their indispensable contributions to this study.
To start with, there are Prof. John Serio of the Center
for Liberal Studies at Clarkson University who helped
me master the word processor used in redrafting my
dissertation as a book; Clarkson University for
granting me research money to meet the expenses
incurred by this project; the staff of Potsdam
College's Clerical and Duplicating Services; and both
Mmes. Lisa Voss and Margaret Woodall for indexing,
proofreading and making editorial suggestions.

There is Fr. Armand A. Maurer, the supervisor of
this study at the dissertation stage. He was patient,
thoughtful and unfailingly encouraging throughout.
There is Prof. Herbert W. Richardson, its director, who
has since become a friend as well as a mentor. It is
he who brought Edwards' neglected Northampton texts to
my attention and suggested that they merited study.
Herbert Richardson is a master teacher and an
incomparable illuminator of texts, a role going beyond
their mere clarification to a penetration of their
unsuspected larger import. Discussing with him
Edwards' writings--as well as other matters--typically
resulted in my having a series of edifying eureka
experiences. But his greatest pedagogical virtue is
building confidence in his students. He teaches by
encouragement, by giving you a conception of what you
could become and then urging you on your way. He has

an uncommon knack for identifying and maximizing your intellectual strengths. It can as well be said of him what was said of Emerson by one of the latter's auditors: "He makes you feel as if you were as good as he."

I owe the next greatest debt to my wife, Louise M. Seidel, who suffered through and typed the final draft of this study at the dissertation stage. She evinced faith in the project when I lacked it, and without her tireless promptings I doubt that it could have been completed.

I owe a debt that can never be remitted to my mother, Eileen M. Hall, who went well beyond her maternal duty in solicitude for her son. She has ever reminded me of the lesson in tenacity which Robert Bruce is said to have learned from a spider.

Finally, but far from least, I owe a comparable debt to Maxwell L. Hall, my father by adoption, who brought me as an adolescent to the country where I was to hear of Jonathan Edwards, and to whom I dedicate this book.

CHAPTER I
THE DISAGREEMENT OVER JONATHAN EDWARDS
AS A SOCIAL AND POLITICAL THINKER

Whether Jonathan Edwards had anything socially or politically worth saying is still at issue in Edwards scholarship. The traditional opinion is that he did not, duly noted as follows by Perry Miller, late dean of Edwards scholars: "Edwards' attitude toward society, it has been generally concluded, was detachment or downright indifference."[1] As evidence of which Miller cites the following passage of Edwards:

> We ought wholly to subordinate all our other business, and all temporal enjoyments to this affair of travelling to heaven. Journeying towards heaven, ought to be our only work and business, so that all we have and do, should be in order to that. When we have worldly enjoyments, we should be ready to part with them, whenever they are in the way of our going toward heaven.[2]

Evidence of Edwards' subordination of politics to religion is to be found in his *A Farewel-Sermon* where he declares that "the mutual concerns of a christian minister and his church and congregation, are . . . , of much greater moment than the temporal concerns of the greatest earthly monarchs, and their kingdoms or empires."[3] The opinion that Edwards was detached from or indifferent toward society, and subordinated politics to religion, is held by such as Anson Phelps Stokes, who claims that Edwards was "a theologian and a mystic, and cared little about political matters";[4] H. Richard Niebuhr, who says that "Jonathan Edwards seems scarcely to have been aware of the political problem";[5] Gerhard T. Alexis, who maintains that "except for the occasional piece, like a funeral sermon for a magistrate, Edwards writes as though almost totally preoccupied with 'things of religion,' civil matters neither constituting a real problem nor possessing vital interest";[6] and Joseph G. Haroutunian who maintains:

> For him [Edwards] religion was independent of the problems of social morality and civil government. He ignored the social principles in the Calvinistic idea of theocracy, and made Calvinistic piety a matter which concerned primarily the relation of the individual soul to God.[7]

On the other hand, the revisionist opinion is that he did have something socially or politically worth saying; this is held, among others, by Miller and his student, Alan Heimert. Paul J. Nagy sympathetically cites as follows Heimert's reassessment of the social significance of Edwards' thought:

> What Miller more or less implies of Edwards, Heimert makes explicit: that there is 'the primacy of a social vision in his thinking,' and that when sufficiently examined, such key notions as benevolence, virtue, and being-in-general lead to the conclusion that 'in substance the God of Jonathan Edwards was a supremely excellent Christian commonwealth.'[8]

A reason that Edwards' status as a social philosopher is at all in doubt is that he left us no treatise--no canonical text--on social or political philosophy. Yet Miller sees significance even in the fact that "in Edwards, social theory seems conspicuous by its absence."[9] He explains that

> in the history of ideas omissions are as significant as inclusions. When men cease, as by a tacit conspiracy, to talk about something which has long been central in their tradition, the historian must begin to ask certain questions which are the most difficult of all questions, because answers

> can be found only amid silences or at best in
> indirect revelations that require for their
> interpretation the most exacting tact.[10]

Thus, commentators who claim that Edwards did have a
social theory of sorts must infer it from texts
seemingly quite remote from social and political
concerns--a somewhat dubious procedure at best.
Complicating the issue further is that different
commentators, in support of their interpretations,
commonly seize upon different topics or passages (while
ignoring others) in Edwards' work, and neglect even to
consider, much less rebut, interpretations contrary to
theirs. Conspicuously absent from Edwards' scholarship
in general is an acknowledgement of and dialogue with
others holding opposite viewpoints. Often, scholars who
are oblivious to each other will interpret the same
topic or text in opposed ways.

Since a purpose of our study is to arbitrate this
disagreement, we need to begin, preliminary to
formulating our own position, by reviewing and imposing
some order on the welter of opinions on either side. We
shall do this by sorting out the topics recurrent in
discussions of Edwards' socio-political thought and by
considering what has been said about them. The
typically recurring topics deemed socio-politically
significant in connection with Edwards are the
following: (1) theocracy, (2) the covenant, (3)
revivalism, (4) sociology, (5) social criticism, (6)
redemption, (7) piety, and (8) consent. Let us start
with the first.

Edwards and Theocracy

Those, like Herbert W. Schneider and Alexis, who
argue against Edwards' socio-political relevance, base
their argument on his alleged abandonment of theocracy,
the principle of Puritan polity in New England. But not
all agree that Edwards abandoned theocracy.

The earliest among them is Ralph Barton Perry, who
holds that Edwards was a theocrat who sought "the
revival of flagging zeal and the reconquest of dissent"
within New England's collapsing Holy Commonwealth in
order "to restore the ascendancy of the strict faith
over the minds and institutions of New England": in
effect, "a theocratic reinvigoration." Perry's view is
that Edwards used the revivals to manipulate the people
into accepting the rule of a theocratic oligarchy on
the premise that "it is necessary that the remnant of
the faithful should lash itself into fury, and then
keep itself and the community at large at a high pitch
of crusading enthusiasm by perpetual excitation."[11] The
result is "an oligarchy in which a ruling class derives
a specious appearance of general support from an
admixture of hysteria with sullen conformity."[12] His
view, then, is based on a sociological interpretation
of the Great Awakening as a reactionary movement
leading to the consolidation of an oligarchy; this
interpretation, though, is questionable, especially in
light of Miller's and Heimert's interpretations of it
as a progressive movement leading to the establishment
of a republic. Most recently Patricia Tracy, echoing
Perry, associates Edwards' endorsement of theocracy
with his millennialism, and finds theocratic elements

in his funeral eulogy, *A Strong Rod Broken and Withered*
(hereinafter cited as *A Strong Rod*):

> Jonathan Edwards wanted to renew the
> effectiveness of the church as a centralizing
> institution, as he thought it had been when
> 'Pope Stoddard appeared to rule Northampton.
> Clearly, he would have liked to see the
> establishment of a theocracy--that desire
> grew in part from his millennialism, or
> contributed to it, and informed his strange
> description, in the funeral sermon, of
> Colonel John Stoddard as a minister as well
> as a magistrate. [13]

However, as we shall see, her claim is based on an
exceptional reading of this sermon.

On the other side, Schneider argues that Edwards
abandoned the traditional New England theocracy,
together with the socio-political philosophy it
engendered, by psychologizing those doctrines that had
formerly been the foundation of Puritan social
philosophy. Edwards thus turned religion, erstwhile an
objective and public affair, into a subjective and
private one:

> In Jonathan Edwards religion was essentially
> a kind of private experience; he succeeded in
> doing what Anne Hutchinson had in a manner
> unsuccessfully attempted. For in New
> England..., religion had been an objective
> social institution, preoccupied with public
> concerns; Edwards, however, transformed it
> into an inner discipline of the emotions. The
> gospel of the divine sovereignty, of
> election, of predestination, and of the
> Covenant of Grace, which the New England
> Puritans had constructed into a social and
> political philosophy, was now transferred to
> the inner life of the soul. . . . Edwards was
> surprisingly blind to the political
> philosophy of the Holy Commonwealth. . . .
> The theocracy was dead and Edwards apparently
> saw the practical futility of the political
> philosophy which it had generated. [14]

Miller, agreeing with Schneider that the early Puritans
had objectified religion by giving it a social and
institutional form, explains how they did it:

> The founders sought, in their ecclesiastical
> and political structure, to institutionalize
> phases of the inner life. The forms of the
> church and the procedures of the state, the
> very lay-out of the town fields, were
> arranged to accommodate the processes of the
> spirit. Theologians, Hooker and Shepard no
> less than Cotton and Norton, always come from
> their psychological analyses, through the
> stages of preparation, justification,
> exaltation, and sanctification, to a social
> program which for them was inherent in the
> stuff of divine grace. The results were such
> social institutions as the Congregational
> discipline, the restricted membership, the
> church covenant, the limited franchise, and
> the sumptuary legislation.[15]

Schneider's point is that Edwards reversed this
process.

Alexis similarly argues that Edwards discarded
theocracy: "Do we find in Jonathan Edwards an advocate
and conveyor of a theocratic ideal? The answer, it
seems to me, is no." The reason, according to Alexis,
is that "in Edwards the vital link in the theocratic
ideal is missing: the agency of the saints in
expressing God's will for the whole of culture";[16]
there "seems to be some difficulty in finding in
Edwards any proposals, however divinely originated, for
his contemporary culture."[17] Alexis bases his case for
Edwards' discarding theocracy on the latter's doctrine
of election and partial separation of church and state.
Alexis indicates that the predestinarianism of Edwards'
doctrines of election, and the millennium, is hardly a
mandate for socio-political change:

> Viewed against the background of an eternal
> ostracism of the damned, or even the coming
> of a millennial rule of the saints such as
> Edwards confidently expected, any charge to
> the elect to effect a transformation of the
> political order in their time seems to lose
> outline and specification. Altering the
> present complexion of things seems no
> essential preliminary step to the
> inauguration of that thousand-year period of
> earthly peace and joy or to that heavenly joy
> from which most of the present world must be
> forever excluded. Ours remains a day of
> Satan's kingdom . . , and when that kingdom
> is overthrown it will not be by authority of
> princes (transformed political power) or by
> the wisdom of the learned (secular knowledge)
> but by the Holy Spirit.[18]

Though Alexis does concede that Edwards allows that
"the saints now on earth may have some part in bringing
the advent of Christ's kingdom about, not by some new
strategy, not by trying to change the way of the world
outwardly, but by intensifying their task of
conversion."[19] It is curious, however, that Alexis
should argue from Edwards' doctrine of election that he
abandoned the theocratic ideal, given that this
doctrine is definitive of the preeminently theocratic
traditions of Puritanism and Calvinism. Alexis does not
explain why that doctrine should be construed as
evidence of only Edwards' abandoning theocracy.

As to Edwards' understanding of the relation
between church and state, Alexis quotes Stokes who says
that Edwards was "insisting that the Church and the
State were very different, and that the Church should
be exalted as a spiritual and not a political
institution."[20] Alexis himself says that Edwards melded
Calvin's principle of cooperation between the civil and
the ecclesiastical powers with Roger Williams'

principle of their radical separation: "Edwards neither
expects rulers to be active protectors of the church
and guarantors of religious unity nor does he insist
upon complete separation of the two realms."[21] After
all, he did expect the civil authorities to lend their
imprimature to the revivals, e.g. "Can it be pleasing
to God, that the civil authority have not so much as
entered upon any public consultation, what should be
done to advance the present revival of religion, and
great reformation that is begun in the land."[22]
Curiously, Alexis cites as evidence of Edwards' partial
separation of powers the very sermon Tracy cites as
evidence of his integration of them. Alexis there finds
Edwards extolling as political virtues "'great ability
for the management of public affairs,' a noble
disposition, resoluteness, integrity with piety, and a
complex of such happy circumstances as good family and
education, wealth, and maturity"--qualifications
secular enough, in Alexis' opinion, for even a deist
like Benjamin Franklin to qualify. As far as Edwards is
concerned, says Alexis, "piety is a quality simply to
be hoped for"[23] in the master politician. Alexis
interprets Edwards' indifference to the Puritan ideal
of the Holy Commonwealth as significant of his
indifference to civil polity generally. Alan Heimert,
incidentally, also interprets this as being politically
significant; but significant, instead, of Edwards'
commitment to a civil polity that is at the foundation
of the American Republic.

Alexander Allen considers Edwards a leading
advocate of the radical separation of church and state.
He thus understands Edwards as reverting to Augustine
on this matter by repudiating both Wycliffe's then

entrenched theory of "dominion by grace"--according to
which political authority, as much as ecclesial, comes
directly and exclusively from God--and any theories,
notably those of Calvin and the early Puritans, which
subordinated the state to the church:

> Church and state were drifting apart, and
> Edwards . . . furnished the formula for their
> withdrawal and separation. In accordance with
> his sharp and ruthless distinction between
> common and special grace, the state is
> deprived of a truly divine or supernatural
> character, while the church becomes the
> exclusive home of the spiritual.[24]

M. Darrol Bryant, arguing from Edwards'
ecclesiology, agrees with Schneider and Alexis that
Edwards rejected Puritan theocracy. According to
Bryant, Edwards, 'in rejecting the Half-way Covenant,
rejected the notion of a Holy Commonwealth where
'citizens' and 'saints' were one, where the boundaries
of the state were identical to the boundaries of the
church";[25] furthermore, he had "an eschatological
understanding of the church which entails an
abandonment of a Holy Commonwealth as an historical
possibility and the desacralization of politics."[26] *A
Strong Rod*, in Bryant's reading, shows just how little
civil polity figures in Edwards' larger theological
vision. By delineating the qualifications for
magistracy that he does, notes Bryant, Edwards is
emphasizing the purely *natural* character of the civil
order, thereby divorcing politics from redemption and
undermining theocracy.

Edwards and the Covenant

There are fundamentally two kinds of covenant
operative in Judeo-Christianity, viz. the covenant of
works and the covenant of grace. They are described by
Nagy as follows:

> The original compact with Adam was a covenant
> of works, in which God agreed to reward him
> upon the performance of certain prescribed
> duties. Having failed in this, an agreement
> called the covenant of grace was drawn up
> with Adam's descendants through Abraham.
> Salvation was guaranteed upon fulfillment of
> the only act man, in his fallen state, was
> now capable of--faith in the mediatorship of
> Christ. The covenant of grace was basic to
> New England theology.

This covenant, moreover, "took on a corporate character
because the Puritans noticed in the Old Testament that
God had made the agreement with the people as a
whole."[27] However, the corporate character of the
covenant did not preclude the individual's personal
relationship to God through the covenant: "while God
works within covenantal relationships of communities--
His people--each member of that community stands
individually before the countenance of God (coram
Deo)."[28] The covenant of grace, then, became the
principal social category in the canon of Puritan
theology. So those arguing against Edwards' relevance
as a social thinker cite his alleged abandonment of the
covenant as a theological category.

Among them is Peter Y. DeJong who maintains that,
"instead of restoring the covenant conception to its
true and legitimate place in the church on the basis of
the original confessions,... Edwards did perhaps

more than anyone else toward preparing for the complete
and final eradication of this idea from New England
religious life,"[29] thereby enervating classical Puritan
communalism. Similarly, Miller (though not arguing
against Edwards' socio-political relevance) states that
Edwards "threw over the whole covenant scheme" and
"declared God unfettered by any agreement or
obligation,"[30] the social significance of which,
according to Heimert, was preparation for a new kind of
social order, i.e. "a union of Americans, *freed from
the covenant relationships of the parochial past..*"[31]
(Italics mine.)

On the other side, however, Conrad Cherry contends
that "far from throwing over covenant theology, Edwards
was quite dependent upon it; in fact, there is every
indication that he had difficulty freeing himself from
its categories even at the points where he discerned
their shortcomings...."[32] And Carl W. Bouge agrees in his
exhaustive study of Edwards' doctrine of the covenant:
"Edwards taught the doctrine of the covenant of grace.
claiming he abandoned the covenant of grace."[33]

Edwards and Revivalism

Roland A. Delattre finds vast political
significance in Edwards' legacy. Echoing the sentiments
of Miller and Heimert, Delattre claims that Edwards,
through his apologetics for and critiques of the
revivals of the Great Awakening, decisively influenced
the course of the American Revolution:

> He displays hardly any interest in politics
> or in the institutional arrangements and
> forms essential to political life. And yet
> his interpretation of the religious life and

12

the Great Awakening, of which he was a major
spokesman, exercised such an enormous
influence upon the course of the American
Revolution that some historians now portray
the Revolution as in considerable measure a
continuation of the religious revolution of
the Awakening through political means--a
political extension of the religious
revolution set in motion by the Awakening.[34]

Delattre explains that the Great Awakening, through the
instrumentality of Edwards,

helped prepare the ground for the Revolution
by challenging established patterns of local
ecclesiastical authority and colonial
political authority even as it contributed
significantly to the development of
intercolonial communication and unity. In
addition, many who associated themselves with
Edwards tended to espouse a more radically
egalitarian, libertarian, and fraternal view
of the religious life--and thus also of the
social and political life--than did their
more socially conservative opponents, whether
orthodox, liberal, or deist.[35]

Examples of these associates of Edwards are his
student, Samuel Hopkins, who was moved by his
Edwardsean convictions to preach against slavery from
his pulpit in Newport; and Isaac Backus, the
Jeffersonian, who "deployed Edwardsean rhetoric in his
arguments for religious liberty."[36] Delattre claims
further that Edwards similarly influenced the
evangelical revival and reform movements of the
subsequent century: "the political influence of Edwards
continued to be felt among Americans through the
tradition of revivalism and the benevolence movements
of evangelical protestantism in the nineteenth century
and also the twentieth century."[37] Delattre, though,
does qualify this by pointing out that some of the
excesses of later revivalism, such as its "arrogant

cultural and political imperialism in the name of a
presumed identity between God's redemptive activity in
history and the purposes of the new Republic," mark
"the distance from Edwards' vision traveled by many who
invoke his name."[38] Alexis makes a similar demur
concerning H. Richard Niebuhr's attribution of later
social movements to the Awakening:

> H. Richard Niebuhr, among others, has
> attributed to this revival period an aroused
> social consciousness that led eventually to
> programs of "the kingdom in deed": missionary
> movements, humanitarian causes, abolitionist,
> charitable, and educational enterprises, and
> more. These long-range consequences of the
> Great Awakening were not engineered or even
> foreseen by Jonathan Edwards.[39]

Perry Miller is one of those historians, mentioned
by Delattre, depicting the American Revolution as "a
political extension of the religious revolution set in
motion by the Awakening," and construing Edwards'
championship of the revivals as helping to transform
the American socio-political order. Miller interprets
the Great Awakening of 1740 as the culmination of the
churches' more open admissions policy instituted in
their adoption of the Half-Way Covenant:

> It was the point at which the method of
> owning the covenant became most widely and
> exultingly extended, in which the momentum of
> the appeal got out of hand, and the
> ministers, led by Jonathan Edwards, were
> forced by the logic of evolution not only to
> admit all those who would come, but to excite
> and to drive as many as possible, by such
> rhetorical stimulations as 'Sinners in the
> Hands of an Angry God,' into demanding
> entrance.[40]

As such, the Great Awakening constituted "a veritable
crisis in the indigenous civilization";[41] it involved

"all the interests of the community, and the
definitions that arose out of it were profoundly
decisive and meaningful."[42] One such consequence,
according to Miller, was the radical redefinition of
both civil and ecclesial authority.

Miller specifies as follows how the Awakening
challenged "established patterns of local
ecclesiastical authority." He dubs as "political
scholasticism" the old way of New England church
polity, according to which popularly elected officials
were bound by, not the people's will, but what they
perceived as a set of absolute, abstract, and divinely
revealed mandates quite distinct from the exigencies of
the electorate. According to the new way opened up by
the revival, however, the body politic demanded that
its own, more pragmatic needs be heeded. During the
Great Awakening, New England Congregationalism ceased,
in Miller's phrase, to be "a silent democracy in the
face of a speaking aristocracy,"[43] a turn of events
that alarmed establishmentarians like Charles Chauncy
and the Harvard faculty, inveterate opponents of the
revivals (and Edwards).

Though Edwards was himself an aristocrat at heart-
-one "born to the purple, to ecclesiastical authority,"
with no interest in democracy and social revolution--
nevertheless, "he was the man who hammered it home to
the people that they *had* to speak up, or else they were
lost." In short, according to Miller, Edwards was not a
political scholastic:

> What he realized . . . was that a leader
> could no longer stand before the people
> giving them mathematically or logically
> impregnable postulates of the eternally good,
> just, and honest. . . . By 1740 the leader
> had to get down amongst them, and bring them

by actual participation into an experience
that was no longer private and privileged,
but social and communal.[44]

Miller cites as evidence of Edwards' political anti-
scholasticism the oft cited *A Strong Rod*, which Miller
reads as Edwards' political interpretation of the
revivals. Edwards is here maintaining that

the leader has the job of accommodating
himself to the realities of human and, in any
particular situation, of social, experience.
. . . He cannot trust himself to *a priori*
rules.... There are requirements imposed by
the office; . . . They are the need for
knowing the people, the knack of properly
manipulating and operating them, the wit to
estimate their welfare, and the cunning to
foresee what may become their calamity.[45]

Miller, moreover, discerns in this sermon the germ of a
utilitarian political ethic:

The more one studies Edwards, the more one
finds that much of his preaching is his
condemnation, in this language of welfare and
calamity rather than of 'morality,' of the
rising and now rampant businessmen of the
Valley. It is precisely here--that the get-
rich-quick schemes of his contemporaries were
wrong not from the point of view of the
eternal values but from that of the public
welfare.[46]

On Miller's view, then, colonial Americans,
through their communal experience of the revivals and
Edwards' interpretation of them, happened upon a
nascent utilitarianism more or less simultaneously with
Hutcheson and Hume. The Great Awakening signaled "the
end of the reign over the New England and American mind
of a European and scholastical conception of an
authority put over men for the good of men who were
incapable of recognizing their own welfare,"[47] by
emboldening the colonists "to contend that the guiding

rule of this society will be its welfare, and the most
valuable knowledge will be that which can say what
threatens calamity to the state."[48] Little wonder,
then, that the "pundits of Boston and Cambridge," such
as Edwards' arch-antagonist Chauncy, "shuddered with a
horror that was deeper than mere dislike of the antics
of the yokels,"[49] for "they sensed that the religious
screaming had implications in the realm of society."[50]

Following Miller, Heimert portrays Edwards as a
prophet of the American Revolution. He boldly propounds
the thesis that Edwards "provided pre-Revolutionary
America with a radical, even democratic, social and
political ideology," and that the evangelical Calvinism
that Edwards espoused "embodied, and inspired, a thrust
toward American nationalism."[51] Sacvan Bercovitch,
moreover, makes a similar claim concerning Edwards'
"Americanism": "Edwards drew out the protonationalistic
tendencies of the New England Way. He inherited the
concept of a new chosen people, and enlarged its
constituency from saintly New England theocrats to
newborn American saints."[52] In Heimert's view, "the
revival and the evangelical impulse" in the Great
Awakening, abetted by Edwards, "pressed to the goal of
a more beautiful social order--which meant, in the New
World, a union of Americans."[53] Heimert finds support
for his thesis in A *Strong Rod* where, in agreement with
Miller, he believes, is to be found "the sources of the
American democratic impulse."[54] One of them, according
to Heimert, is Edwards' enumeration of "qualifications
for magistracy not immediately derivable from the
Calvinist moral law." Heimert sees the political
significance of this sermon in Edwards' exalting

Stoddard, not just as a paragon of virtue, but as one
who proved it by militating against selfishness:

> Yet when Edwards remarked that Stoddard not
> only acted the part of a man of 'public
> spirit,' but set himself against all of a
> narrow, private spirit, and went on to imply
> that Stoddard was presumably among the elect,
> he had made a perhaps more formidable
> contribution to the American political
> process. . . . One opposed selfish men, in
> the final analysis, not only because they
> were sinners, but because by engaging in such
> an enterprise, one could thereby prove
> himself truly virtuous. This insight of
> Edwards, . . . would prove sufficiently
> compelling to serve as the dynamic of the
> democratic political process through the era,
> not only of Jefferson and Jackson, but among
> remnants of God's people to the close of the
> public career of William Jennings Bryan.[55]

Against Heimert, however, Bryant contends that
Edwards "forges a complex of symbols which press toward
a transcendent Kingdom rather than a worldly kingdom,"
which provides not "an ideology for American
nationalism" but rather "a commentary on and critique
of formative elements in the American tradition."[56]
Bryant indicates, for example, that Edwards, though
initially a partisan of revivalism and always
sympathetic to its cause, nevertheless became its most
trenchant critic. Bryant by no means denies the
"primacy of a social vision" in Edwards' thought, but
only Heimert's characterization of it as civil society.
That vision, according to Bryant, is not of a temporal,
political order, but of "the transcendent Kingdom of
God witnessed to on earth, not by political society,
but by the *communion of saints.*"[57] Bryant writes:

> Edwards' vision was not empty of social
> content, but it is not the content which
> Heimert finds. Heimert wants to find in

> Edwards' eschatology and ecclesiology a
> sanction for the movement towards socio-
> political change. Edwards, however, sought a
> spiritual community which would bear witness
> to the transcendent sovereign over all
> things, the Divine Governor.[58]

It is that witnessing "spiritual community," or the
church, not the state (however enlightened), that is
"the social content of Edwards' theology":[59]

> The church, for Edwards, was the community
> which witnessed to an eschatological, rather
> than historical, hope: the fulfilment of the
> divine-human drama. That hope always
> transcended every historical time and rested
> not in a human agency but in the sovereignty
> of God.[60]

Edwards as Sociologist

Miller thinks that Edwards evinces striking
sociological discernment in three sermons preached at
different times during the revivals of the 1730's and
early 1740's. They seem to Miller "to be full of acute
observations about the Northampton community, and also
to show, in the organization of the remarks, a sense of
a pattern of human relations."[61] Thus, in one of them,
when Edwards addresses the moral predicament of
colonial culture, he shows his awareness of the organic
interconnectedness of social groups. Decrying the
"prodigious prevalency of infidelity and heresy"[62] in
England, he warns that England's apostasy "has a very
threatening aspect upon" her American colonies because
they, being dependent on the mother country, "are upon
many accounts exceeding liable to be corrupted by
them."[63] In another, Edwards applies himself to the
moral condition of his own colonial town of
Northampton, lamenting the social ill of "contention

and party spirit" (which Edwards interprets as the
societal effect of God's withdrawal), returning with
renewed virulence after its brief quiescence at the
height of the Awakening. In so doing, notes Miller,
Edwards gives "an exhaustive if somewhat terrifying
picture of a rural community in eighteenth-century New
England."[64] And in the third of these sermons, on the
doctrine that "the saving mercy of God in Christ
extends to all sorts of persons," Edwards logically
adjusts his discourse to the differences in age, sex
and class within his congregation, effectually
presenting, in Miller's words, "a sociological analysis
of Northampton."[65]

This latter sermon especially, for Miller, "shows
a highly developed sense of the groups and types that
make up the community." It further suggests to him a
reason Edwards never wrote a treatise on society, as he
did on sundry theological topics: "Edwards did not need
to speculate about the nature of society, as he did
about the will or original sin, because rather than
having none, he had all too clear a conception of how
it was constituted." And we might add another reason,
that because Edwards' conception of society, unlike his
conception of original sin, the will, and virtue, was
uncontroversial, it did not call for a defense from the
press. Edwards implicitly assumes, according to Miller,
"that the social pattern is status, in which all
persons are types determined by their position in the
community, exactly as in their inward life they are
determined by their moral ability." Edwards "conceived
of grace as operating within a social setting, just as
it operated in particular persons through a
psychological mechanism." That the "social pattern is

status" is, according to Miller, "a major premise, in all his thinking."[66]

However, Alexis thinks that Miller overstates the case for Edwards' being a nascent sociologist on the basis of these three sermons, because they "fail most remarkably to demonstrate anything but the most obvious divisions of the congregation. . . . Social awareness on this level is rudimentary and must have been employed chiefly and perhaps only for rhetorical effectiveness."[67]

Another commentator, Karl Dieterich Pfisterer, believes that Edwards' sociological acumen is evinced in his revival writings, which painstakingly document and describe the religious experiences of "multitudes of all kinds of capacities, natural tempers, education, customs and manners of life"[68] represented by his local society: "Edwards did justice to this variety in the style of *A Faithful Narrative* by giving as complete a description of the variety of these responses as possible. He took every kind in society seriously."[69] In Pfisterer's view, "the rise of the revival from a local to a regional--and eventually to a provincial and national--phenomenon seemed to have brought him as many insights and questions in looking at the world as if he had dealt with other than European cultures as it happened in the European Enlightenment."[70]

Edwards as Social Critic

Heimert pays homage to Edwards' percipience as a social critic in his seeing the incipient mercantilism of his day as a moral problem:

> However, Edwards' analysis of his society
> went well beyond the standard rubrics of
> vices. In his diagnosis too he moved ahead of
> many of his contemporaries by discovering at
> the heart of New England's illness the
> commercial frenzy of the period. To this
> Edwards attributed men's 'dishonesty' in
> their dealings with one another. . . . Where
> Edwards went further was in tracing to
> 'covetousness' the 'envy' and the
> 'backbitings' that were the bane of nearly
> every New England town, and also the land and
> currency disputes that divided many a
> community against itself.[71]

According to Heimert, Edwards' vision of the Christian
utopia of the millennium served as the standard against
which to judge the shortcomings of his own society:

> Still, Edwards' image of the good society
> stood in marked judgment on the erratic and
> often ruthless individualism, the divisions
> and contentions, of colonial American
> society. When Edwards informed his
> Northampton congregation that the saints
> would one day 'all be one society,' or that
> they would be 'united together without any
> schism,' he was implicitly remarking on all
> the local animosities which the Awakening but
> temporarily numbed.[72]

Heimert goes on to assert that Edwards' "good society"
was a united *American* society which would be the
historical realization of millennial society: "Slowly,
but nonetheless surely, the vision of the *Work of
Redemption* was transformed into an ideal of continental
union."[73]

Following Heimert's lead, Robert B. Westbrook
similarly regards Edwards as a social critic and
visionary. Westbrook attributes the dearth of social
commentary by Edwards, and thus his apparent
indifference to contemporary society, to his fixation
on the Christian ideal of society in the millennium.

Edwards' sociology is normative rather than
descriptive:

> for Jonathan Edwards had, if not a
> substantial social theory, an imposing social
> vision. The fact that his comments on the
> society of New England were few and far
> between indicates not a lack of concern with
> society but a lack of concern with imperfect
> society. Edwards' social thought was
> selfconsciously normative.[74]

Like Heimert and Westbrook, Bryant claims that
Edwards conceives the Kingdom of God, as embodied in
the eschatological societies of the millennium and of
heaven, as "the constant horizon of criticism of the
public and private orders." Though unlike Heimert,
Bryant maintains that Edwards conceives of that horizon
as extending over *any* public order, even the civil
polity of the American Republic. For the "quest for the
Kingdom of God," says Bryant, "neither undergirds the
movement towards political society, nor sanctifies its
aspirations."[75] In Bryant's view, Edwards provides a
"theological critique of culture," and not, as Heimert
contends, "an ideological apology for the American
Republic."[76] According to Bryant, the
"otherworldliness" of Edwards' speculations on the
millennium and heaven is

> the basis of a critique of the quest for
> power, particularly, the tendency of civil
> society to confuse its aspirations with the
> intentions of the Divine Sovereign. For
> Edwards, God is the agent and goal of the
> Kingdom of God and, vis-a-vis that Kingdom,
> all other kingdoms stand judged, not
> legitimized.[77]

More particularly, Edwards seems to have believed that
"through the testament of the church," the temporal
witness of the promised Kingdom, "civil society would

be simultaneously reminded of its tendencies to idolize its own undertaking and, freed from bondage to its own idols, allow the realm of experience to come into its own as the legitimate guide and teacher of civil society."[78]

Paul K. Conkin goes further, asserting that even Edwards' metaphysics was antithetical to the social and economic individualism of his day: "His organic metaphysics, his unending interest in the corporate whole, was diametrically opposed to the rampant individualism, in politics and economics, that was developing in his lifetime."[79]

Edwards' Social Conception of Redemption

"The theme (both implicit and explicit) of all Edwards' thinking," according to Nagy, "is the theological message that redemption is social, and that society is the instrument as well as the end of salvation."[80] This is logical if, as Cherry says, Edwards used the covenant of grace as a theological category from which he could not extricate himself. The corporateness of the covenant implies the redemption of the covenanting group:

> The covenant thereby came to be an instrument for forging together a community of visible saints whose redemption was effected through the gathered church. Eventually the covenant was extended to include sinners as well, so that it now became the instrument for the broadened task of forging a political community. The purpose of such a community was not merely the realization of political and civil goals but the achievement of the spiritual salvation of the corporate whole. Edwards took this extension into full consideration in his account of redemption.[81]

We must demur, though, at the last statement in
this passage. The extension of the covenant "to include
sinners" that Nagy speaks of refers to the Half-Way
Covenant, the more lax policy on church admissions
instituted by Solomon Stoddard. However, as will be
plain enough from our forthcoming discussion in the
fifth chapter, Edwards rescinded the Half-Way Covenant
of his grandfather, thereby deliberately excluding
visible sinners from the "community of visible saints."
Thus, Edwards did not take "this extension into full
consideration," other than to reject it; consequently,
consonant with Bryant's interpretation of Edwards'
ecclesiology, Edwards emphatically did not regard the
covenant of grace as "the instrument for the broadened
task of forging a political community."

According to Nagy, the social character of
Edwards' conception of redemption is most apparent in
his last, posthumously published *Two Dissertations: I.
Concerning the End for Which God Created the World. II.
The Nature of True Virtue* (hereinafter cited as
Concerning the End and *True Virtue* respectively). It is
also apparent, according to Heimert, in Edwards' *A
History of the Work of Redemption. Containing the
Outline of a Body of Divinity, in a Method Entirely New*
(hereinafter cited as *Work of Redemption*), a theme of
which is, in Heimert's words, "that the redeeming work
of the Holy Spirit concerned not individuals merely but
society"[82]--oddly enough, though, Heimert agrees with
Miller that Edwards abandoned the covenant idea.
Edwards thereby helped foster, in Heimert's view, that
optimism toward the future which would become a
hallmark of social thought in America during the next
century:

From the delivery of these sermons [the
original format of the *Work of Redemption*]
may be dated the historical optimism that was
to be the Awakening's most distinctive
legacy. The thought of American Christianity
was turning away from past glories and toward
the future--and, even more impressively, from
the individual to the greater community.[83]

Edwards' Conception of Piety

Sidney Mead, Alexis and DeJong, among others, all
portray Edwards as a quietist, for whom piety is quite
divorced from society or politics. John E. Smith and
Heimert, though, dissent from this traditional view,
seeing instead enormous social implications in Edwards'
understanding of piety.

For Mead, Edwards' theology "in principle pushed
the doctrine of justification by faith alone to an
absolute separation of salvation from one's life in the
'natural world.'" He thinks Edwards makes this
"perfectly clear" in the following passage from *A
Treatise concerning Religious Affections* (hereinafter
cited as *Religious Affections*), where Edwards affirms
the absolutely supernatural origins and character of
authentic piety or grace:

> It is evident, that these gracious influences
> which the saints are subjects of, and the
> effects of God's Spirit which they
> experience, are entirely above nature,
> altogether of a different kind from any thing
> that men find within themselves by nature, or
> only in the exercises of natural principles;
> and are things which no improvement of those
> qualifications, or principles that are
> natural . . . will ever bring men to; because
> they not only differ from what is natural,
> and from every thing that natural men
> experience, in degree and circumstances, but
> also in kind; . . . And this is what I mean,
> by supernatural, when I say that gracious

affections are from those influences that are
supernatural.[84]

Mead interprets this excerpt as Edwards' theological
mandate for quietism:

> This theology obviously legitimated the
> privatization of religion, and by completely
> divorcing salvation from all "qualifications,
> or principles that are natural," gave the
> convert the possibility of disengagement with
> honor from active participation in the
> political and social life of his society.[85]

Mead enlists the authority of Alexis in support of this
position, who interprets Edwards' stand on
qualifications for full Communion as evidence of his
sundering of personal piety from social activism:

> Edwards' attempt to return to the earlier
> requirement of a public profession of faith
> as a requirement for church membership, far
> from being a move to reinvigorate the rule of
> the saints in public affairs, can be
> interpreted as evidence of his preoccupation
> with the meaningfulness of the spiritual
> realm.[86]

DeJong, moreover, considers that Edwards severed piety
from the social order by overly emphasizing the
relationship of the person to God at the expense of his
relationship to others:

> Edwards at times seemed to divorce religion
> from daily life. . . . Moreover, in his
> various treatises he conceived of religion
> too much in terms of the individual's
> relation to God. In his concern for defining
> the Biblical theory of Christian experience,
> he lost sight of the relationships in which
> the individual stood. Thus religion to him
> came to mean largely the fellowship of the
> soul with God to the exclusion of the rest of
> life.[87]

This is a criticism of Edwards, writes DeJong, that
"seems to be quite general."[88] He thus cites Earnest S.

Bates' opinion that Edwards' conception of religion, being individualistic and subjective in character, is wholly divorced from secular and social concerns, thereby deviating from traditional Calvinism:

> He [Edwards] drew Calvinism up out of the murk of this world into an atmosphere high above considerations of politics and earthly advantage, while in rising into this realm of universal principles he unconsciously deprived Calvinism of that urge to righteous power which was its actual basis. He moved back and forth between the two poles of the individual and the universal, and in neglecting the intermediate stages of social activity he facilitated the withdrawal of religion into the limited field of individual conduct to concern itself above all with the subjective consciousness.[89]

On the other hand, John E. Smith avers that, in Edwards' conception, piety is more than a state of mind or a fellowship with God; it necessarily expresses itself objectively and externally by changing the social order:

> Religion, much as it concerns the heart in Edwards' view, is not to be confined to an internal feeling or state of mind. Religion, though it is ultimately an intangible relationship between the individual and God, must express itself objectively and thus assume public shape. In order for this to take place, changes must be wrought in the surrounding universe. If it is true that a man must not only be in right relations with God, but also show this through an outward and visible form of life, then the entire social order must ultimately be affected.[90]

Whereas Heimert, ignoring the equally important contemplative side to Edwards' conception of piety, asserts that, for Edwards, piety is essentially a form of social activism. This is what Heimert says about Edwards' chief text on the nature of authentic piety:

"The *Religious Affections* . . . was an exhortation to Edwards' readers to be up and doing, and to the ministers of the colonies to urge their people on their way."[91]

Edwards' Concept of *Consent*

Nagy and Delattre both amplify the socio-political resonances of Edwards' central, axiological category of *consent to being*. Consent, for Edwards, is definitive of the structure of reality (hence an ontological category), beauty (hence an aesthetic category), and virtue (hence a moral category).

Nagy construes Edwards' idea of consent as "the leading metaphor in the light of which all of Edwards' thought is to be understood."[92] He understands the social significance of Edwards' category of consent as conciliation among opposites: "at the imaginative center" of Edwards' vision is an Emersonian "each and all" doctrine "in which there is a dynamic and ever-continuing reconciliation of opposites, of the part with the whole, the singular with the universal, of the individual with society, and that this process of reconciliation is governed by a subtle dialectic which . . . Edwards sought to unravel."[93] Consent, then, is "a standpoint for achieving reconciliation when the reconcilers are isolated," and thus "it is not too difficult to discern a reconciliation of opposites permeating the metaphysical thinking of Edwards."[94]

Delattre construes beauty, the aesthetic manifestation of consent, as "the decisive concept of his [Edwards'] onotological philosophy of being, of his theology, and of his interpretation of the structure and dynamics of the moral and spiritual life." In sum, beauty is Edwards' "primary model of order."[95] Delattre understands the political significance of Edwards' category of consent as intrinsic to its meaning: Edwards' "definition of beauty and sensibility in terms of consent and dissent suggests a systematic relevance of his aesthetically articulated ontology and ethics to the political life of selves and communities--for consent is a political as well as an aesthetic concept."[96] Delattre, in fact, defines "politics" in terms of consent: "Politics is the activity through which men exercise together, by mutual or common consent, their governance over that portion of reality marked by human presence."[97]

Miller, Conkin and Cherry all see social consequences in Edwards' theory of virtue, the moral manifestation of consent. According to Miller, "Jonathan Edwards expounded how disinterested benevolence would enhance the good of the community, . . . the benevolent God who led the Americans to independence was interpreted as a Being who shepherded this whole community into a heritage of social prosperity."[98] And according to Conkin:

> Concerned with such "basic" ideas as true virtue, Edwards never gave any extended theoretical attention to social, political, or economic problems. He believed that his definition of virtue would place in proper perspective all the mundane matters of earthly life and certainly never hesitated to make a practical application in his weekly sermons, condemning village sins in too vivid detail for his own popularity. Implicit in his ethical theory, as well as in earlier Puritanism, was a strong public consciousness. In fact, Edwards made the relationship between private and public good

> an analogue of the relation between natural
> and true virtue.[99]

And Cherry discerns in Edwards' agapistic ethics the
seed of political activism: "certainly the burden of
his argument would have been to participate more in the
political process and to be more influential and not to
hold back."[100] And in company with others, Cherry sees
Edwards' ethics as having helped give rise to
abolitionism and other reform movements of the
nineteenth century.

We now might make the following critical
observations on this spate of scholarly opinions about
Edwards' socio-political significance, which partially
explains the difficulty in determining the fact, nature
and extent of Edwards' social and political philosophy:
(a) Different commentators latch onto different topics
in attempting to prove the same point. Thus, some
(Schneider and Alexis) focus on Edwards' abandonment of
the theocratic ideal, whereas others (Mead and DeJong)
focus instead on his presumably quietistic theory of
piety as evidence of what they deem Edwards' socio-
political irrelevance. (b) Alternatively, they seize
upon the same topic in attempting to prove opposite
points. Thus, commentators who focus on Edwards' theory
of piety find evidence of either his social
indifference (DeJong, Alexis, and Mead) or his social
relevance (Smith and Heimert). (c) In other cases, they
read the same text in contrary ways. In *A Strong Rod*,
for example, Tracy finds a sanction for theocracy,
while most (Alexis, Heimert, and Bryant) find no such
thing. (d) Or, different commentators see conflicting
implications in the same interpretation of a given
text. Though both interpret the funeral eulogy for

Stoddard as sanctioning the separation of church and
state, Alexis understands it as implying Edwards'
rejection of socio-political philosophy generally,
whereas Heimert understands it as implying his
rejection of only the socio-political philosophy
associated with the Holy Commonwealth. (e) On the other
hand, commentators might read a text selectively,
excerpting and interpreting passages out of context,
and in this way reaching opposed conclusions; hence,
Mead reads *Religious Affections* as a statement of
quietism, whereas Heimert reads it as a plea for
activism. (f) Edwards scholars sometimes seem oblivious
to one another, not acknowledging, much less rebutting,
interpretations contrary to theirs. They thereby fail
to establish that ongoing and cumulative tradition of
argumentation that is a hallmark of scholarship. Thus,
Mead neglects even to acknowledge alternative
interpretations of Edwards' conception of piety (Smith
and Heimert), though published well before his own. (g)
Still, other commentators fail to acknowledge those
sharing their opinions, and thus not establishing a
continuity of scholarly reflection on the subject. For
example, Tracy, though writing years after Perry, does
not mention that he shared her view of Edwards as a
theocrat.

     To summarize: Arguments over the socio-political
relevance of Edwards' thought typically cluster about
Edwards vis-a-vis the topics of theocracy, the
covenant, revivalism, sociology, social criticism,
redemption, piety, and *consent*. Those arguing against
its socio-political relevance cite one or another of
the following: Edwards' alleged indifference to
theocracy--the political philosophy regnant in his

culture--and to the covenant--the basis of Puritan
communalism--and his presumably quietist theory of
piety. However, Edwards' indifference to theocracy
could be construed alternatively, as Heimert suggests,
as his indifference to the polity of the Holy
Commonwealth only, not to political theory generally.
Whereas Heimert construes Edwards' presumed rejection
of the covenant scheme as politically relevant inasmuch
as it was a preamble to a new kind of political order,
i.e. "a union of Americans freed from the covenant
relationships of the parochial past." Others, though,
claim that Edwards was committed to the theocratic
ideal and, presumably, the political philosophy it
entailed. On the other side, those arguing for the
socio-political relevance of Edwards' thought typically
cite one or another of the following topics (all of
which, curiously, are ignored by those arguing against
it): the social implications of his theory of piety,
his social conception of redemption, the socio-
political resonances of his category of consent, his
sociological insight and social criticism, and his
involvement with the socially and politically
significant revivals of the Great Awakening.

This disagreement over Edwards' status as a social
and political thinker--together with its attendant
issues such as his positions on theocracy and the
covenant--can be settled, however, through a careful
reading of four texts of his dating from the last three
years of his pastorate in Northampton. Their
abbreviated titles,[101] with dates of publication, are
as follows: *Humble Attempt* (1747), *Life of Brainerd*
(1749), *Humble Inquiry* (1749),[102] and *A Farewel-Sermon*
(1751). Traditionally, though, these texts have been

unjustifiably neglected or even disparaged by Edwards scholars as indicated by their typically scanty, perfunctory, or erroneous remarks on them. Had these texts been taken seriously by more scholars, the aforementioned disagreement might have been avoided. It is to a consideration of these texts, then, that we shall now turn.

CHAPTER I

NOTES

[1]Perry Miller, "Jonathan Edwards' Sociology of the Great Awakening," *The New England Quarterly*, XXI, NO. 1 (1948), pp. 51-52.

[2]Jonathan Edwards, *The True Christian's Life, a Journey towards Heaven*, in *The Works of President Edwards*, IV (8th ed.; New York, 1851), pp. 576-577, quoted ibid., p. 52.

[3]Jonathan Edwards, A Farewel Sermon , in *The Works of President Edwards*, ed. by E. Hickman, I (London, 1834), cciii.

[4]Anson Phelps Stokes, *Church and State in the United States*, I (New York, 1950) p. 241.

[5]H. Richard Niebuhr, *The Kingdom of God in America* (Chicago, 1937), p. 123.

[6]Gerhard T. Alexis, "Jonathan Edwards and the Theocratic Ideal," *Church History*, XXXV, NO. 1 (1966), p. 329.

[7]Joseph G. Haroutunian, *Piety Versus Moralism: The Passing of the New England Theology* (New York, 1932), p. xxi.

[8]Paul J. Nagy, "The Beloved Community of Jonathan Edwards," *Transactions of the Charles S. Peirce Society*, VII, NO. 2 (1971), p. 94.

[9]Miller, "Edwards' Sociology," p. 51.

[10]Ibid., p. 53.

[11]Ralph Barton Perry, *Puritanism and Democracy* (New York, 1944), p. 343.

[12]Ibid., p. 344.

[13]Patricia J. Tracy, *Jonathan Edwards, Pastor: Religion and Society in Eighteenth-Century Northampton*, American Century Series (New York, 1980), p. 190.

[14]Herbert Wallace Schneider, *The Puritan Mind* (New York, 1930), pp. 106-107.

[15]Miller, "Edwards' Sociology," p. 51.

[16]Alexis, "Theocratic Ideal," p. 343.

[17]Ibid., p. 334.

[18]Ibid.,pp. 340-341.

[19]Ibid., p. 341.

[20]Stokes, *Church and State*, I, 241, quoted ibid., p. 330.

[21]Alexis, "Theocratic Ideal," p. 331.

[22]Jonathan Edwards, *Some Thoughts concerning the Revival, in The Works of President Edwards*, ed. by Sereno E. Dwight, IV (New York, 1829-30),p. 146, quoted ibid., p. 331.

[23]Alexis, "Theocratic Ideal," p. 330.

[24]Alexander Viets Griswold Allen, *Jonathan Edwards*, American Religious Leaders (Boston, 1896), p. 255.

[25]Marcus Darrol Bryant, "History and Eschatology in Jonathan Edwards: A Critique of the Heimert Thesis" (unpublished Ph.D. dissertation, Institute of Christian Thought, University of St. Michael's College, 1976), p. 293.

[26]Ibid., p. 256.

[27]Nagy, "Beloved Community," p. 97.

[28]Carl W. Bogue, *Jonathan Edwards and the Covenant of Grace* (Cherry Hill, New Jersey, 1975), p. 173.

[29]Peter Y. DeJong, *The Covenant Idea in New England Theology, 1620-1847* (Grand Rapids, Michigan, 1945), p. 151.

[30]Perry Miller, *Errand into the Wilderness* (Cambridge, 1956), p. 98.

36

[31]Alan Heimert, *Religion and the American Mind: From the Great Awakening to the Revolution* (Cambridge, Mass., 1966), p. 95.

[32]Charles Conrad Cherry, *The Theology of Jonathan Edwards: A Reappraisal* (Garden City, New York, 1966), p. 123.

[33]Bogue, *Jonathan Edwards*, p. 87.

[34]Roland Andre Delattre, "Beauty and Politics: A Problematic Legacy of Jonathan Edwards," in *American Philosophy from Edwards to Quine*, ed. by Robert W. Shahan and Kenneth R. Merrill (Norman, Oklahoma, 1977), p. 20.

[35]Ibid., pp. 21-22.

[36]Ibid., p. 22.

[37]Ibid., pp. 20-21.

[38]Ibid., p. 22.

[39]Alexis, "Theocratic Ideal," p. 333.

[40]Perry Miller, "Jonathan Edwards and the Great Awakening," in *The Great Awakening: Event and Exegesis*, ed. by Darrett Bruce Rutman (Huntington, New York, 1977), p. 147.

[41]Ibid., p. 143.

[42]Ibid., p. 141.

[43]Ibid., p. 150.

[44]Ibid., p. 151.

[45]Ibid., pp. 153-154.

[46]Ibid., p. 154.

[47]Ibid., p. 155.

[48]Ibid., p. 156.

[49]Ibid., p. 155.

[50]Ibid., pp. 155-156.

[51]Heimert, *American Mind*, p. viii.

[52]Sacvan Bercovitch, *The American Jeremiad* (Madison, Wisconsin, 1978), p. 105.

[53]Heimert, *American Mind*, p. 95.

[54]Ibid., p. 302.

[55]Ibid., p. 303.

[56]Bryant, "History and Eschatology," quoted in Nancy Manspeaker, *Jonathan Edwards: Bibliographical Synopses* (New York, 1981), p. 24.

[57]Bryant, "History and Eschatology," p. 254.

[58]Ibid., pp. 308-309.

[59]Ibid., p. 270.

[60]Ibid., p. 293.

[61]Miller, "Edwards' Sociology," p. 53.

[62]Ibid., p. 54.

[63]Ibid., p. 55.

[64]Ibid., p. 57.

[65]Ibid., p. 62.

[66]Ibid., p. 62.

[67]Alexis, "Theocratic Ideal," p. 332.

[68]Jonathan Edwards, *Some Thoughts concerning the Revival*, in *The Works of Jonathan Edwards*, ed. by C. C. Goen, IV (New Haven, 1972), 317, quoted in Karl Dietrich Pfisterer, *The Prism of Scripture: Studies on History and Historicity in the Work of Jonathan Edwards*, Anglo-American Forum, Vol. I (Bern, 1975), p. 189.

[69]Pfisterer, *Prism of Scripture*, p. 189.

[70]Ibid., p. 192.

[71]Heimert, *American Mind*, p. 33.

[72]Ibid., p. 99.

[73]Ibid., p. 100.

[74]Robert B. Westbrook, "Social Criticism and the Heavenly City of Jonathan Edwards," *Soundings*, LIX, No. 4 (1976),p. 396.

[75]Bryant, "History and Eschatology," p. 267.

[76]Ibid., p. 250.

[77]Ibid., pp. 309-310.

[78]Ibid., p. 309.

[79]Paul K. Conkin, "Jonathan Edwards: Theology," in his *Puritans and Pragmatists: Eight Eminent American Thinkers* (New York, 1968), p. 71.

[80]Nagy, "Beloved Community," p. 97.

[81]Ibid., pp. 97-98.

[82]Heimert, *American Mind*, p. 34.

[83]Alan Heimert and Perry Miller, eds., *The Great Awakening: Documents Illustrating the Crisis and Its Consequences*, The American Series, NO. 34 (Indianapolis, 1967), p. xxiii.

[84]Jonathan Edwards, *Religious Affections*, in *The Works of President Edwards in Eight Volumes*, IV (Worcester, 1808), 133, quoted in Sidney E. Mead, *The Old Religion in the Brave New World: Reflections on the Relation between Christendom and the Republic*, The Jefferson Memorial Lectures (Berkeley, 1977), p. 52.

[85]Mead, *Old Religion*, p. 53.

[86]Alexis, "Theocratic Ideal," p. 343.

[87]DeJong, *Covenant Idea*, p. 198.

[88]Ibid., p. 239.

[89]Ernest Sutherland Bates, *American Faith: Its Religious, Political, and Economic Foundations* (New York, 1940), p. 208, quoted Ibid., p. 239.

[90]John E. Smith, "Jonathan Edwards: Piety and Practice in the American Character," *The Journal of Religion*, LIV, No. 2 (1974), p. 176.

[91]Heimert, *American Mind*, p. 132.

[92]Nagy, "Beloved Community," p. 95.

[93]Ibid., pp. 94-95.

[94]Ibid., p. 95.

[95]Roland André Delattre, "Beauty and Sensibility in the Thought of Jonathan Edwards: An Essay in Aesthetics and Ethics" (Ph.D. dissertation, Yale University, 1966), quoted in Manspeaker, *Bibliographical Synopses*, p. 52.

[96]Roland André Delattre, "Beauty and Politics: Toward a Theological Anthropology," *Union Seminary Quarterly Review*, XXV, No. 4 (1970), p. 402.

[97]Ibid., p. 414.

[98]Perry Miller, *Nature's Nation* (Cambridge, Mass., 1967), p. 285.

[99]Conkin, "Jonathan Edwards," p. 71.

[100]Charles Angoff, ed., *Jonathan Edwards: His Life and Influence*, The Leverton Lecture Series (Rutherford, New Jersey, 1975), p. 57.

[101]Their more extended titles are as follows:

An Humble Attempt to Promote Explicit Agreement and Visible Union of God's People in Extraordinary Prayer for the Revival of Religion and the Advancement of Christ's Kingdom on Earth, pursuant to Scripture-Promises and Prophecies concerning the Last Time An Account of the Life of the Late Reverend Mr. David Brainerd, Minister of the Gospel . . . .

An Humble Inquiry into the Rules of the Word of God concerning the Qualifications Requisite to a Compleat Standing and Full Communion in the Visible Christian Church.

A Farewel-Sermon Preached at the First Precinct in Northampton, after the People's Publick Rejection of Their Minister . . . .

[102]A companion piece to *Humble Inquiry* is *Misrepresentations Corrected, and Truth Vindicated, in a Reply to the Rev. Mr. Solomon Williams's Book* . . . . (1752). In this work, as its title suggests, Edwards sought to refute Williams' objections to his stand on qualifications for Communion. *Misrepresentations Corrected* is of interest to us insofar as it clarifies points made in *Humble Inquiry*, our reason for occasionally citing it.

CHAPTER II

THE NEGLECTED NORTHAMPTON TEXTS
AND EDWARDS' SOCIO-POLITICAL THOUGHT

In the first section of this chapter, we attempt
an explanation of the traditional neglect and
disparagement of the four Northampton texts, discuss
the consequences of this state of affairs for Edwards
scholarship, and consider the benefits of their
reclamation; in the second, we put these texts in the
context of Edwards' life and thought; and, in the third
section, we clarify what it is that we are looking for
in the texts, describe how we shall find it, and set
out the limits and benefits of our study.

1

Though an explanation of scholars' neglect of the
texts in question can be only conjectural, two
plausible reasons do suggest themselves; namely, their
character and content, and the traditionally narrow
focus of most Edwards scholarship. First, the character
and content of these texts would explain their being
slighted and relegated to the periphery of the Edwards
corpus. They are occasional pieces about apparently
dated and parochial matters of merely historical
interest like public prayer for the millennium and
requirements for church membership. As such, they
seemingly lack any substantive philosophical or
theological interest. Second, Edwards scholars usually
have focused narrowly on his early philosophical works,
notably the "Natural Philosophy"[1] and "The Mind," at

the expense of the others, which would account for the
neglect of the Northampton texts. And they have done so
for no better reasons than bias, and their peculiar
view--mistaken it turns out--that these philosophical
writings epitomize Edwards' thought.

Consider first their biases. Scholars have been
biased toward "Natural Philosophy" and "The Mind," two
private notebooks of Edwards never intended for
publication, but containing his boldest philosophical
speculations which were occasioned by his study of
Newton and Locke. Now the reason for their bias is not
hard to find. The pioneers of modern Edwards
scholarship at the turn of the century, who were
largely responsible for the recovery of Edwards and set
the tone for all subsequent scholarship on him, were
preponderately philosophers[2] and thus, understandably,
more interested in investigating his more philosophical
works. Two things about these notebooks particularly
struck these commentators. One was their philosophical
precocity. They were traditionally thought to have been
written during Edwards' adolescence, and so seemed to
reveal "an intellectual prodigy which has no
parallel."[3] A second thing was that these books
revealed an apparently more attractive portrait of
Edwards as an ingenious philosopher, quite at odds with
the portrait of him as a dogmatic theologian and fire-
breathing evangelist popularly known from the rest of
his work. It was this second thing that was the
principal reason for the enormous scholarly vogue that
has been enjoyed by these texts ever since their
discovery by philosophers in the last century. They
provided a much needed antidote to the popular
caricature of Edwards as "the virtual embodiment of the

sulphurous side of Calvinism"[4] without which he "might
have lapsed into an obscurity which he does not
deserve, simply because his published titles bear to
the modern mind the *odium theologicum*."[5] These works,
then, virtually redeemed Edwards' reputation, at least
among the philosophers. And this brings us to the
second bias of the early Edwards scholars--their bias
against theology, especially Calvinist.

Their antitheological bias is evident in the too
common regret among these scholars that Edwards
apparently gave up philosophy and science for theology.
Thus, Moses Coit Tyler regretted that Edwards, rather
than fulfilling the enormous promise of his
philosophical notebooks, became an apologist for "that
ganglion of heroic, acute, appalling dogmas commonly
named after John Calvin. To the defense of that
theology, in all its rigors, in all its horrors,
Jonathan Edwards brought his unsurpassed abilities as a
dialectician."[6] Both Tyler and Charles van Doren
believed that Edwards' scientific genius was
"sacrificed to the religious passion."[7] According to A.
V. G. Allen, F. J. E. Woodbridge, and Vernon L.
Parrington, Edwards was essentially a speculative
philosopher who was distracted by theology:
"Psychologists have yet to discover . . . what it was
that turned Jonathan Edwards from his critical
philosophy to the dark theology that he adopted."[8]
Another characterized Edwards' intellectual biography
as "the perversion, and ultimately the extinction of
one of the most remarkable intelligences ever to have
appeared in the New World."[9] Even today persists the
myth of Edwards as a tragic figure, "an American
Pascal."[10]   Thus we have the typical opinions that

44

Edwards, after writing his early notebooks, became a
"servant of sterile doctrine,"[11] that he had "a greatly
gifted mind who squandered his talents on theological
trifles,"[12] and that this was "the tragedy of Edwards's
intellectual life: the theologian triumphed over the
philosopher, circumscribing his powers to ignoble
ends."[13]

Consider now the entrenched opinion in Edwards
scholarship--only recently refuted--that his "Natural
Philosophy" and "The Mind" together constitute the
epitome of his thought; that the ideas contained
therein he maintained, with minor variations, until the
end of his life; that from them he never departed
because his thought never developed. Now this rather
startling conclusion was reached through the attempt to
solve the problem of interpreting these private
notebooks raised by their disclosure of an Edwards
quite different from the one found elsewhere in his
corpus. Thus, the Edwards found elsewhere did not
evince the prodigious scientific curiosity of the one
in the private notebooks. Nor did he later allude to
the idealism delineated in those early notebooks.
Edwards scholars at the turn of the century sought to
solve this problem of interpretation by looking for
traces of the private notebooks in Edwards' late works.
These they claimed to have found, and on this basis
concluded that the notebooks are indeed of a piece with
the late works. Their conclusion, then, that the
"Natural Philosophy" and "The Mind" "may be trusted,
since it is generally agreed that the philosophical
views here expressed were essentially maintained by
Edwards to the end of his life,"[14] which was drawn at
the inauguration of the modern era of Edwards

scholarship, has been uncritically accepted and reaffirmed by virtually all later Edwards scholars.

Hence, because of their bias toward philosophy and against theology, and their view of Edwards' early philosophical notebooks as the epitome of his thought, Edwards scholars have focused so narrowly on these works and esteemed them so highly. Allen, whose celebrated *Life and Writings of Jonathan Edwards* inaugurated the modern era of Edwards scholarship, sought the very "*key* to Edwards's thought, his theology, his preaching, and, in a manner, the very type of his piety"[15] in the private notebooks. Even today, in the recent "renaissance" of Edwards scholarship, these books are the focus of attention since allegedly "the best of Edwards is his private notebooks."[16] And because of the disproportionate attention given to them, the rest of Edwards' oeuvres, particularly the later Northampton texts, has been woefully neglected.

To review: The unconscionable neglect by Edwards scholars of some of his Northampton texts is explicable by the occasional character of the texts themselves and their ostensible lack of philosophical or theological interest; and by the traditionally narrow focus of most Edwards scholarship on his "Natural Philosophy" and "The Mind" because of the antitheological bias of the pioneers in the field, their predilection for Edwards' philosophical works, and their view of Edwards' private notebooks as epitomizing his thought.

Their chronic neglect of a significant portion of the Edwards corpus has led scholars to seriously misconstrue him either by utterly misconceiving his social-political philosophy or, more commonly, by

denying that he had any such thing--indeed, that he had
nothing at all worth saying about society or politics.
Thus, they have erroneously placed Edwards in the royal
line of New England theocrats, claimed that he rejected
the idea of the covenant, styled him a quietist and
theological individualist who utterly divorced religion
from the world and its social and political concerns,
or, on the other hand, proclaimed him a proto-American
nationalist and herald of the American Revolution.
Interestingly, the above stances have implications for
social/political philosophy; thus, to discuss Edwards
with respect to any of them is to discuss him socio-
politically and to imply that he had something worth
saying in that regard. Yet, not all scholars have thus
misconstrued Edwards, which has resulted in the spate
of contradictory opinions about Edwards in the
literature which we surveyed in the first chapter.

The reclamation of Edwards' neglected Northampton
texts will have four beneficial results. One is the
decisive refutation of many long entrenched canonical
opinions about Edwards' social and political
philosophy. Thus, these texts will enable us to
establish once and for all the following propositions:
(1) that Edwards was emphatically not a theocrat but
might even have been sympathetic to the separation of
church and state; (2) that he unambiguously affirmed
the idea of the covenant; (3) that far from being a
quietist and theological individualist sundering
religion from society and politics, Edwards insisted
that the litmus of true religion is its transfiguration
of the world at large; (4) that his vision of the
redeemed society, contrary to being chauvinistic and
exclusive, is radically international and inclusive,

and that to hail Edwards as a harbinger of the American
revolution is perhaps to ignore the subtlety and
conservatism of his political thought; and, most
importantly, that there is indeed a social-political
philosophy implicit in Edwards' thought--one that is
articulate, sophisticated, suggestive and contrary to
the socio-political theory regnant in his day.

A second result will be an indication of when, and
perhaps why, Edwards modified his earlier definition of
virtue expressed in "The Mind." In *Life of Brainerd* and
Humble Inquiry, Edwards seems to be both iterating his
early conception of Christian love formulated in
Religious Affections and adumbrating his later one
expounded in *True Virtue*, thereby making *Life of
Brainerd* and *Humble Inquiry* apparently transitional
texts. Thus, these texts lend further support to the
revisionist view that Edwards' thought developed.
Moreover, in the circumstances and period of their
writing, we might even find an explanation of this
development.

A third result will be a shift in the focus of
Edwards scholarship from (traditionally) his very
earliest and latest works to those in between. Focusing
the published works from his last years in Northampton
has ample justification. For one thing, Edwards
intended them for publication, unlike "Natural
Philosophy" and "The Mind." It is ironic that Edwards
scholars have made these works the starting point of
their scholarship. Second, the later Northampton texts
date from years of personal and social crises in
Edwards life, and thus have at least biographical and
historical importance. Third, four of these texts
concern the nature and practice of piety, both

individually and corporately, which was, on Edwards'
own admission, the greatest preoccupation of his
intellectual life. Indeed, three of them are related
thematically to one of Edwards' greatest books,
Religious Affections, his most sustained and systematic
account of the nature of true piety, insofar as they
either illustrate, or defend the implementation of,
principles contained therein. And fourth, on one of
these texts, namely *Humble Inquiry*, Edwards staked not
only his livelihood, career and reputation, but the
very cause of true religion as well.

Finally, a fourth result of retrieving Edwards'
neglected Northampton texts will be the disclosure of
Edwards as not only a social thinker but very much a
social reformer as well. Thus, *Humble Attempt*, in
addition to delineating his vision of the ideal human
society, expresses his hope that it, through divine-
human cooperation, will be established on earth;
explains what Christians can and must do to help bring
it about; and exhorts them to do so. And *Humble Inquiry*
contains Edwards' blueprint for transforming his own
congregation into a type and vanguard of that society.

2

Now, before undertaking our reading of these
Northampton texts to settle the disagreement over
Edwards' status as a social and political thinker, we
need to consider them in their context of Edwards' life
and thought, thereby serving to illuminate them
further. Specifically, we shall locate them in the
contexts of his life's story, of the period when they
were written, and of the Edwards' corpus. To that end,

it is convenient to divide Edwards' intellectual life
into four creative periods according to his major
preoccupations, and the problems addressed in his
writings, at various times. The first period (1716-26)
covers his student years at Yale, his short pastorate
in New York City, and the two years of his tutorship at
Yale; the second (1726-42), the first sixteen years of
his pastorate in Northampton; the third (1743-50), his
last seven years in Northampton and the time in which
he wrote the texts under consideration; and the final
period (1751-58), his years of missionizing in
Stockbridge and his too brief tenure as president of
the College of New Jersey (later Princeton).

Before looking at his last years in Northampton,
the productions of which are the focus of our study, we
shall look briefly at the other periods of his life--
the major works from which have received more scholarly
attention--as a setting for the critical period of
1743-50. Between 1716 and 1726, Edwards was most
preoccupied with philosophy and science. It was then
that he formulated his own form of idealism, and
planned to write a major treatise on natural
philosophy.[17] This vast project, unfortunately, was
never brought to fruition, much to the chagrin of such
as Tyler and van Doren. From this period date his
precocious notebooks, "Natural Philosophy" and "The
Mind,"[18] presumably studies for his projected
treatises, and the works upon which his posthumous fame
has largely rested. However, though he abandoned the
writing of his projected philosophical system, he did
not cease philosophizing altogether. The private
notebooks he kept up throughout his life, not to
mention his major theological works, are richly laden

with philosophical speculations, possibly fragments of
that unfinished system.

In 1726, Edwards was called to Northampton as the
colleague and, three years later, the successor of his
grandfather, the venerable and highly esteemed Solomon
Stoddard, who died in 1729. The first sixteen years of
his ministry there were relatively felicitous. This was
the period of a general religious awakening that
extended from Scotland to the American colonies--the
revivals of 1734-35 and the Great Awakening of 1740-43.
Against their detractors, Edwards thought these
movements of spiritual renewal were a genuine work of
the Holy Spirit and a harbinger of the millennium, and
so enlisted enthusiastically in their cause as promoter
and apologist. The revivals were the occasion of his
writing the works for which he received fame in his own
life-time: *A Faithful Narrative of the Surprising Works
of God* . . . (hereinafter cited as *Faithful Narrative*)
(1736), *The Distinguishing Marks of a Work of the
Spirit of God* (hereinafter cited as *Distinguishing
Marks*) (1741), *Some Thoughts concerning the Present
Revival of Religion in New-England* (hereinafter cited
as *Some Thoughts*) (1742), and *Religious Affections*
(1746). The last-named treatise, which is a reply to
Chauncy's and others' animadversions on revivalism,
distinguishes carefully between religion and
religiosity. It seeks to demonstrate that the
"experimental" religion nurtured by the revivals could
not be dismissed outright as mere "enthusiasm," but is
in fact true religion. Throughout these works, Edwards
developed a theory of religion in which he gives the
emotions prime of place not only as the very essence of
the religious life, but as clues to its authenticity as

well. However, the religion he describes is not a mere
wallowing in blind hyper-emotionalism, but is infused
by the light of a fully enlightened understanding. It
is noteworthy that, around 1731, Edwards conceived of
yet another major project, "A Rational Account of the
Main Doctrines of the Christian Religion Attempted,"
which would have been a demonstration that theology is
the queen of the liberal arts and sciences.[19] However,
this too was abandoned.

In 1751, Edwards and his large family made their
trek into the wilderness of western Massachusetts to
spread the gospel to the Indians. This opens the last
great creative period of his life. During this time he
was mainly preoccupied with countering with his pen
various attacks on the tenets of evangelical Calvinism.
Thus, in *A Careful and Strict Enquiry into the Modern
Prevailing Notions . . . of Freedom of Will*
(hereinafter cited as *Freedom of Will*) (1754), a
trenchant reply to the Arminian position on the
subject, he argues that though our choices are not
freely made, we are nonetheless culpable for them. His
The Great Christian Doctrine of Original Sin Defended
(hereinafter cited as *Original Sin*) (1758) is a
sustained and disturbing reply not only to John
Taylor's treatise[20] on the same subject, but to all
those who held the then fashionable doctrine of man's
innate goodness. However, Edwards' twin dissertations,
True Virtue and *God's End* (written in 1755 but
posthumously published in 1765), seem not to have had a
polemical purpose but signal a return to the
metaphysical speculations of his youth. The first of
them is a fundamental revision of his theory of
religion delineated earlier in *Religious Affections* as

well as, in the name of a radically theocentric ethics,
a refutation of the moral sense theories of Hutcheson
and Shaftesbury. While the second attempts an answer to
the perennial question of why there is something rather
than nothing.

   We turn now to the critical period of 1743-50
which, compared to the other periods of Edwards' life,
is conspicuous by its turbulence. It was, for Edwards,
a time of crises in both his personal life and the
society at large. At the personal level, Edwards
suffered several shocks. The Great Awakening, the
movement Edwards had seen so much promise in and had
expended such a great deal of his energy on, devotedly
taking it up as a cause and championing it from the
press, was massively opposed by the "Old Lights." In
1743, Charles Chauncy, a minister at Boston's First
Church, virulently attacked from the press[21] Edwards'
apologia for the revivals, and charged Edwards with
enthusiasm, something that Edwards himself abhorred and
from which, in his revival writings, he painstakingly
distinguished what he thought the authentic religious
experiences issuing from the Awakening. Furthermore,
Edwards, for his advocacy of the Awakening, had
incurred the enmity of no less a light than Samuel
Johnson who was an eminent philosopher, a correspondent
and disciple of Bishop Berkeley, and an arch anti-
revivalist. It must have chagrined Edwards, had he
known of it, and certainly dealt a blow to the prestige
of his cause when, in the same year as the publication
of Chauncy's attack, Oxford conferred a doctorate on
Johnson for his polemics against the revivals.[22]

   Four years later, Edwards was the victim of two
personal tragedies. In 1747, David Brainerd, his dear

friend whom he greatly admired and whose memoirs and
biography he carefully edited and published, died in
his house at thirty years of age. Nine months later,
Edwards' daughter, Jerusha, "the flower of the
family,"[23] joined him in the grave at the age of
seventeen. From 1747 on, Edwards' relationship with his
congregation and the town turned progressively sour.
Acrimonious squabbles ensued over his salary, his
public censure of certain youths for reading "bad"
books, and, finally and most serious of all, the issue
of requirements for church membership.

It also worth speculating on further pressures on
Edwards at this time. In 1747, Edwards was forty-four
and so entering his middle age. By then he had labored
for twenty-one continuous years in the shadow of the
imposing figure of his grandfather Solomon Stoddard,
whose successor in the Northampton church Edwards had
become. Might the pressure of having to define and
assert his own identity in the face of his blood-
relation to Stoddard, together with the latter's
daunting reputation, helped induce Edwards in this year
to repudiate publicly Stoddard's Half-Way Covenant as
the principle of membership in the Northampton church?
And then there was the case of David Brainerd, who was
expelled from Yale for impugning the piety of a
professor of divinity there. Brainerd's remarks were an
expression of his religious zeal and his sympathy for
revivalism, then a controversial matter. Thus,
Brainerd's expulsion could be seen by those sympathetic
to the revivals as a brave act of self-denial for the
cause of true religion. Was Edwards perhaps "convicted"
by Brainerd's courage and zeal in the cause of
religion, of which Edwards then could offer no example

of his own?[24] For in 1747, Edwards did set just such an
example, risking all for the sake of a religious
principle, with full foreknowledge of its consequences,
by revoking the Half-Way Covenant. And, in 1751,
Edwards turned down the offers of pulpits elsewhere,
and instead betook himself and his family to
Stockbridge, settling in the vast solitudes of the
Berkshires "as deep into America as though in 1851 a
man had gone, let us say, from Albany to the
Dakotas."[25] There, like Brainerd, he was a missionary
to the Indians, a task for which he was suited neither
by training nor temperament. Were these actions of
Edwards in middle-life a sort of atonement for what he
thought was backwardness on his part in actively
furthering the cause of true religion? Was he here
emulating Brainerd while declaring his independence of
Stoddard?

Exacerbating Edwards' personal problems were the
changes in the larger society occurring during the
1740's which, for a person of Edwards' persuasion,
constituted a crisis. Northampton was then in the
throes of secularization. The unifying hegemony of the
traditional theocracy had disintegrated, and an ethos
of rampant individualism had usurped the place of
Puritan communalism. Consequently, the social milieu
became more and more competitive and factious. Tracy
writes:

> By the 1740s, despite the briefly
> spiritualizing effects of the latest revival,
> Northampton became more worldly and
> contentious--a normal eighteenth-century
> town. Amid the inexorable social changes, we
> can see the fragmentation of a once
> integrated body into a mere geographical
> collection of competitive individuals. . . .
> In the loss of a unity once imposed by

> hardship and ideology there came also the
> separation of morality, and especially piety,
> into an isolated corner of everyday life.[26]

The Northampton community had lapsed into the
irreligion, immorality, and social discord that so
disfigured it in the late 1720's, the period in which
Edwards commenced his ministry in Northampton. It was
as if the religious revivals of 1734-35 and of the
Great Awakening in 1740-43, together with their
socially ameliorative effects, had never occurred.

By contrast, during the periods of revival,
religion and morality flourished in Northampton, and
the social concord Edwards longed for prevailed. In a
letter of 30 May 1735, Edwards mentions the social
amelioration effected by the recent revivals:

> I have observed that the Town for this
> several years have gradually been Reforming;
> There has appeared Less & Less of a party
> spirit, & a contentious disposition, which
> before had Prevail'd for many years between
> two Parties in the Town.[27]

This halcyon time, unfortunately, was short-lived. The
Holy Spirit withdrew from the town, only to be replaced
by the old "party spirit." Thus in a letter of 19 May
1737, Edwards writes:

> The work that went on so swiftly and
> wonderfully while God appear'd in might &
> irresistible power to carry it on, has seemed
> to be very much at a stop in these (Valley)
> towns for a long time, and we are sensibly by
> little and little, more and more declining.
> ...Contention and a party spirit has been
> the old iniquity of this town; and . . . has
> of late manifestly revived.[28]

Between 1740-43, however, there occurred another and
more powerful revival, the Great Awakening, which was

given impetus by George Whitefield's evangelizing in the American colonies during the autumn of 1740.

Edwards himself enlisted as an evangelist in this movement, becoming its most articulate, albeit critical, spokesman. It was during these revivals that Edwards preached the jeremiads *Sinners in the Hands of an Angry God* (for which he is chiefly, and perhaps unfortunately, remembered in the popular mind) and *The Future Punishment of the Wicked Unavoidable and Intolerable*. He was at the zenith of his public career and influence in the summer of 1741. The Great Awakening, according to Miller, was "Edwards' greatest moment."[29] And with the publication of *Distinguishing Marks* and *Some Thoughts*, his major works from the early 1740's, Edwards established a reputation for himself as an incomparable apologist for evangelical Calvinism.

Following the pattern of the earlier revivals in the mid-1730's, the Great Awakening eventually waned, leaving the New England Church torn between champions and opponents of revivalism. Soon after 1742, Northampton again became spiritually moribund with Edwards gradually losing his moral authority in the town. "By the late 1740s," writes Tracy, "Edwards seemed to be left without means to turn his people's attention toward God again. He had tried inspiring them to piety, and he had tried bald discipline; both had failed."[30]

This is the background against which Edwards published his major but neglected works in the second half of the decade. Each one in some way addressed what for Edwards were the contemporary religious and moral crises and the social divisiveness they incurred. In *Humble Attempt*, Edwards sought, as is made plain in its title, "to promote explicit agreement and visible union of God's people in extraordinary prayer for the revival of religion and the advancement of Christ's kingdom on earth." In other words, it was an ecumenical attempt to close the schisms that had rent the church so badly in the aftermath of the Great Awakening, and to trigger yet another revival with its resultant spiritual and social blessings. The publication of the *Life of Brainerd* was occasioned by the premature death of David Brainerd. Edwards hoped that publicizing a sterling example of Christian piety as actually lived and practiced by a particular individual would serve to inspire others and fan the embers of their faith. *Humble Inquiry* represents his attempt to rekindle the piety in the members of the church by making its visibility the requirement for membership in complete standing. By requiring a profession of faith in word and deed as the qualification for full Communion, Edwards reversed the more liberal and popular ecclesiastical polity of Solomon Stoddard, his grandfather and revered predecessor in the Northampton church. It was his restrictive policy on church admission, when the privileges of church membership were coveted as signs of social status, that catalyzed public opinion against Edwards, forcing his resignation from the Northampton pulpit in 1750. *A Farewel-Sermon* was Edwards' valedictory address to his congregation on the occasion of his dismissal, a witness of his failure to implement the social ideal of a pious society in Northampton.

Though these four works of Edwards from the last three years of his Northampton pastorate have not received the scholarly attention they deserve, they are

by no means negligible or peripheral. These texts are
linked by theme and aim to two of Edwards' major and
most acclaimed texts, viz. *Religious Affections* and
True Virtue, and are profoundly concerned with one of
the persistent themes of Edwards' life and thought--
namely, the nature of true piety or virtue. The
question of its nature is addressed in the earliest of
Edwards' major published works--the sermon, *A Divine
and Supernatural Light* and the aforementioned
Distinguishing Marks. Whereas it receives Edwards'
most sustained and systematic answer in his massive
treatise, *Religious Affections*, and another (though
significantly modified) answer in his much later
dissertation, *True Virtue*. Now the neglected texts
from the late 1740's likewise address various aspects
of the question of true religion. They are thereby
concerned with a central preoccupation of Edwards' life
and thought, and stand in a significant relationship to
Religious Affections and *True Virtue* which epitomize
distinctive stages of his theory of religion. Thus if
Religious Affections and *True Virtue*, together with
Distinguishing Marks and *Some Thoughts*, are concerned
with delineating the nature of true piety or virtue,
then *Humble Attempt*, the *Life of Brainerd*, and *Humble
Inquiry* are concerned respectively with its
promulgation, illustration, and social embodiment.
These latter texts constitute, as it were, a set of
practical appendices to the treatise of 1746 and the
posthumously published dissertation.

Moreover, along with *A Farewel-Sermon*, they are
even more significant in two other ways: First, two of
them, the *Life of Brainerd* and *Humble Inquiry*, together
signal a crucial transition in Edwards' moral

philosophy. And second, they cumulatively disclose the social dimension of Edwards' thought. With the exception of the *Life of Brainerd*, they are his only published works that in their entirety focus the social group. Thus, *Humble Attempt* concerns societies of prayer as an instrument of redemption, and millennial society as the penultimate goal of the history of redemption. *Humble Inquiry* is about the visible church as the earthly paradigm of a pious society and the prototype of millennial society. *A Farewel-Sermon* is concerned with the church congregation, together with whole nations and generations, as defendant and plaintiff in the court of the Last Judgment. Even the *Life of Brainerd*, through ostensibly about an individual, indirectly concerns the proper moral relationship of the individual to the group.

3

We are now ready to apply Edwards' four neglected Northampton texts to the related tasks of settling the disagreement over Edwards' status as a social thinker-- together with its attendant issues such as his positions on theocracy and the covenant--and demonstrating that embedded in Edwards' thought, and undergirding the "imposing social vision" Westbrook attributes to him, are the rudiments of not only a social and political philosophy but also a philosophical sociology.

However, questions might be raised at this point over our distinction between Edwards' *social and political philosophy* and his *philosophical sociology*, and our qualification of the latter as "philosophical."

So in order to determine what we are attributing to
Edwards, we shall now clarify the meaning of the terms
"social and political philosophy" and "philosophical
sociology" and the distinction between them.

Whitaker T. Deininger has provided the following
four definitions of "social and political philosophy":

1. any thoughtful discussion "about the nature
and functions of society";

2. "the creation of ideal standards and utopian
schemes against which, as it were, to 'measure'
existing social and political institutions and values";

3. "that special branch of moral philosophy
concerned with showing what ought to be the goals
sought by men in their social and political affairs";

4. "the attempt to discover and to make precise
the fundamental nature of Justice."[31]

Robert A. Nisbet has identified the distinctive and
central concern of sociology as *the nature of the
social bond*[32] or, more precisely, "the mechanisms and
processes through which human beings become members of
the social order and by which they remain members."[33]
Now the domains of social philosophy and sociology, in
these conceptions of them, are indistinguishable at
some points: Deininger's first definition of "social
philosophy" can apply equally to "sociology" as broadly
understood by Nisbet. However, they might be
distinguished as follows: First, sociology, unlike
social philosophy, aspires to being normatively neutral
with respect to its subject-matter; consequently, only
the first of the above definitions of "social
philosophy" apply to it. Second, the methods of
sociology are more rigorously empirical than those of
social philosophy; the latter can be highly speculative

and intuitive, though no less theoretic, in its approach.

We have qualified Edwards' sociology as *philosophical* because officially there is no science of sociology before Auguste Comte. Prior to the early nineteenth century, society, or social behavior, was not being studied deliberately, systematically and empirically. An aspect of Edwards' social thought is sufficiently "sociological" in the modern sense, inasmuch as it anticipates some fundamental concepts distinctive of modern sociology, to warrant its distinction from social philosophy. On the other hand, it is also sufficiently intuitive and speculative to warrant its distinction from modern social science-- hence, its designation as "philosophical." Presumably, Edwards' sociology is to scientific sociology much as Locke's psychology, for example, is to scientific psychology.

However, there is a methodological problem in trying to identify a social and political philosophy, much less a philosophical sociology, in Edwards' thought. Edwards never published a canonical treatise, or even a part of one, on any of these subjects. And nothing like them appears even in germinal form (as far as we know) in his private notebooks where he usually first developed his ideas. The closest Edwards comes to an explicitly theoretical treatment of society is in a few sporadic jottings from his *Miscellaneous Observations on Important Theological Subjects*. Nevertheless, a rudimentary socio-political philosophy and philosophical sociology is discernible in Edwards' thought. Our methodological task, therefore, is to make them explicit. We shall do this by reading the four

Northampton texts in light of contemporary sociological theory. This will enable us to identify certain of Edwards' ostensibly philosophical-theological concepts as being distinctively sociological categories in disguise, and so translate them into the idiom of modern sociology.

Thus, we shall demonstrate that implicit in *Humble Attempt* is what amounts to both *descriptive* and *normative* theories of society. Edwards' descriptive theory belongs to the domains of social philosophy and philosophical sociology alike, as conceived by Deininger and Nisbet, for it is a theory as to "the nature and functions of society," particularly "*the nature of the social bond*." Edwards' normative theory of society belongs squarely to the domain of social philosophy, as defined by Deininger, for he has a theory as to the nature of the ideal society and so is concerned with "the creation of ideal standards and utopian schemes." In *Humble Attempt*, we shall find Edwards' vision of the Christian utopia, his metaphor for which is the Kingdom of God. From the *Life of Brainerd* we shall explicate an Edwardsean theory of membership or citizenship in the ideal society, Edwards' metaphor for which is Gethsemane.[34] This theory falls within the pale of social philosophy insofar as that is "concerned with showing what ought to be the goals sought by men in their social affairs." Edwards' theory of citizenship makes more determinate the nature of his social ideal by suggesting that it is an authentic community made up of genuine individuals united by the bond of mutual benevolence. The *Life of Brainerd*, then, complements *Humble Attempt*: as the latter's socio-theoretic focus is the group, its focus is the individual. We then shall show that *Humble Inquiry* implicitly contains, as it were, a strategy for implementing in microcosm the social ideal envisioned in *Humble Attempt*. Edwards' metaphor for the historical form of the ideal community is the church. Finally, we shall see that latent in *A Farewel-Sermon* is a theory of justice as the normative form of society, Edwards' metaphor for which is the Last Judgment. Edwards' theory of justice, obviously, has socio-philosophical significance inasmuch as it is an "attempt to discover and to make precise the fundamental nature of justice," especially as it pertains to the social order.

Put succinctly, what we shall demonstrate is that the above texts treat of different aspects of Edwards' ideal social vision and the problem of its concrete realization within the precincts of Northampton. And it was precisely Northampton's resisting his attempt to remould it into a microcosm of millennial society that occasioned Edwards' writing them at all, thereby prompting him to bring to the surface those elements of his socio-political thought that might otherwise have remained hidden. Tracy corroborates this in her description of the last fifteen years of Edwards' Northampton ministry, from the last third of which these texts date, in terms of an ever-widening discrepancy between Edwards' social ideal and the social reality around him:

> The story of Edwards' last fifteen years in Northampton might be summed up as his own holding fast to an ideal vision of community life and ministerial influence that seemingly became a reality in 1734-35, while the community continued to grow economically and socially away from the ability or the desire to participate in such a mode of life. [35]

Each of the four subsequent chapters (the third
through the sixth chapters) takes up one of the
Northampton texts in chronological order. Each chapter
is divided into four sections corresponding to
different aspects of the text, viz. (1) its historical
background, (2) its exposition, (3) scholarly
evaluations and interpretations of it, and (4) its
implications for social and political philosophy. We
begin by briefly covering the social and historical
circumstances occasioning the text's publication, and
Edwards' motives and aims in writing it. We then
present the text's contents, but confining ourselves to
those which either help settle the scholarly conflicts
over Edwards' significance as a social thinker or
suggest the elements of social thought. Next we
consider how the text has been evaluated and
interpreted. In order to expose interpretations that
contradict the text or help us choose between
conflicting ones, we shall juxtapose them with relevant
passages from the text itself. We shall look for
patterns of interpretation. Last we explicate the
elements of socio-political thought latent in the text,
building wherever possible on the interpretive insights
of others. The final chapter resolves the scholarly
disagreement over Edwards' status as a socio-political
thinker; synthesizes the various elements of social-
political thought previously unearthed from the four
texts into a coherent socio-political theory; and
describes Edwards' philosophy of community.

As we excavate Edwards' social thought in the
texts from the 1740's, we shall see that it is
determinate enough to admit comparison with the social
thinking regnant in both the eighteenth and the

nineteenth centuries. Thus, so as to render Edwards'
social theory the more determinate, we shall
demonstrate at appropriate points in our study that it
contrasts fundamentally with the individualistic and
mechanistic presuppositions of the social contract
theory as classically formulated by Thomas Hobbes, and
prefigures the holism and organicism distinctive of
nineteeth-century sociology as represented by Auguste
Comte and Herbert Spencer.

We shall now indicate the limits of our study. It
is not intended to be a contribution to the history of
either sociology or social philosophy. Nor does it
pretend that Edwards is principally a social
philosopher or a sociologist. This study was prompted
solely by the scholarly disagreement over whether
Edwards' thought is socio-theoretically relevant, which
it hopes to arbitrate. To this end, therefore, it
undertakes to establish definitely, against the
traditional interpretation, only *that* Edwards has a
nascent socio-political philosophy and philosophical
sociology latent in his system.

Our study should prove beneficial in the following
ways: (1) by providing a new angle of vision on
Edwards' philosophical-theology; (2) by enabling us to
graft, and thereby reclaim, some hitherto neglected and
problematic texts of Edwards' into the main body of his
work; (3) by allowing us to relate Edwards in an
illuminating way to the mainstream of European social
thought; (4) by suggesting a continuity, with respect
to their common social theme of community, between
Edwards and other American thinkers, such as Josiah
Royce, Henry James Sr., and George Herbert Mead; and,
(5) by indicating the perhaps unsuspected relevance of

Edwards' social philosophy to the present human
condition, prophetically epitomized in this passage
from Benjamin Disraeli's *Sybil*:

> There is no community in England; there is
> aggregation, but aggregation under
> circumstances which make it rather a
> dissociating than a uniting principle.[36]

CHAPTER II

NOTES

[1]*Natural Philosophy* is also known as *Notes on Natural Science*, the title given by Dwight. See Wallace Earl Anderson, "Editor's Introduction," in *The Works of Jonathan Edwards*, ed. by John E. Smith, VI (New Haven, 1980), p. 1, n. 1.

[2]Nancy Manspeaker, "Did Jonathan Edwards' Thought Develop? A Comparison of the Doctrine of Love Expressed in His First and Last Writings" (unpublished Ph.D. dissertation, Institute of Christian Thought, University of St. Michael's College, Toronto, 1983), p. 11.

[3]Allen, *Jonathan Edwards*, p. 6, n. 1, quoted ibid., p. 9.

[4]Isaac W. Riley, "The Real Jonathan Edwards," *Open Court*, 22 (1908), 705, quoted in Manspeaker, "Did Edwards' Thought Develop?," p. 8.

[5]H. G. Townsend, ed., *The Philosophy of Jonathan Edwards from his Private Notebooks* (Eugene, Oregon, 1955), p. xix, quoted in Manspeaker, "Did Edwards' Thought Develop?," p. 8.

[6]Moses Coit Tyler, *A History of American Literature, 1607-1765* (New York, 1879), I, 183, quoted in Manspeaker, "Did Edwards' Thought Develop?," pp. 10-11.

[7]Rufus Suter, "An American Pascal: Jonathan Edwards," *Scientific Monthly*, 68 (1949), 388, quoted in Manspeaker, "Did Edwards' Thought Develop?," p. 27.

[8]Gilbert Seldes, "Jonathan Edwards," *The Dial*, 84 (1928), 43, quoted in Manspeaker, "Did Edwards' Thought Develop?," p. 28.

[9]R. A. Horne, "The Atomic Theory of Jonathan Edwards," *Crane Review*, 3 (1961), 65, quoted in Manspeaker, "Did Edwards' Thought Develop?," p. 32.

[10]Suter, "An American Pascal," p. 388.

[11]Horne, "Atomic Theory," p. 67, quoted in Manspeaker, "Did Edwards' Thought Develop?," p. 33.

[12]W. Glyn Evans, "Jonathan Edwards: Puritan Paradox," *Bibliotheca Sacra*, 124 (1967), p. 57, quoted in Manspeaker, "Did Edwards' Thought Develop?," p. 32.

[13]Vernon L. Parrington, *Main Currents in American Thought* (New York, 1927), I, 158, quoted in Manspeaker, "Did Edwards' Thought Develop?," p. 32.

[14]Henry C. King, "Jonathan Edwards as Philosopher and Theologian," *Hartford Seminary Record*, 14 (1903), 25, quoted in Manspeaker, "Did Edwards' Thought Develop?," p. 20.

[15]H. Norman Gardiner, "The Early Idealism of Jonathan Edwards," *Philosophical Review*, 9 (1900), 574, quoted in Manspeaker, "Did Edwards' Thought Develop?," p. 12.

[16]Robert C. Whittemore, "Jonathan Edwards and the Theology of the Sixth Way," *Church History*, 35 (1966), 73, quoted in Manspeaker, "Did Edwards' Thought Develop?," p. 13.

[17]Anderson, "Editor's Introduction," p. 30.

[18]Ibid., pp. 2-3.

[19]Ibid., p. 36.

[20]The title of Taylor's treatise is *The Scripture-Doctrine of Original Sin, Proposed to Free and Candid Examination*. Its date of publication seems to have been either 1738 or 1740. See Clyde A. Holbrook, "Editor's Introduction," in *The Works of Jonathan Edwards*, ed. by John E. Smith, III (New Haven, 1970), p. 2.

[21]The title of Chauncy's treatise is *Sensible Thoughts on the State of Religion in New England, a Treatise in Five Parts*. See C. C. Goen, "Editor's Introduction," in *The Works of Jonathan Edwards*, ed. by John E. Smith, IV (New Haven, 1972), p. 80.

[22]Elizabeth Flower and Murray G. Murphey, *A History of Philosophy in America*, I (New York, 1977), p. 85.

[23]Clarence H. Faust and Thomas H. Johnson, eds., *Jonathan Edwards: Representative Selections, with Introduction, Bibliography, and Notes*, American Century Series (Revised ed.; New York, 1962), p. 425.

[24] I am indebted for these insights to Herbert W. Richardson.

[25] Edwards M. Griffin, *Jonathan Edwards*, University of Minnesota Pamphlets on American Writers, No. 97 (Minneapolis, 1971), p. 14.

[26] Tracy, *Jonathan Edwards*, pp. 147-148.

[27] Letter, Jonathan Edwards to Benjamin Colman, May 30, 1735, printed in Faust and Johnson, eds., *Jonathan Edwards*, p. 73.

[28] Letter, Jonathan Edwards to Benjamin Colman, May 19, 1737, quoted in Tracy, *Jonathan Edwards*, p. 124.

[29] Perry Miller, *Jonathan Edwards*, The American Men of Letters Series (New York, 1949), p. 171.

[30] Tracy, *Jonathan Edwards*, p. 169.

[31] Whitaker Thompson Deininger, *Problems in Social and Political Thought, a Philosophical Introduction* (London, 1969), pp. 6-7.

[32] Robert A. Nisbet, *The Social Bond: An Introduction to the Study of Society* (New York, 1970), p. 18.

[33] Ibid., p. 45.

[34] Our using the image of Gethsemane as a metaphor for understanding Edwards' conception of true citizenship was prompted by William Robertson Nicoll's classifying Edwards' edition of Brainerd's biography and literary remains as a "Gethsemane book." For Nicoll's appreciation of this text, see his *The Seen and the Unseen* (London, n.d.), pp. 30-31.

[35] Tracy, *Jonathan Edwards*, p. 122.

[36] Benjamin Disraeli, Earl of Beaconsfield, *Sybil, or the Two Nations*, in *Novels and Tales by the Earl of Beaconsfield with Portrait and Sketch of His Life*, Hughenden Edition, VIII (London, 1881), pp. 74-75.

CHAPTER III

THE SOCIAL IDEAL OF JONATHAN EDWARDS:
A DESCRIPTIVE AND NORMATIVE THEORY OF SOCIETY

Historical Background

Edwards' *Humble Attempt* is his *apologia* for an
ecumenical proposal of some Scottish ministers, among
whom were friends of his, that Christians everywhere,
of whatever persuasion, join with them and their
brethren in their renewed commitment to the united and
regular *"prayer that our Lord's kingdom may come,"*[1] as
had been the custom in Scotland and elsewhere since
1744. They clearly stated that the scope of their
appeal is not "restricted to any particular
denomination or party" but includes all who "have at
heart the interest of vital Christianity."[2] The authors
of the Memorial suggested that the proposed concert of
prayer be continued for seven years, on the
recommendation of Edwards himself who had communicated
his sentiments to one of its promoters.

Edwards was especially receptive to the idea,
having earlier proposed something similar for the
revival of religion:

> I have often thought it would be a thing very
> desirable, and very likely to be followed
> with a great blessing, if there could be some
> contrivance that there should be an agreement
> of all God's people in America, that are well
> affected to this work, to keep a day of
> fasting and prayer to God; wherein we should
> all unite on the same day in humbling
> ourselves before God for our past long
> continued lukewarmness and unprofitableness.[3]

He was very sympathetic to the cause of God's Kingdom, as is evident from this entry in his *Personal Narrative* of 1739: "My heart has been much on the advancement of Christ's kingdom in the world."[4] And he considered prayer "one great and principal means of carrying on the designs of Christ's kingdom in the world"; he believed that "when God has something very great to accomplish for his church, 'tis his will that there should precede it the extraordinary prayers of his people."[5] Edwards described himself as being "almost constantly in ejaculatory prayer," and especially "for the advancement of Christ's kingdom in the world."[6]

The Memorial's call for united prayer to revive religion was opportune, for the New England Church was rent by rampant schisms and bitter disputes over doctrine, symptoms of its decline, which Edwards decried in *Humble Attempt* as follows:

> And how lamentable is the moral and religious state of these American colonies? Of New England in particular? . . . What fierce and violent contentions have been of late among ministers and people, about things of a religious nature? . . . How many of our congregations and churches rending in pieces? . . . How strong and deeply rooted and general are the prejudices that prevail against vital religion and the power of godliness, and almost everything that appertains to it or tends to it?[7]

Edwards' sentiments are corroborated by an anonymous Connecticut divine who proclaimed: "Christian Brethren have their Affections widely alienated; . . . --Many Churches and Societies are broken and divided."[8] Conflict, moreover, was not confined to the Church. Edwards, in a letter from 1751, recalled that at the time his congregation had engaged in "some mighty

contests and controversies" over power and economic
status which "were managed with great heat and
violence."[9] And in a sermon preached in May of 1737
during an ebb in Northampton's first revival, he
deplored the "party spirit," too long the bane of the
town:

> Contention and party spirit is the old
> iniquity of this town. It has been a
> remarkably contentious town. I suppose for
> these thirty years people have not known how
> to manage scarcely any public business
> without dividing into parties. Though it be a
> great disgrace to a town, yet it is too
> notorious to be denied of this town.[10]

These contentions stemmed from a roughly half-century
old "settled division of the people into two
parties,"[11] the smaller one being an affluent and
powerful elite and the larger a poorer and powerless
proletariat. The decadent mid-forties represented a
reversion to the old days, before the revivals of 1734
and the so-called Great Awakening of 1740, when New
Englanders were distinguished, in the judgment of
another anonymous divine, by their "want of Brotherly
Love," a condition Edwards greatly lamented. Conflict
and discord, moreover, were rife among nations at the
time. The Jacobite Rebellion and the French and Indian
War were both threatening, to Edwards' alarm, a
Catholic hegemony in the Old and New Worlds. In
speaking of the "great commotion and tumult among the
nations"[12] in *Humble Attempt*, Edwards specifically
cited Prince Charles Edward's invasion of England in
1745 and the recent Catholic persecutions of the
Huguenots in France:

> The fresh attempts made by the antichristian
> powers against the Protestant interest, in
> their late endeavors to restore a popish

government in Great Britain, the chief
bulwark of the Protestant cause; as also the
persecution lately revived against the
Protestants in France, may well give occasion
to the people of God, to renewed and
extraordinary earnestness in their prayers to
him, for the fulfillment of the promised
downfall of Antichrist, and that liberty and
glory of his church that shall follow.[13]

By contrast, during the seasons of revival from
1734 to 1735 and throughout 1740, social concord
prevailed in Edwards' local community, a circumstance
that Edwards duly reported in a letter from May of 1735
documenting the first series of revivals in the
Connecticut River Valley:

Persons are soon brought to have done with
their old quarrels; contention and
intermeddling with other men's matters seems
to be dead amongst us. I believe there never
was so much done at confessing of faults to
each other, and making up differences, as
there has lately been.[14]

He likewise observed that the people "generally seem to
be united in dear love and affection one to another,
and to have a love to all mankind," and confessed never
to have seen "the Christian spirit in love to enemies
so exemplified in all my life as I have seen it within
this half year."[15] And, in a letter from December of
1743, Edwards documented the social harmony prevailing
in Northampton during the Great Awakening of 1740:

A party spirit has more ceased: I suppose
there has been less appearance these three or
four years past, of that division of the town
into two parties, that has long been our
bane, than has been these thirty years; and
the people have apparently had much more
caution, and a greater guard on their spirit
and their tongues, to avoid contention and
unchristian heats, in town meetings and on
other occasions.[16]

Pfisterer describes what happened in Northampton during
1735 as the flickering emergence of authentic
community, normally only dreamt of in utopian
literature and social theory:

> Here the perennial dream of and aspirations
> toward community itself as communion rather
> than as coercion had become a datable event
> in church history. . . . , both literary and
> social theory are confronted with community
> as it became incarnate in space and time for
> a brief period in the revival at
> Northampton.[17]

Edwards explains theologically this contrast
between "awakened," and both pre- and post-awakened
Northampton in terms of God's presence or absence in
history. Edwards postulated a prelapsarian age wherein
"all was in excellent order, peace, and beautiful
harmony"; but upon man's apostacy, God withdrew himself
from him, with the consequential "succession of a state
of the most odious and dreadful confusion" persisting
down to the present. Putting social discord in the
broadest historical perspective, Edwards interpreted it
as just a recent manifestation of the "discord and
confusion" endemic to humankind since the Fall.[18] Yet,
God had promised to restore the world to its
prelapsarian order. Just as God had formed chaos into
cosmos in his work of creation, so would he form
chaotic society into an harmonious community in his
work of redemption. Edwards thus interpreted social
concord, and the revivals with which it was correlated,
as a sign of God's once again drawing nigh to man as a
token of his ancient covenant promise. In the above-
mentioned sermon from 1737, Edwards actually correlated
social unity, or the lack thereof, with the influences
of the Holy Spirit:

> When the Spirit of God was of late so
> remarkably poured out, this spirit seemed to
> cease. But as God has withdrawn, this hateful
> spirit has again put forth his head; and of
> late, time after time, that old party spirit
> has appeared again, and particularly this
> spring.

And he specifically diagnoses contentiousness in the
individual as being the symptom of the want of piety:

> I appeal to the experience of all who are now
> my hearers, whether at such times as when
> their spirits have been heated with a spirit
> of opposition and a desire of disappointing
> others, or the like, their souls have not
> been destitute and instead of flourishing in
> grace and comfort, and the light of God's
> countenance all has not gone down and
> languished.[19]

Edwards identifies the root of factiousness in society
as the pride and excessive self-interest of individual
persons: "When men's outward interests or their pride
is touched, I have no reason to think from any thing
which at present apears but they will contend, and
create strife and division in the town."[20] Edwards, in
fact, blamed much of the social discord following upon
the revivals on spiritual pride and "intemperate,
unhallowed zeal"--vices, ironically, spawned by
revivalism itself.

   This 1737 sermon, incidentally, one of those cited
by Miller as evidence of Edwards' sociological acumen,
refutes the claim of some that Edwards was oblivious to
society and sundered piety from social concerns.
Edwards here is acutely aware of society, and plainly
states that individual piety or virtue, or the absence
thereof, registers "seismographically" in the social
sphere. Vital piety, the sort espoused by him and
fostered by the revivals, is ultimately to be judged by

its social fruits; thus, Edwards feared that it might
be discredited because of the social behavior in
"awakened" Northampton:

> No town in America is so much like a city set
> on a hill, to which God has in so great a
> degree entrusted the honour of religion....
> It has also been very much noticed by pious
> and learned persons in other parts of the
> land. And they have been greatly affected by
> it. They have spoken of it, how wonderfully
> God makes Northampton a place of wonders. But
> when they hear after all that has been done
> for us, that we have strifes and contentions,
> what a wound will this be to the honour of
> this kind of religion, which we profess?[21]

Edwards, himself anathematizing hypocrites and
fanatics, dreaded that they in Northampton stood in
danger of being dismissed as "a parcel of hypocrites
and enthusiasts, and whimsical deluded people."[22] So
closely is the condition of society linked in Edwards'
mind to the moral and spiritual condition of its
individual members, he asserts that Godless men cannot
but be factious: "I have now no hope but that they will
quarrel still, unless God takes their hearts in hand
and makes them much better men than ever yet they have
been."[23] C. C. Goen explains the conciliatory spirit of
the revivals socio-psychologically as the result of a
person's acquiring a new identity based on love in the
experience of conversion, which is his reconciliation
with God:

> As one submitted humbly, love displaced fear
> and furnished a new ground of confidence;
> i.e. one acquired a new identity. When this
> happened on a wide scale, social conflicts
> were healed and people were united in
> 'affection one to another,' as Edwards
> abundantly testified.[24]   p. 77

Edwards, along with others, interpreted the
spiritual renascence and social concord of the Great
Awakening as the overture to the golden age of the
millennium: "the dawning, or at least a prelude, of
that glorious work of God, so often foretold in
Scripture, which in the progress and issue of it, shall
renew the world of mankind."[25] So successful was the
revival that Edwards, in one atypically unguarded
moment, exultingly proclaimed: "The New Jerusalem in
this respect has begun to come down from heaven, and
perhaps never were more of the prelibations of heaven's
glory given upon earth."[26] He even dared suggest that
"there are many things that make it probable that this
work will begin in America."[27] However, by the time of
his writing *Humble Attempt*, he was considerably more
reserved in his millennial prognostications.

Despite the widespread social discord following in
the wake of the Awakening, Edwards nevertheless
remained sanguine; he steadfastly believed that,
"notwithstanding the thick and dark clouds that so soon
follow that blessed sunshine that we have had," God
would indeed "revive his work, and that what has been
so great and very extraordinary is a forerunner of a
yet more glorious and extensive work."[28] However,
Edwards believed that God would do so only on the foot
of the prayers of his people, from "'the clefts of the
rock, in the secret places of the stairs'; in a low and
obscure state, driven into secret corners."[29]

Edwards, then, saw the concert for prayer
commended in the Memorial as a way to reverse New
England's spiritual declension and, in particular,
foster social harmony. Incidentally, it is an
interesting comment on Edwards' relations with his

town, and their receptivity to his ideas, that his attempt to garner support for the Memorial met with difficulty. According to Stephen J. Stein, "as of November 1745, however, he had mostly discouraging news to report concerning the union. . . . The concert was far from an overwhelming success in Northampton."[30]

Let us now briefly consider the background to the Scottish Memorial. As in New England, the church in Scotland towards the mid-eighteenth century was rent by deep schisms and embittered doctrinal disputes which Edwards did not fail to deplore in Humble Attempt: "The Church of Scotland has very much lost her glory, greatly departing from her ancient purity, and excellent order; and has of late been bleeding with great and manifold wounds, occasioned by their divisions and hot contentions."[31] There were controversies and splits not only between the establishmentarians and both the evangelicals and moderates, but also among the ecclesiastical authorities themselves.

The evangelical cause in the Scottish church had been spurred by Thomas Boston's advocacy of The Marrow of Modern Divinity (1645). Boston and his followers, adhering to the Calvinist tenet of predestination, nevertheless took seriously the great commission of the gospel.[32] In the first half of the eighteenth century, the area of Cambuslang in Scotland lent its name to a spate of remarkable revivals virtually coinciding with those of the Great Awakening in Northampton--a coincidence that Bishop Söderblom, Gifford Lecturer for 1931, explains as follows: "the yearning for salvation and the sense of God's nearness break forth at certain epochs simultaneously with over-mastering power and

with effects that are felt centuries and millenniums
later."[33] This quickening evangelical movement in the
Church of Scotland, however, was strenuously opposed by
the ecclesiastical authorities. In 1720, the General
Assembly of Scotland decreed *The Marrow of Modern
Divinity* heretical; as a result, the "Marrow" men
seceded from the national church in 1740.[34] The
eighteenth century in Scotland was to witness many such
conflicts between the individual conscience and the
church.

Moderatism, a liberal movement inspired by the
Enlightenment and advocated by Francis Hutcheson who
hoped to revolutionize theology, surfaced as a force to
be reckoned with in the Scottish church towards the
middle of the eighteenth century. This movement,
predictably, was also anathematized by the church
establishment. John Simson, another Moderate and
professor of divinity in Glasgow, was in fact charged
with heresy by the ecclesiastical courts, and was
colorfully described in a contemporary account as "a
hotchpotch or bagful of Arian, Arminian, Socinian,
Pelagian, old condemn'd damnable errors."[35]

The seventeenth century, moreover, saw the
hegemony of the Church of Scotland itself split into
the competing factions of episcopalianism and
presbyterianism, a breach left unhealed by the
religious settlement proposed by William of Orange.
From a meeting of the General Assembly in 1690,
according to Arthur Fawcett,

> There emerged a heterogeneous mixture of
> covenanting ministers who had bravely borne
> hardships, and of prelatic clergy, 'vicars of
> Bray,' whose convictions about episcopacy
> were not sufficiently strong to induce them
> to abandon their livings. From these earliest

days there was a serious cleavage within the
national church, a dichotomy which was to
widen and separate the two groups even more
as the years went by.[36]

Against such a background of civil and
ecclesiastical strife Edwards' vision in *Humble Attempt*
of the Great Society of the millennium seems that much
more vivid, significant, urgent and poignant. His near
obsession with disunity in society is the obverse side
of his fixation on community.

Exposition

Edwards' purpose in writing the *Humble Attempt*
was "to persuade such as are friends to the interests
of Christ's kingdom, to a compliance with the proposal
and request made in that Memorial."[37] It is in three
parts: In the first, the Scripture (Zech. 8:20-22)
informing the treatise is expounded and a brief account
is given of the concert for prayer proposed in the
Memorial; in the second, incentives are provided for
complying with the memorial's proposal; and in the
third part, objections to that compliance are
anticipated and met.

Edwards interprets Zechariah's prophecy as
foretelling "that *last* and greatest enlargement and
most glorious advancement of the church of God on
earth." [38] This is yet to be fulfilled since, on
Edwards' survey of history, no such event as prophesied
has yet occurred; moreover, the tenor of this prophecy
agrees with that of others in scripture which obviously
concern the end time.

This future enlargement and advancement of the church will be precipitated, according to Zechariah, by the prayer of God's people. Edwards makes some interpretive comments on the prophet's understanding of prayer. One is that prayer is a duty of God's people.[39] The second is that its object should not be "the favor or mercy of God," but his "manifestations and communications of himself by his Holy Spirit."[40] The third is that the supplicants will be a multitude from all over the world, who "shall be given much of a spirit of prayer,"[41] and through their ever widening and intensifying concert of prayer will spark a general revival of religion--like the Great Awakening though vastly larger--which will vivify and prosper the church. The understanding is that the church and the cause of religion languish when God is absent from his people, but are revived when he is present with them. Edwards' fourth comment is that prayer for the kingdom should be united and public, conducted by a "visible union"[42] of God's people formed by their express agreement and joint resolution. Finally, his fifth comment is that such prayer should be "thoroughly performed," with the supplicants being "speedy, fervent, and constant in it." Edwards understands Zechariah to be endorsing such a concert of prayer for the millennium as "a *becoming* and *happy* thing" which is "acceptable to God"[43] and guaranteed to succeed. Therefore, he concludes, God's people should join such a concert as proposed in the Memorial.

The second part of *Humble Attempt* contains nine incentives for its readers to comply with the Memorial's proposal and enter into a concert of prayer for the revival of religion, with the attendant

advancement of Christ's kingdom on earth. These
incentives concern either (1) the merit itself of
concerted prayer, (2) the reality and desirability of
its ends and effects, (3) the example of nature's
pursuing these very ends, (4) Scripture's encouragement
of prayer for the kingdom, or (5) the contemporary
condition of the world. We shall now look more closely
at those aspects of each of them relevant to our aim of
explicating Edwards' socio-political thought.

Edwards presents as one incentive the merits of
concerted prayer, which are its beauty, its
anthropological soundness, and its general
salutariness. "How condecent [suitable or appropriate],
how beautiful, and of good tendency would it be," he
rhapsodizes, "for multitudes of Christians, in various
parts of the world, by explicit agreement, to unite in
such prayer as is proposed to us."[44] He extols social
union in prayer as beautiful because "union is one of
the most amiable things, that pertains to human
society; yea, 'tis one of the most beautiful and happy
things on earth, which indeed makes earth most like
heaven."[45] And it is especially so in the church.
Edwards cites Scripture to the effect that unity is
"the peculiar beauty of the church of Christ."
Moreover, social union in prayer, as a pious or
religious union, is more beautiful than any secular
union:

> A civil union, or an harmonious agreement
> among men in the management of their secular
> concerns, is amiable; but much more a pious
> union, and sweet agreement in the great
> business . . . of religion; the life and soul
> of which is love.[46]

And for Edwards, a "union or agreement in prayer is
especially becoming, when Christians pray for that
mercy, which . . . tends to the relief, prosperity and
glory of the whole body, as well as of each individual
member."[47]

Furthermore, social union is anthropologically
sound since it is consonant with man's instinctual
gregariousness and the exigencies of his environment:
"And this [union] is agreeable to the nature that God
has given men, disposing them to society; and the
circumstances God has placed them in, so many ways
obliging and necessitating them to it." God created
humanity with a common nature, thereby teaching us
"that it becomes mankind all to be united as one
family."[48]

Edwards offers as further inducement the salutary
effects of a concert of prayer for the kingdom. First,
it would make for a greater bonding of the
participants, and both foster and exemplify their
benevolence and public spiritedness: "It would tend
very much to promote union and charity between distant
members of the church of Christ, and a public spirit
. . . ; as well as be an amiable exercise and
manifestation of such a spirit." Second, it would
nurture mutuality and intimacy among them: "Union . . .
in the duty of prayer, in praying one with and for
another, and jointly for their common welfare, . . .
tends to promote mutual affection and endearment."
Third, it would increase their attention, activity and
responsiveness with respect to the cause of true
religion and the kingdom:

> It would engage 'em to more attention to such
> an affair, . . . , more ready to use
> endeavors to promote that which they, with so

> many others, spend so much time in praying
> for, and more ready to rejoice and praise God
> when they see or hear of anything of that
> nature or tendency:

And fourth, concerted prayer for the kingdom would
enliven the personal piety of all those involved, since
it would "naturally lead each one to reflect on
himself, and consider how religion flourishes in his
own heart, and how far his example contributes to the
thing that he is praying for."[49]

Edwards offers as a second incentive for his
readers to enter into a concert of prayer the reality
and desirability of its effects and ends. He describes
the surpassing gloriousness of the time whereof
Zechariah speaks which the faithful stand to enjoy.
Then the divine glory will be fully and ever manifest,
and "both God will be greatly glorified, and his saints
made unspeakably happy in the view of his glory." Now
on Edwards' reading of Scripture, the millennial glory
will manifest itself four ways. Intellectually, the
millennium will be the epoch of unprecedented and
universal enlightenment, of a "vast increase of
knowledge and understanding, especially in divine
things." Morally, it will be the era of remarkable
sanctity which will pervade all aspects of life--even
the mundane and everyday ones of daily survival,
commerce, and politics--with holiness being "as it were
inscribed on everything, on all men's common business
and employments, and the common utensils of life."[50]
Indeed, "vital piety shall take possession of thrones
and palaces, and those that are in most exalted
stations shall be eminent in holiness."[51]

Socially, the millennium will be the age of the
good society par excellence, being the inversion of

contemporary earthly society inasmuch as (in Edwards'
paraphrase of Ps. 113:7-8)"the poor shall be raised
from the dust, and the beggar from the dunghill, and
shall be set among princes, and made to inherit the
throne of God's glory." The millennial age will be one
of intensive and extensive social concord, of
"wonderful union, and the most universal peace, love
and sweet harmony." Specifically, that union will
embrace the church, for then "the church of God shall
not be rent with a variety of jarring opinions" and
"all [shall] agree in worshiping God in his own
appointed way." And the union will be international in
scope, for then "the whole earth shall be united as one
holy city, one heavenly family, men of all nations
shall as it were dwell together, and sweetly correspond
one with another as brethren and children of the same
father." In sum, this "whole great society shall appear
in glorious beauty, in genuine amiable Christianity,
and excellent order."[52]

Finally, respecting the larger natural order, the
millennium will be a period of "great temporal
prosperity," of "great health"[53] and of "long life,"
when "the earth shall be abundantly fruitful" and "the
world shall be delivered from that multitude of sore
calamities that before had prevailed." Above all, it
will be a time of "universal joy on earth" such that
"the very fields, trees and mountains shall then as it
were rejoice, and break forth into singing," and of
"extraordinary joy in heaven."[54]

Generally considered, the glory of the millennium
marks, for Edwards, the penultimate fulfillment of
God's promises in the covenants of grace and
redemption, and thus the penultimate end of human

redemption. God the Father covenants with God the Son
to accept the faithful as being in the Son, whereas God
the Son covenants with the faithful to redeem them
through God the Holy Spirit. The Holy Spirit, and the
new life he makes possible, is what Christ promises in
his covenant with his people:

> The Father provides and gives the Redeemer,
> and the price of redemption is offered to
> him, and he grants the benefit purchased; the
> Son is the Redeemer that gives the price, and
> also is the price offered; and *the Holy
> Spirit is the grand blessing, obtained by the
> price offered, and bestowed on the redeemed*
> [italics mine].[55]

Now the millennium, according to Edwards, is "the *chief*
time of the bestowment of this blessing"[56] and thereby
of the fulfillment of the covenant promise.

Edwards tenders as a third incentive for his
readers to join in the concert of prayer the example of
the whole nonhuman creation's eagerly awaiting and
travailing to bring on the millennium, which marks the
fullness of its redemption as well. Paraphrasing St.
Paul, he writes, "The 'whole creation' is, as it were,
earnestly waiting for that day, and constantly groaning
and travailing in pain to bring forth the felicity and
glory of it."[57] This is so because all nature is
implicated in the Fall, and thus contaminated and
perverted by sin and subject to human misuse and abuse.
As Edwards puts it, "This visible world has now for
many ages been subjected to sin, and made as it were a
servant to it, through the abusive improvement that
man, who has the dominion over the creatures, puts the
creatures to."[58]

Yet nature is similarly implicated in man's
redemption; even now it is tending toward the

millennium, the time of its restoration and denouement:
"Though the creature is thus subject to vanity, yet it
don't rest in this subjection, but is constantly acting
and exerting itself, in order to that glorious liberty
that God has appointed at the time we are speaking of."
Edwards' view of the world is thoroughly teleological
in which every event conspires to usher in the
millennial age: "All the changes that are brought to
pass in the world, . . . , are ordered in infinite
wisdom in one respect or other to prepare the way for
that glorious issue of things."[59]

Edwards finds a fourth incentive for God's people
to be much in united and regular prayer for the kingdom
in Scripture's specifically encouraging it and strongly
assuring us of its efficacy. He notes that Christ
himself commends praying in unison, "an holy union and
communion of his people being that which. . .he came
into the world to bring to pass, . . .[and] one chief
end of the whole affair of our redemption by him."[60]
Further, according to Edwards, God puts himself
virtually at the disposal of his people respecting
their importunities for the outpouring of his Spirit in
the advancement of his kingdom, and remains poised to
grant them: "God, . . .,is pleased to represent
himself as it were at the command of his people, with
regard to mercies of this nature, so as to be ready to
bestow them whenever they shall earnestly pray for
them."[61]

Finally, Edwards notes, as a fifth incentive for
his readers to comply with the Memorial's proposal,
that the moral morass of the contemporary world vividly
proves man's radical powerlessness to ameliorate it
himself--much less to realize the stupendous benefits

of the millennium, thereby showing his utter dependence
on God: "The insufficiency of human abilities to bring
to pass any such happy change in the world as is
foretold, or to afford any remedy to mankind, from such
miseries as have been mentioned, does now remarkably
appear." Edwards saw evidence of this in the parodoxes
of his own age of Enlightenment. Despite its vaunted
intellectual accomplishments, never, thought he, had
religion and morality ebbed so low as then:

> Great discoveries have been made in the arts
> and sciences, and never was human learning
> carried to such a height, as in the present
> age; and yet never did the cause of religion
> and virtue run so low, in nations professing
> the true religion.[62]

He saw further evidence of man's chronic moral
inability in the religious excesses--the fanaticism,
delusions, gullibility, spiritual pride, militant zeal,
and factiousness--attending the Great Awakening, which
he thought showed how awry even a divine work can go
when employing flawed human instruments who forget
their fallibility and need of God.

We turn next to some of Edwards' rebuttals of
possible objections to compliance with the Memorial's
proposal which are of interest, among other things, for
the light they shed on Edwards' idea of a pious union
in prayer.

One objection addressed by Edwards is the
proposal's "whimsicalness"[63] in supposing that the
prayers of many offered up at the same time are thereby
more forceful than an equivalent number at different
times. Edwards replies that this objection is based on
a misunderstanding; nowhere is it stated or implied, in
either the proposal itself or supporting arguments,

that prayers are more likely to be heard if uttered simultaneously. However, this is far from denying that it is "very expedient"[64] for prayers to be recited in unison. Edwards subsequently explains the expediency of instituting times for united prayer.

People formally agreeing to pray together at an appointed time would be psychologically expedient in two ways. First, it might remind them of and reinforce their commitment to the agreement:

> If there should be only a loose agreement or
> consent to it as a duty,...that
> Christians should be much in prayer for the
> revival of religion,...without agreeing
> on particular times, how liable would such a
> lax agreement be to be soon forgotten, and
> that extraordinary prayerfulness, which is
> fixed to no certain times, to be totally
> neglected?[65]

And second, it "may tend to encourage and assist those in praying, that are united in prayer."[66] According to Edwards, the awareness that others are concurrently engaged with us in a common enterprise is especially affecting because, given our mental constitution, the realization that certain events are contemporary gives them a poignancy and force they would not otherwise have:

> The consideration of things being present...
> does especially affect human nature....
> if a man could be certainly informed, that
> his dear child at a distance, was now under
> some extreme suffering; or that an absent
> most dear friend, was at this time thinking
> of him, and in the exercise of great
> affection towards him,...; would not
> those things be more affecting . . . , for
> being considered as things that are in
> existence, at the present time, than if
> considered as at some distance of time,
> either past or future?[67]

Furthermore, people's praying at the same time makes for "the *visibility* of their union in such prayer," which is a desirable thing since such union is itself "truly beautiful."[68] Union in prayer becomes visible, according to Edwards, by people's praying in the same place at the same time or, if they are widely separated, at least at the same time.

A second objection Edwards addresses is the charge that compliance with the Memorial's proposal smacks of "Pharisaism,"[69] or a sanctimonious exclusivity, as "it would look like affecting singularity, and open distinction from others of God's professing people, in extraordinary religion."[70] Edwards' replies that this charge is groundless since the ecumenicism of the proposal is stated plainly enough in the text of the Memorial itself, i.e. the concert "may by no means be understood, as restricted to any particular denomination or party, . . . ; but to be extended to *all*, who . . . have at heart the interest of vital Christianity."[71]

> The very design of the Memorial, is not to promote singularity and distinction, but as much as possible to avoid and prevent it. The end of the Memorial is not to confine and limit the thing proposed...; but on the contrary to extend it, and make it as general among professing Christians as possible.[72]

Furthermore, adds Edwards, that the Memorial was drawn up and published at all, inviting Christians everywhere to join in the concert that had been practiced in Scotland by a relative few, puts pay to the charge of Pharisaism.[73]

Finally, a third objection Edwards meets is that since, according to a prophecy recorded in Revelation about the "slaying of the witnesses," the millennium

will be preceded by a period of terrible tribulation
for and persecution of the church "wherein the
generality of God's people must suffer so extremely,"[74]
it hardly behooves the faithful to pray for the
hastening of an event which must be preceded by their
own demise. Edwards' answer is that the aforementioned
prophecy "is not an event that remains yet to be
fulfilled,"[75] having been fulfilled in the time
immediately following the Reformation in the form of
Rome's myriad machinations against the Protestant
cause, a point he proceeds to demonstrate exegetically.
However, though the church is not to suffer the
calamities foretold in this prophecy, Edwards does
caution that it must still do terrible battle with the
forces of evil with the consequent suffering of its
members:

> There is yet remaining a mighty conflict
> between the church and her enemies, the most
> violent struggle of Satan and his adherents,
> in opposition to true religion, and the most
> general commotion that ever was in the world,
> since the foundation of it to that time; and
> many particular Christians, and some parts of
> the church of Christ, may suffer hard things
> in this conflict.[76]

But throughout it all the church will prevail, and in
the end the evil forces will be utterly extirpated.

Evaluations & Interpretations

For Alexander Allen, *Humble Attempt* "is a book of
less interest and value than those we have been
reviewing; but it has importance as presenting his
views on the subject of prayer, as also a glimpse of
his attempt at a philosophical interpretation of

history."[77] But for Alfred Aldridge, this book "now has
value only as a curiosity."[78] Arthur Cushman McGiffert,
though declaring that "his [Edwards'] books were not
just tracts for the times, useful today and forgotten
tomorrow,"[79] deems *Humble Attempt* the exception to this
rule because of its unoriginality. In contrast to his
fellow commentators, Samuel Miller effusively praises
this treatise: "Instead of making his 'Humble Attempt'
a pamphlet of twenty or thirty pages, as most men would
have done, he made it a volume; rich, instructive,
carefully reasoned, and of permanent value."[80]

Perry Miller, surprisingly, gives short shrift to
Humble Attempt, dismissing it as so much "propaganda"
and "old-fashioned chiliasm."[81] However, he does see
significance in Edwards' millennialism, as treated
elsewhere in his corpus. Its significance becomes
apparent, according to Miller, when it is read in light
of the political radicalism inherent in millennial
thought from the beginning and made manifest by
Anabaptists and the Puritan sectaries in the English
Civil War.[82] In that light, Edwards' millennialism can
be seen as a vision of and a demand for a new and more
just human order, and part and parcel of his
condemnation of mercantile ethics (yet another
expression of Arminianism): "Edwards' exposition of the
millennial expectation, . . . was the proclamation of a
radical thesis..., and which alone..., was
powerful enough to check the depredations of the river
gods." Miller emphasizes that Edwards makes explicit,
and insists, that the millennium signals "a thousand-
year administration of social justice."[83]

Heimert, however, is the first historian to have
taken this text seriously, and to have seen its larger

socio-political significance. All recent
interpretations of this work are indebted to Heimert's
interpretation, being so many sympathetic
amplifications or critiques of it. It is with this
interpretation, then, that we shall begin. Heimert, as
we have seen, politicized Edwards' eschatology. He
interprets Edwards as having nationalized the
millennium by envisioning it as a "union of Americans."
Thus, Heimert writes in one place that "the vision of
the *Work of Redemption* was transformed into an ideal of
continental union." And in another, that "the revival
and the evangelical impulse pressed to the goal of a
more beautiful social order--which meant, in the New
World, a union of Americans."

Bryant thinks "our reading of Edwards requires
that we acknowledge a discontinuity between his pre-
and post-1742 writings,"[84] as evidence of which he
quotes the following passage from *Humble Attempt*: "It
[a union in prayer] would tend very much to promote
union and charity between *distant members of the church
of Christ*, and a public spirit, and *love to the Church
of God*, and concern for the *interest of Zion*."[85]
(Italics mine.) There is nary a hint here or anywhere
in *Humble Attempt* of a specifically *American* or
colonial union, nor any national union for that matter-
-not even the British Empire of which Edwards was an
unquestionably proud and loyal subject. But there is a
plain enough emphasis here and throughout the text on
ecclesiastical union--not just a regional or national
one, but a broadly *ecumenical* one at that. As Bryant
writes, "Perhaps Heimert's reading is consistent with
Americolatry, but Edwards' concern was a union in

prayer as an expression of the universality of the church in relation to its eschatological end."[86]

Edwards' radical universalism, amply attested by *Humble Attempt*, is evident in his inclusive conception of not only the union in prayer itself (as Bryant notes) but also the union of millennial society, the ultimate goal of the concert for prayer and part of Edwards' eschatological hope. Thus, Edwards imagines in *Humble Attempt* that the concert might consist of "great multitudes in *different parts of the world*"[87] and thereby precipitate "an accession of many of the *chief nations of the world* to the church of God."[88] (Italics mine.) Edwards, significantly, further conceives of the millennial Kingdom as being the last best hope of not just Christians, but *all* men, i.e. "It is becoming of Christians, . . . , to be much in prayer for that public mercy, wherein consists the welfare and happiness of the whole body of Christ..., and the *greatest good of mankind*."[89] (Italics mine.) In Edwards' conception, the union of millennial society is not a merely American, but a preeminently international union. Thus, in *Humble Attempt*, Edwards envisions the millennium as an era when "the *whole earth* shall be united as one holy city, one heavenly family, *men of all nations* shall as it were dwell together, and sweetly correspond one with another as brethren and children of the same father." (Italics mine.) And, in the *Work of Redemption*, he similarly imagines that then "shall *all the world* be united in one amiable society. *All nations, in all parts of the world, on every side of the globe*, shall then be knit together in sweet harmony."[90] (Italics mine.)

The radical inclusiveness of Edwards' vision is
further corroborated by his hope that the millennium
will bring about a universal intellectual enlightenment
and an enormous proliferation of knowledge, even in the
uncivilized world, with philosophers, scientists and
theologians turning up among the aboriginal populations
of Africa, Asia, Australia and America. Again, in the
Work of Redemption, Edwards writes:

> Then all countries and nations, even those
> which are now most ignorant, shall be full of
> light and knowledge. Great knowledge shall
> prevail every where. It may be hoped, that
> then many of the Negroes and Indians will be
> divines, and that excellent books will be
> published in Africa, in Ethiopia, in Tartary,
> and other now the most barbarous countries;
> and not only learned men, but others of more
> ordinary education, shall then be very
> knowing in religion.[91]

And he likewise rhapsodizes about the universality of
the millennial enlightenment in this entry from his
Miscellanies:

> How happy will that state be when neither
> divine nor human learning shall be confined
> and imprisoned within only two or three
> nations of Europe, but shall be diffused all
> over the world...; when the most
> barbarous nations shall become as bright and
> polite as England, when ignorant heathen
> lands shall be packed with most-profound
> divines and most-learned philosophers.

Most significantly, according to Edwards' conception,
the millennial union will embrace, along with "the
chief nations of the world," the lesser, "barbarous"
nations. In the millennium,

> the distant extremes of the world shall shake
> hands together and all nations shall be
> acquainted, and they shall all join the
> facets of their minds in exploring the
> glories of the Creator, their hearts in

loving and adoring Him, their hands in
serving Him, and their voices in making the
welkin ring with His praise![92]

Now is this that vision of a "union of Americans"
Heimert attributes to Edwards? Edwards' universalism is
fully manifest in the anthropology that undergirds his
account of millennial society: In *Humble Attempt*,
Edwards states that "God has 'made of one blood *all
nations of men*'"; therefore, he enjoins the moral that
"it becomes *mankind all* to be united as one family."[93]
(Italics mine.) Furthermore, in an entry from his
Miscellanies, Edwards states that a purpose of God's
redemption is that the *"whole earth* may be as one
community."[94] (Italics mine.)

The universality of Edwards' vision, however, has
not been lost on two of his commentators. Westbrook,
who, interestingly, acknowledges the influence of
Heimert's interpretation of "Jonathan Edwards' social
vision," writes:

> The radical universalism of Edwards' vision
> is clear; there is no tolerance here for
> provincialism or nationalism. Edwards'
> community of saints is to be an international
> society of benevolent individuals, a 'nation'
> above nations and above national sentiment.[95]

And Conkin says, "He [Edwards] was unalterably
committed to the greatest community, a community that
stretched beyond either national or racial boundaries
to include all mankind, and far beyond that to include
the source and totality of being."[96]

Aside from representing Edwards' conception of
millennial society as that of an exclusively American
society, Heimert says something else that, in light of
the conciliatory tenor of Edwards' millennialism, is
quite astonishing:

> But as the Calvinist mind amply proved
> whenever an appropriate occasion arose, both
> local and international schism was tolerable,
> even to be encouraged, so long as it brought
> within nearer view the union of God's people
> in America.[97]

But how credible is this with respect to Edwards, given his jeremiads in *Humble Attempt* and elsewhere on "both local and international schism," civil and ecclesial? And where does Edwards ever recommend schisms, within either secular society or the church, as the means of prosecuting the work of redemption or bringing "within nearer view" the pervasive social union of the millennium? Edwards, in fact, strenuously and persistently abhors schisms of any kind or extent. Does he not roundly condemn in *Humble Attempt* the "great outward calamities, in which the world is involved" because of the strife among nations, and the "fierce and violent contentions" schismatizing the church in Scotland and New England? In contrast, the millennium will be preeminently an epoch of "the most universal peace, love and sweet harmony"; there

> shall then be universal peace and a good
> understanding among the nations of the world,
> instead of confusion, wars, and bloodshed...
> . Then shall malice, and envy, and wrath,
> and revenge, be suppressed every where; and
> peace and love shall prevail between one man
> and another.[98]

It is clear from *Humble Attempt* that Edwards considers union itself, in the form of union in prayer, as the only legitimate means to redemptive union.

Heimert, furthermore, in his interpretation of Edwards' millennialism, not content with portraying Edwards as a proto-American nationalist, even more remarkably turns him into something resembling a closet

Arminian. Consider, for example, the following of
Heimert's statements: That the argument of *Humble
Attempt* "contained within itself the premise that
mankind could create within itself the very desires
that were to accomplish and constitute the earthly
Kingdom";[99] that

> Edwards' crucial premise--that God is 'at the
> command of the prayer of faith and in this
> respect, as it were, under the power of his
> people'--was, for all its modifications, a
> clear declaration that the achievement of
> millennial society was dependent on the
> collected will of God's people.[100]

And that "what Edwards was seeking to impress on the
evangelical mind generally was the vision of a future
that could be brought into being through the harmonious
cooperation of all men."[101] This "Arminian"
interpretation of Edwards' millennialism is significant
since it is the basis of the belief that Edwards'
Humble Attempt provided that impulse for an "optimistic
activism" on behalf of programs of social reform.
Edwards certainly does say in *Humble Attempt*, as
Heimert quotes him, that God is as it were, "under the
power of his people"[102] with regard to their concerted
prayers for the Kingdom. However, with respect to his
discussion in the same work of the need for a union in
prayer in redressing turpitude, Edwards talks about
"our entire and absolute dependence"[103] on God, and the
"insufficiency of human abilities to bring to pass any
such happy change in the world as is foretold, or to
afford any remedy to mankind, from such miseries as
have been mentioned." Moreover, it should be kept in
mind that, for Edwards, the *immediate* object of the
"prayer of faith" is not the Kingdom as such, but
rather "those great effusions of the Holy Spirit, *which*

shall bring on that advancement of Christ's church and kingdom."[104] (Italics mine.) Therefore, in Bryant's words, "the coming of Christ's Kingdom is wholly in the hands of a Sovereign God."[105]

Bryant's interpretation of *Humble Attempt* is explicitly a critique of Heimert's. Bryant understands this work as being Edwards' response to the contentiousness and schisms spawned by the Great Awakening. Edwards, according to Bryant, sought through the concert to ground the unity of the church in the will of God, and to orient the church towards its proper eschatological end, i.e. the Kingdom of God, of which it is the witness:

> Against the divisiveness and confusions of
> the Great Awakening, Edwards sought to
> restore the universal and eschatological
> nature of the church through the Union of
> Prayer. . . . The church, as a community
> gathered in prayer, exemplified a union
> grounded, not in human strength nor in human
> wills, but in the Sovereignty of God. In
> prayer, the church orients itself towards the
> proper object of its hope: The Kingdom of
> God.[106]

Another interpretation of *Humble Attempt* takes its cue from Edwards' revisionist reading of the prophecy concerning the "slaying of the witnesses" as already having been fulfilled. This reading, exegetically excising what might have been a stumbling block to people's acceding to the concert, marks Edwards' significant departure from the traditional premillennialist view of history. According to it, the millennial age would be inaugurated cataclysmically with the literal second-coming of Christ. The premillennialist view was of the Kingdom's coming as a *deus ex machina* which would obtrude upon history,

short-circuiting the course of nature and nullifying
natural laws. However, Edwards believed that the
millennial age would end, not begin, with the second-
coming. Edwards' *post*-millennialist view, a modern
development in millennial thought deriving from the
eschatological speculations of Sir Isaac Newton, is of
the millennium as an event evolving inexorably but
gradually through the normal processes of history and
nature, with human institutions and the laws of nature
remaining intact. In short, the postmillennialist
historicized the millennium as something emergent
within rather than supervenient upon history.[107]

In contrast to premillennialism, with its grim
scenario of an imminent apocalypse, postmillennialism,
with its more sanguine view of an oncoming golden age
immanent in history and precipitated by human endeavor
rather than supernatural catastrophe, naturally made
for optimism. In the words of C. C. Goen, "Edwards
foresaw a golden age for the church on earth, within
history, and achieved through the ordinary processes of
propagating the gospel in the power of the Holy
Spirit."[108] And, in Heimert's opinion, "perhaps
Edwards' most impressive achievement was to purge
Calvinist millenarianism of all those seventeenth-
century elements which were symptoms of cosmic
despair."[109] Stephen Stein writes, "Edwards was
persuaded that praying Christians could exert a
powerful influence upon the fortunes of the church and
the world."[110] Moreover, it was Edwards'
postmillennialism that led sociologist Robert Nisbet to
classify him as one who helped give legitimacy to the
the idea of progress.[111] Edwards' doctrine of the
immanency of the millennium is regarded as the

watershed of American utopianism, the secular and
corrupt form of postmillennialism, which would enjoy
its heyday in the coming century: "though direct
evidence may be lacking," according to Goen, "it is
difficult to believe that Edwards' historicizing of the
millennium did not furnish a strong impetus to
utopianism in America."[112] Consequently, *Humble Attempt*
is interpreted as a source-book of this utopian
optimism. However, this interpretation of the text
needs to be tempered by Edwards' own qualification of
his remarks on the prophecy in Revelation. He makes it
clear that, though the predicted general massacre of
God's people is past, there still remains a time of
tribulation and strife for the church. This, of course,
is the apocalypse; but it will occur after the
thousand-year period of peace and properity, and this
time the forces of darkness will be decisively
vanquished:

> 'Tis true, there is abundant evidence in
> Scripture, that there is yet remaining a
> mighty conflict between the church and her
> enemies, the most violent struggle of Satan
> and his adherents, in opposition to true
> religion, and the most general commotion that
> ever was in the world, since the foundation
> of it to that time; and many particular
> Christians..., may suffer hard things in
> this conflict: but in the general, Satan and
> Antichrist shall not get the victory, nor
> greatly prevail; but on the contrary be
> entirely conquered, and utterly overthrown,
> in this great battle.[113]

In summary: *Humble Attempt* attests strikingly to
"the primacy of a social vision" in Edwards' thought,
the preponderant, and indisputable, view of recent
commentators. Their disagreement is really over the
extent and nature of Edwards' "imposing social vision,"

i.e. whether it is exclusive or inclusive, temporal or
spiritual. For Heimert, it is the worldly and
nationalist vision of "a union of Americans." Whereas
for Bryant, *et alia*, it is the transcendent and
universal vision of a "spiritual community" which, for
Conkin, is inclusive even of "the source and totality
of being." However, *Humble Attempt*, among other texts,
decisively settles this conflict by corroborating
Bryant's observation that "Edwards' vision was not
empty of social content, but it is not the content
which Heimert finds." It is to the rich mother-lode of
this social content, starting with its outcroppings in
Humble Attempt, to which we shall now turn.

Implications for Social & Political Theory

From our reading of *Humble Attempt*, we shall show
in the first part of this section that, and how, society
is a significant idea in Edwards' thought. In the
second part, we shall demonstrate that Edwards has a
conception of two fundamentally different types of
society represented by his distinction between pious
and civil union and implied by his esteeming pious
union as the more beautiful. In the course of
explicating Edwards' distinction between pious and
civil union, we shall see that he has theories of how
each type of society is constituted, viz. through
either cordial or natural consent, and mediated, i.e.
through conversation. Finally, in the third part, we
shall see that Edwards' distinction between pious and
civil union, his equation of the former with primary
beauty, and his ideas of consent and conversation can
be formulated into a rudimentary but coherent and

suggestive theory--both *descriptive* and *normative*--of
the nature and function of society.

The Significance of Society

It is evident from *Humble Attempt* that society
holds enormous significance for Edwards. It has
axiological significance inasmuch as social union has
intrinsic value as "one of the most beautiful and
happy things on earth," with the "whole great society"
of the millennium appearing in "glorious beauty" and
"excellent order"; and it has extrinsic value as
something "agreeable to the nature that God has given
men, disposing them to society." Society has
theological significance inasmuch as forms of it are
the means and end of redemption, viz. the concert of
prayer and millennial society respectively. The
millennium represents the penultimate stage in the
history of redemption[114] and, significantly, it is when
the whole world shall be "united in one amiable
society." The millennial virtues he celebrates as an
incentive for prayer are preeminently social ones. They
include the sanctification of commerce, i.e. "holiness
should be as it were inscribed on everything, on all
men's common business and employments," and of
politics, i.e. "vital piety shall take possession of
thrones and palaces"; church union , i.e. "the church
of God shall not be rent with a variety of jarring
opinions"; and, above all, international accord, i.e.
"the most universal peace, love and sweet harmony," for
in the millennium "the whole earth shall be united as
one holy city, one heavenly family." Edwards, then,

conceives of redemption, as represented by the
millennium, in conspicuously social terms. He also
conceives of the means of redemption socially. Edwards
promulgated the concert for prayer, itself a pious
society, as the indispensable way of ushering in the
millennial age:

> God speaks of himself as standing ready to be
> gracious to his church, and to appear for its
> restoration, and only waiting for such an
> opportunity to bestow this mercy, when he
> shall hear the cries of his people for it,
> that he may bestow it in answer to their
> prayers.[115]

Edwards was greatly distressed at social discord,
particularly and routinely condemning the factionalism
so deeply entrenched in Northampton. In his estimation,
not the least of the benefits of the Great Awakening he
so scrupulously documented was the exorcism of the
party spirit that had bedevilled the town for over a
quarter of a century: "I suppose there has been less
appearance these three or four years past, of that
division of the town into two parties, that has long
been our bane, than has been these thirty years." And
he commends the accord among the townspeople fostered
by the earlier revivals of 1734-35, when they generally
seemed "to be united in dear love and affection one to
another." Edwards hoped that the concert of prayer
would continue the conciliatory work begun by these
revivals.

The Types of Society

Edwards defines "civil union" as "an harmonious
agreement among men in the management of their secular
concerns," and "pious union" as a "sweet agreement in

the great business . . . of religion; the life and soul
of which is love." Edwards' distinction between the two
types of social union is sociologically significant in
three ways: (1) it represents, minimally and obviously,
the most rudimentary kind of social taxonomy; (2) more
profoundly, it represents the fundamental
classification of society as either secular or
religious in type; (3) and less obviously but just as
importantly, it presupposes a theory of social bonding,
of how each type of society is constituted or cemented,
viz. through either natural or cordial consent, and of
how the order or unity of each is mediated, i.e.
through conversation. As we shall see, Edwards'
distinction between pious and civil union, then,
amounts to the first principles of a latent
philosophical sociology.

The Kinds of Consent

Nowhere in *Humble Attempt*, or elsewhere for that
matter, does Edwards make clear the distinct ways in
which the two types of society are constituted, which
is the ground of their distinction. That is, Edwards
does not explain the nature of society in general, or
the nature of religious and of civil society in
particular. However, Edwards does equate social union
with beauty, and pious union with the greater beauty.
This is the clue from which we shall work to Edwards'
theory of the social bond, and thence to the ground of
his distinction between civil and religious society and
his conception of the nature and function of each.
We know from our reading of *Humble Attempt* that
for Edwards "union is one of the most amiable things,

that pertains to human society," or "one of the most
beautiful and happy things on earth." Now latent in
Edwards' equation of social union with beauty, and his
concept of beauty, is a theory of the social bond. In
"The Mind," Edwards defines "beauty" generically as
"the consent of being to being." His corollary to this
is that "the more the consent is, and the more
extensive, the greater is the excellency, [i.e. the
beauty]."[116] Thus, the "beauty of the world consists
wholly of sweet mutual consents."[117] Since social union
is beauty, it too consists of such "mutual consents."
Therefore, society is constituted or unified by consent
among its members; that is, the social bond is consent.
Nagy has already drawn attention to the "social
connotation" of Edwards' category of consent which is
its presupposition of a plurality of beings and their
union. "One alone, without any reference to any more,
cannot be excellent," insists Edwards, "for in such a
case there can be no manner of relation no way, and
therefore, no such thing as consent."[118] Consent is,
for Edwards, "the molecular cement of society,"[119] or
that which binds individual persons into a social unit.
"Agreement" is a synonym for "consent," as in the
"harmonious agreement" constitutive of civil union and
the "sweet agreement" constitutive of pious union.
Other synonyms would be "contract" and "covenant."
Thus, the social contract would be an instance of the
"harmonious agreement among men in the management of
their secular concerns," and the covenant of grace
would be an instance of their "sweet agreement in the
great business . . . of religion."

Now Edwards declares in *Humble Attempt*, "A civil
union..., is amiable; but *much more* [italics mine]

a pious union." Indeed, he esteems millennial society,
a paradigm of pious union, as "'the perfection of
beauty.'"[120] Furthermore, he characterizes as
"harmonious" the agreement formative of civil union,
but as "sweet" that of pious union. This suggests a
further distinction in Edwards' mind between two kinds
of beauty, or consent, corresponding to his distinction
between the two types of social union, thereby
promising further to enrich our account of Edwards'
theory of the social bond and to clarify his
distinction between civil and religious society.

We find in *True Virtue* that Edwards does in fact
distinguish between two kinds of beauty that can belong
to society. "There is a beauty of order in society," he
says, "besides what consists in benevolence, or can be
referred to it, which is of the secondary kind." This
secondary kind of beauty in society is exemplified
"when the different members of society have all their
appointed office, place and station, according to their
several capacities and talents, and every one keeps his
place, and continues in his proper business." He
considers this "beauty of order in society" essentially
an aesthetic beauty, of the same kind as the beauty of
order in architecture:

> In this there is a beauty, not of a different
> kind from the regularity of a beautiful
> building, or piece of skilful architecture,
> where the strong pillars are set in their
> proper place, the pilasters in a place fit
> for them, the square pieces of marble in the
> pavement, the panels, partitions, and
> cornices, etc. in places proper for them.[121]

Edwards defines secondary beauty as "a mutual consent
and agreement of different things, in form, manner,
quantity, and visible end or design; called by the

various names of regularity, order, uniformity,
symmetry, proportion, harmony, etc."[122] Material things
can thus consent or agree no other way, according to
Edwards, "but by equality, or by likeness, or by
proportion."[123] He cites as further examples of
secondary beauty "the mutual consent of the different
parts of the periphery of a circle," or "the beautiful
proportion of the various parts of a human body or
countenance," or "the sweet mutual consent and
agreement of the various notes of a melodious tune."[124]

There is accord between Edwards' theory of
secondary beauty and the aesthetic theories of
Hutcheson and Berkeley.[125] Edwards notes that his
theory is "the same that Mr. Hutchinson [sic]...,
expresses by uniformity in the midst of variety."
Hutcheson's theory, according to Edwards, is that
beauty

> is no other than the consent or agreement of
> different things in form, quantity, etc. He
> observes, that the greater the variety is in
> equal uniformity the greater the beauty.
> Which is no more than to say, the more there
> are of different mutually agreeing things,
> the greater is the beauty.[126]

Edwards' theory also subsumes Berkeley's theory of
beauty as utility. He remarks that "the beauty which
consists in the visible fitness of a thing to its use"
is not distinct from that consisting in consent:

> The answerableness of a thing to its use is
> only the proportion and fitness of a cause or
> means to a visibly designed effect, and so an
> effect suggested to the mind by the idea of
> the means. This kind of beauty is not
> entirely different from that beauty which
> there is in fitting a mortice to its tenon.

Edwards, moreover, analyzes utility into a "twofold"
agreement or consent, or a "double" beauty: the
agreement between means and end, and the agreement
among the means as having a common end:

> When the beauty consists in unity of design,
> or the adaptness of a variety of things to
> promote one intended effect, in which all
> conspire, as the various parts of an
> ingenious complicated machine, there is a
> double beauty, as there is a twofold
> agreement and conformity. First, there is the
> agreement of the various parts to the
> designed end. Secondly, through this designed
> end or effect, all the various particulars
> agree one with another as the general medium
> of their union, whereby they, being united in
> this third, are all united one to another.[127]

Edwards' formula for secondary or aesthetic beauty,
then, enables him to synthesize the ostensibly
incompatible formulae of Hutcheson and Berkeley by
disclosing not only their compatibility but also their
fundamental relatedness.

Thus, as consent or agreement, the secondary
beauty of society consists in good order--or unity in
variety--and utility, and might be analyzed on Edwards'
principles into the following relations: (a)
correspondence, or the agreement of aptitude to
function; (b) *expediency*, or the agreement of function
to end; (c) *complementariness*, or the agreement among
various functions with respect to some end; (d)
adaptation, or the joint agreement of several functions
to some common end or ends, and thereby to each other.

However, there can be another kind of beauty in
society, according to Edwards, which "consists in
benevolence." This he calls "primary" beauty to
distinguish it from secondary. Edwards defines primary
beauty as love: "all the primary and original beauty

. . . that is among minds is love."[128] He regards love
as *primary* beauty since it is moral beauty, which is
unique and appropriate to persons who, as moral and
spiritual beings, are the crown and end of created
being:

> The union or propensity of minds to mental or
> spiritual existence, may be called the
> highest and primary beauty; being the proper
> and peculiar beauty of spiritual and moral
> beings, which are the highest and first part
> of the universal system, for whose sake all
> the rest has existence.[129]

Edwards considers the two kinds of beauty--primary
and secondary--as distinct but similar. Secondary or
aesthetic beauty is the analogue or image of primary or
archetypal beauty; something is aesthetically beautiful
only so far as it mirrors moral beauty: "It is
sufficient that he [God] makes an agreement of
different things, in their form, manner, measure, etc.
to appear beautiful, because here is some image of an
higher kind of agreement and consent of spiritual
beings."[130] Again,

> It has pleased him [God] to establish a law
> of nature, by virtue of which the uniformity
> and mutual correspondence of a beautiful
> plant, and the respect which the various
> parts of a regular building seem to have one
> to another, and their agreement and union,
> and the consent or concord of the various
> notes of a melodious tune, should appear
> beautiful; *because therein is some image of
> the consent of mind, of the different members
> of a society or system of intelligent beings,
> sweetly united in a benevolent agreement of
> heart.* (Italics mine.)[131]

Edwards observes in "The Mind" how something, insofar
as it exhibits secondary beauty, seems to embody a mind
of its own thereby suggesting primary beauty:

> Sensible things, by virtue of the harmony and
> proportion that is seen in them, carry the
> appearance of perceiving and willing being.
> They evidently show at first blush the action
> and governing of understanding and volition.
> The notes of a tune or the strokes of an
> acute penman, for instance, are placed in
> such exact order, having such mutual respect
> one to another, that they carry with them
> into the mind of him that sees or hears the
> conception of an understanding and will
> exerting itself in these appearances. And
> were it not that we, by reflection and
> reasoning, are led to an extrinsic
> intelligence and will that was the cause, it
> would seem to be in the notes and strokes
> themselves. *They would appear like a society
> of so many perceiving beings, sweetly
> agreeing together.* (Italics mine.)[132]

Similarly, the sweetly concordant notes in music

> are so conformed and have such proportion one
> to another that they seem to have respect one
> to another, as if they loved one another. So
> the beauty of figures and motions is, when
> one part has such consonant proportion with
> the rest as represents a general agreeing and
> consenting together; *which is very much the
> image of love in all the parts of a society
> united by a sweet consent and charity of
> heart.* (Italics mine.)[133]

Alluding to Hutcheson's formulation, Edwards explains
that secondary beauty mirrors primary "because by that
uniformity diverse things become as it were one."
Union, then, is for Edwards the essence of beauty, the
dynamic of which is consent. And "the union of
spiritual beings in a mutual propensity and affection
of heart" is more real than the analogous union of
material things.[134]

It is highly significant of the prominence of the
idea of society in Edwards' thought, and particularly
of his esteem for social union, that in the quotations

above he should virtually identify primary beauty with a kind of society. There Edwards variously compares instances of secondary beauty with "a society of so many perceiving beings, sweetly agreeing together"; to "a society or system of intelligent beings, sweetly united in a benevolent agreement of heart"; and to "the parts of a society united by a sweet consent and charity of heart."

Edwards considers primary beauty superior to secondary beauty in two ways: (a) It is superior in *kind*, inasmuch as it is the archetype or original of which secondary beauty is the copy or derivative; it is that in virtue of which there is secondary beauty at all. (b) It is superior in *degree*, insofar as it allows for a complexity well beyond the pale of secondary beauty: "Spiritual harmonies are of vastly larger extent, i.e. the proportions are vastly oftener redoubled, and respect more beings, and require a vastly larger view to comprehend them."[135]

Since beauty for Edwards is consent, his distinction between two kinds of beauty suggests a corresponding distinction between two kinds of consent. Edwards distinguishes between *cordial* and *natural* consent, corresponding to primary and secondary beauty respectively. Cordial consent, which is "consent" in its "prime and proper sense," Edwards describes as an activity of mind--specifically, of its faculty of inclination. It is a being inclined towards or an approving of something--either a person, in which case it is love, or an impersonal object, in which case it is choice: "There is no other proper consent but that of minds, even of their will; which, when it is of minds towards minds, it is love, and when of minds

114

towards other things it is choice."[136] Such consent is
cordial inasmuch as it involves "the will, disposition,
or affection of the heart." The cordial consent in love
"consists in concord and union of mind and heart."[137]

Natural consent, on the other hand, which is
"consent" in its figurative sense, Edwards describes as
simply any kind of agreement or unity, either within or
among things, involving no exercise of the will or
feeling. Natural consent consists "only in uniformity
and consent of nature, form, quantity, etc." Edwards
cites as an example the consent, or quantitative and
formal agreement, between and within a pair of
congruent equilateral triangles. Natural consent is
analogous to cordial consent but is "entirely a
distinct thing"[138] because "the will, disposition, or
affection of the heart" has no concern in it.

Cordial consent, then, makes for a voluntary or
cordial union, i.e. a "union of mind and heart,"
whereas natural consent makes for a nonvoluntary or
natural union, i.e. any "uniformity and consent of
nature, form, quantity, etc." Now cordial consent *qua*
love, as the "concord and union of mind and heart,"
obviously corresponds to and makes for primary beauty,
which is "the union or propensity of minds to mental or
spiritual existence." Whereas natural consent, as the
"uniformity and consent of nature, form, quantity,
etc." obviously corresponds to and makes for secondary
beauty, which is the "mutual consent and agreement or
different things, in form, manner, quantity, and
visible end or design."

Edwards' distinction between primary and secondary
beauty, particularly as exemplified in society, enables
us to identify the kind of beauty exhibited by each

type of social union, and to determine why the beauty
of pious union is superior to that of civil union. The
beauty of civil union, as the "harmonious agreement
among men in the management of their secular concerns,"
is the "beauty of order in society" or secondary
beauty. Whereas the beauty of pious union, as their
"sweet agreement" in religion, "the life and soul of
which is love," is "what consists in benevolence" or
primary beauty. Consequently, pious union, as primary
beauty, is superior in kind and degree to civil union,
as secondary beauty. Furthermore, Edwards' distinction
between cordial and natural consent, which are
definitive of the two kinds of beauty, enables us to
describe how each type of social union is constituted,
and thereby to understand the ground of Edwards'
distinction between pious and civil union. Thus, a
pious union or society, as primary beauty, is
constituted by the cordial consent of benevolent love,
i.e. "concord and union of mind and heart." Whereas
civil union or society, as secondary beauty, is
constituted by natural consent, i.e. "uniformity and
consent of nature, form, quantity, etc." Edwards'
distinction between the two types of social union,
then, is based on the difference between the modes of
consent from which they emerge.

   We have exposed the theory of social bonding
embedded in Edwards' equation of social union with
beauty and his esteem of pious union as the greater
beauty, and can now formulate it as follows: Consent is
constitutive of any social union or society. In virtue
of "the consent of being to being," or their agreement,
they are one; from their consent emerges a social
aggregate. Cordial consent, when "of minds towards

minds," is constitutive of a pious union or religious society. In virtue of their mutual love, persons are truly one; from their cordial consent emerges a pious society. Natural consent is constitutive of a civil union or secular society. In virtue of the uniformity or regularity of the social order, as "when the different members of society have all their appointed office," the constituents of secular society--such as persons and roles--are functionally one, a natural union analogous to cordial union; from their natural consent emerges a civil society. Cordial consent is the "molecular cement" of a pious society. Natural consent is the "molecular cement" of a civil society. These principles of social cohesion can be more clearly differentiated as follows: Cordial consent, as the benevolent "union of mind and heart," is a consent (union) among *persons*; whereas natural consent, as the "uniformity and consent of nature, form, quantity, etc.," is a consent (union) among the *roles* of persons, and between these functions, as means, and certain ends.

In differentiating the kinds of consent and types of society emerging from them, we are not suggesting that cordial consent is constitutive only of pious society. It is equally constitutive of civil society. There is, however, a difference between the cordial consent formative of pious society and that formative of civil society. Edwards distinguishes between the cordial consent "of minds towards minds," or *love*, and that "of minds towards other things," or *choice*. Thus the cordial consent formative of civil society is choice--all the myriad political, legal and economic choices that are the dynamic of social life. Nor are we

suggesting that natural consent is not constitutive in
some way of pious society. Millennial society, as
Edwards envisions it, would undoubtedly exhibit, in its
commerce and politics, the good order and regularity
distinctive of a successful secular society. We might,
then, distinguish pious and civil society, according to
the mode of their union, in this way: Though each type
of society is constituted by both kinds of consent, one
of them predominates and is essential. Thus, cordial
consent *qua* love predominates and is essential for
pious society, though not for civil society in which
cordial consent *qua* choice and natural consent
predominate and are essential.

Conversation

Edwards does not discuss explicitly how social
bonding is expressed and maintained, or mediated.
Indeed, he does not even discuss explicitly the social
bond as such. However, just as we were able to show
that Edwards has a theory of social bonding embedded in
his equation of social union with beauty, and of beauty
with consent, we can likewise show that he has an
implicit theory of how the social bond is mediated,
which complements his theory of social bonding.
According to Edwards, then, if the social bond is
consent, then its medium is what he calls
"conversation."

Conversation is discussed in passing in the eighth
chapter, "On the Medium of Moral Government--
particularly Conversation," of Edwards' *Miscellaneous
Observations on Important Theological Subjects*; in the
first chapter, "Of God's Moral Government," of his

Remarks on Important Theological Controversies; and in
the fifth chapter, "Heaven," of his *Miscellaneous
Observations*. In these chapters, Edwards makes some
suggestive comments about symbols' being the
indispensable medium of human culture. The
philosophical sociology of these texts, then,
reinforces and complements that of *Humble Attempt* and
so they are invaluable in our explication of Edwards'
social theory.

Edwards defines "conversation" as "intelligent
beings expressing their minds one to another, in words,
or other signs intentionally directed to us for our
notice, whose immediate and main design is to be
significations of the mind of him who gives them."[139]
Conversation presupposes consent while manifesting it
for "in maintaining communication or converse, one must
yield to the other, must comply with the other; there
must be *union of wills*; one must be clothed with
authority, the other with submission."[140] (Italics
mine.) And the "union of wills" manifest in such
mutuality is none other than cordial consent. According
to Edwards, conversation is the medium of consent and
so of social union. It mediates, i.e. expresses and
maintains, the social and moral order. Edwards,
significantly, virtually identifies conversation and
union, as in this passage on the incarnation and faith:

> For, Christ being united to the human nature,
> we have advantage for a far more intimate
> union and conversation with him than we could
> possibly have had if he had remained only in
> the divine nature. So, we being united to a
> divine person, can in him have more intimate
> union and conversation with God the Father,
> who is only in the divine nature, than
> otherwise possibly could be.

Or in this one on the communion of the apostles (and,
by implication, all the elect) in heaven: "The
conversation of Christ's disciples in heaven shall in
many respects be vastly more intimate than it was when
Christ was upon earth; . . . for in heaven the union
shall be perfected."[141]

Conversation is the medium of social union. "The
special medium of union and communication of the
members of the society, and the being of society as
such," maintains Edwards, "is conversation."[142] It is
"the great medium of social concerns,"[143] and he
understands that "the affairs of . . . social union
cannot well be maintained without conversation."[144]
Edwards cites as evidence that conversation is the
necessary medium of the social order the fact that it
is the necessary medium of friendship, which he thinks
the ultimate purpose of society:

> The need of conversation in order properly to
> support and carry on the concerns of *society*,
> may well appear, by considering the need of
> it for answering all the purposes of
> *friendship*, which is one of the main concerns
> of society, in some respects the main social
> concern, and the end of all the rest.[145]

Indeed, conversation is especially essential to
friendship of any social concern:

> Friendship, above all other things that
> belong to society, requires conversation. It
> is what friendship most naturally and
> directly desires. By conversation, not only
> is friendship maintained and nourished, but
> the felicity of friendship is tasted and
> enjoyed.

For Edwards, significantly, "the well-being and
happiness of society is friendship. It is the highest
happiness of all moral agents." And friendship with God

is the chief beatitude of a pious society and
especially requires conversation:

> The happiness of God's moral kingdom
> consists, in an inferior degree, in the
> members' enjoyment of each other's
> friendship; but infinitely more in the
> enjoyment of their Head. Therefore, here
> especially, and above all, is conversation
> requisite.[146]

Friendship with God elicits prayer, our mode of
conversation with him:

> Sincere friendship towards God, . . . , does
> most apparently, directly, and strongly
> incline to prayer; and it no less disposes
> the heart strongly to desire to have our
> infinitely glorious and gracious Friend
> expressing his mind to us by his word, that
> we may know it.[147]

Inasmuch as for Edwards conversation is the medium
of the social order, it is equally the medium of the
moral order: "the *moral* world, and the *conversible*
world, are the same thing."[148] The moral order
presupposes the social: "The *ground* of moral
behaviour, and all moral government and regulation, is
society, or mutual intercourse and social regards."[149]
He equates moral agency with social agency, and regards
moral concerns as preeminently social ones: "Moral
agents are *social* agents; affairs of morality are
affairs of society."[150] Consequently, moral affairs,
being social, must similarly be mediated through
conversation: "Especially do we find conversation
proper and requisite between intelligent creatures
concerning *moral* affairs, . . . ; affairs wherein
especially moral agents are concerned, as joined in
society, and having union and communion one with
another."[151]

Inasmuch as conversation is the medium of social
union in general, in particular it is the medium of
civil union or the political order which for Edwards
consists of the interactions between governors and the
governed: "Moral government in a society is a *social*
affair; wherein consists the intercourse between
superior and inferior constituents, between that which
is original, and that which is dependent, directing and
directed in the society."[152] Edwards considers
conversation necessary for the union between governors
and governed:

> It is needful in a moral kingdom, . . .--that
> there should be conversation between the
> governors and governed. It is requisite that
> the former should have intercourse with the
> latter in a way agreeable to their nature;
> that is, by way of *voluntary signification* of
> their mind to the governed, as the governed
> signify their minds voluntarily one to
> another.[153]

And, conversation is especially necessary between them
because their vertical union is tighter and more
crucial than the horizontal union among the citizens
themselves:

> The head of the society, so far as it is
> united with it on a *moral* ground, is a social
> head. The head belongs to the society, as the
> natural head belongs to the body. And the
> union of the members with the head is
> greater, stricter, and more important, than
> one with another. And if their union with
> other members of the society require
> conversation, much more their greater union
> with the head.[154]

The connection between conversation and civil union is
such that when the latter is sundered the necessity of
conversation is obviated:

> If a particular member of the society were
> wholly cut off, and ceases to be of the
> society--the union being entirely broken--the
> argument for conversation, the great medium
> of social concerns, ceases. So, if the body
> be cut off from the head, or be entirely
> disunited from it, intercourse ceases.[155]

Political conversation, according to Edwards, is
mediatory inasmuch as it consists in the following: On
the part of the governors, it consists, first, in their
proclaiming to the governed the laws and regulations of
the society: "the mind of the rulers should be declared
as to the rules, measures, and methods, to be observed
by the society."[156] Second, it consists in their
enforcing these edicts by promises of rewards and
threats of punishment, inasmuch as promising and
threatening need to be verbally expressed:

> The ruler should enforce the rules of the
> society, by threatening just punishments, and
> promising the most suitable and wise rewards.
> But, without word or voluntary declaration,
> there is no threatening or promising in the
> case, in a proper sense.

And, third, conversation on the part of the governors
consists in their declaring the rationale and purposes
of their policies: "The designs and ends of government
should be made known; it should be visible what is
aimed at."[157] Both the *general* end of government, or
the ultimate end of the government as a whole (the
common good), and its *particular* ends, or the
penultimate ends of its various branches (the ends of
domestic and foreign policy) require declaration:

> It is needful, not only that the general end,
> *viz.* the public good, should be known, but
> also, the particular design of many of the
> principal parts of the administration, among
> which we may reckon the main negociations
> [*sic*], treaties, and changes of affairs, the

> cause and end of wars engaged in, the ground
> of treaties of peace and commerce, the design
> of general revolutions in the state of the
> kingdom, &c.

On the part of the governed, political conversation
consists in their expressing their concurrence with the
civil laws and regulations, either their consent to or
dissent from public policies, their happiness with the
merits of the government, and their respect for the
governors, thereby legitimating and vindicating the
political order. This can be inferred from what Edwards
says about a society in which the governors do *not*
signify their minds to the governed, or make known or
visible their laws, policies, and ends:

> The members have no opportunity to consent or
> concur, to approve or disapprove, to rejoice
> in the goodness, wisdom, and benefit of the
> administration, and to pay proper regards to
> those in whose hands the government is, &c.
> These things are necessary for the
> establishment and confirmation of the
> government.[158]

The necessity of conversation as the medium of
political union, i.e. of the consent between governors
and governed, is implied, according to Edwards, not
only by politics being a social affair, but also by
its very nature. Politics, by definition, concerns
moral agents; and moral agents are beings having
understanding and will, enabling them to act
intentionally and voluntarily. Thus, the governing of
them *qua* moral agents consists in influencing their
wills by informing their understandings:

> The moral government of a society, in the
> very nature of it, implies, and consists in,
> an application to their understandings, in
> directing the intelligent will, and in

enforcing the direction by the declaration made.[159]

Moral government is moral, for Edwards, only so far as it is visible; that is, the governors make known their minds, enabling the governed voluntarily to reply, and thereby making possible the conversation between them:

> The order of government serves to maintain authority, and to influence and rule the subject morally, no further than it is visible. . . . How absurd is it to suppose, that there should be converse and moral government maintained between the head and subjects, when both are intelligent, voluntary agents, without a voluntary communication of minds and expressions, thoughts and inclinations, between the head and the members of the society![160]

Moreover, Edwards considers that the visibility of civil government is necessary for revealing the government's virtue and merit, thereby raising the morale of the individual members of society, and benefiting society as a whole. Thus, "in order to the wisdom, righteousness, and goodness of the administration being properly visible--so far as is requisite for encouraging and animating of the subject, and in order to the suitable convenience, satisfaction, and benefit of the whole society of intelligent agents,"[161] the government's judicial and economic policies and ends must be made public.

Finally, conversation, as the medium of social union in general, is of course the medium of pious union. Now a pious society is both a "vertical" union between God and his people, i.e. "a society that have God for their King, united to them as the Head of the society,"[162] and a "horizontal" union among its members. Conversation mediates the union between God

and man, and consists in revelation on God's part and
prayer on man's:

> Conversation between God and mankind in this
> world, is maintained by God's *word* on his
> part, and by *prayer* on ours. By the former,
> he speaks and expresses his mind to us; by
> the latter, we speak and express our minds to
> him.[163]

And conversation mediates the union of the pious
themselves. Thus, the members of millennial society
will "sweetly correspond one with another as brethren,"
meaning that they "will be abundant in expressing their
love to one to another, not only in words, but in deeds
of charity."[164] The pious enjoy immensely their
conversation. In heaven,

> They shall have great delight in the society
> and enjoyment of one another. We now do not
> know what enjoyment they will have in
> conversing together, and in communicating
> with each other; but doubtless it will be far
> more perfect than any we have now.[165]

The necessity of conversation as the medium of
pious union, i.e. of the conversation between God and
his people, and among his people themselves, it
demonstrated, according to Edwards, by the ends of
redemption, the incarnation, and the creation of man;
and by the fact of God's moral government in the world,
and the nature of the happiness in God's Kingdom. The
end of redemption is the union of mankind with the
Godhead: "This was the design of Christ, to bring to
pass that he, and his Father, and his people, might be
brought to a most intimate union and communion."[166]
The end of the incarnation, the mode of redemption, was
conversation between man and God. "Christ took on him
man's nature for this end, that he might be under
advantage for a more familiar conversation than the

infinite distance of the divine nature would allow of."[167] And the end of man is conversation with God: "the special end for which God has made man, is something wherein he has intercourse with his Creator, as an intelligent, voluntary agent." This is suggested by his capacity for intentional and voluntary behavior:

> The greatest thing that men are capacitated
> for, by their faculties..., is, that
> they are capable of having intercourse with
> their Creator, as intelligent and voluntary
> agents. They are capable of . . . receiving
> instructions and commands from him, and
> capable of obeying and serving him.[168]

This union, then, between God and mankind, which is the end of redemption, is mediated by conversation, the end of the incarnation and of man. In addition, God governs men morally, thereby requiring conversation with them: "God does take care that a good moral government should be maintained over men; that his intelligent, voluntary acts should be all subject to rules; and that with respect to them all, he should be the subject of judicial proceeding."[169] Thus, conversation is as essential to divine government as to human:

> On the supposition, that God has a moral
> kingdom in the world...; in what
> darkness must the affairs of this moral
> kingdom be carried on, without a
> communication between the head and the body;
> the ruler never making himself known to the
> society by any word, or other equivalent
> expression whatsoever, either by himself, or
> by any mediators, or messengers![170]

Edwards' Socio-Political Theory

We are now in a position to start formulating what amounts to a distinctively Edwardsean social and political theory. As we do so, in order better to

understand and appreciate Edwards' own sociological
insights, we shall compare them with the more explicit
sociological concepts of later, classic sociologists
whom he seems to anticipate. The elements of his social
theory which we so far have explicated from *Humble
Attempt* and other, complementary texts, are as follows:

1. A rudimentary and very fundamental social
typology represented by the distinction between a
pious union and a civil union.

2. A conception of the social bond as consent, and
a conception of the different kinds of consent,
viz. cordial and natural, as the ground of the
typology of society.

3. An explanation of the medium of the social bond
in terms of conversation.

4. A theory of utopia in the idea of social union
as a supreme good:

    a. Of a pious union as primary (superior)
    beauty;

    b. Of a civil union as secondary (inferior)
    beauty;

    c. Of a pious union as both the means (the
    concert of prayer) and an end (millennial
    society) of redemption.

The first element above, Edwards' distinction
between pious and civil union, represents a distinction
between religious and secular society. This is a
classic distinction. It intimates Weber's quite similar
distinction between *sacred* and *utilitarian* societies,
besides which, according to Durkheim, "there exists no
other example of two categories of things so profoundly
differentiated."[171] "The essence of the sacred,"
according to Nisbet, "lies in its being considered

beyond the criteria of mere utility, human reason, or
power."[172] Edwards seems to evince a sense of this in
his identifying civil union with the beauty of utility,
a form of secondary beauty, and pious union with the
quite distinct primary beauty of benevolence, and
distinguishes them accordingly.

The second element, Edwards' classification of the
types of society according to the mode of consent,
prefigures the seminal social typology of Ferdinand
Tönnies. To see this, let us look briefly at the
latter's classificatory scheme. Tönnies classifies
social groups according to whether they are examples of
what he calls the *Gemeinschaft-* or the *Gesellschaft-*
type.[173] The principal way of bonding in societies of
the *Gemeinschaft* type is through the exercises of the
so-called "essential" or "natural will" (*Wesenwille*)[174]
of man which, in Melvin Rader's words, "embraces all
instincts, impulses, and feelings that are part of the
organic essence of man."[175] The distinctive
characteristics of such societies are as follows: Their
social relationships are vital, affective and personal
and so "characterized by a high degree of cohesion,
communality, and duration in time."[176] Such social
relationships are holistic and inclusive for they are,
as Raymond Plant puts it, "with the whole man, not with
a man under a particular description or acting from
within a particular role."[177] Persons so related
encounter each other primarily as persons, not roles,
and regard one another as ends in and of themselves. In
the *Gemeinschaft*, or authentic community, social bonds
are nurtured for their own sakes. Rader characterizes
this social type as "a social unity of a deeply organic
character, arising out of the instinctive and essential

nature of human beings."[178] Examples, even paradigms, of societies of the *Gemeinschaft*-type are families, clans, friendship groups, and religious sects and communities.

By contrast, the primary way of bonding in societies of the *Gesellschaft*-type is through the exercises of the so-called "rational" or "selective" will (*Kurwille*)[179] of man which is "deliberate purpose." The distinctive characteristics of such societies are as follows: Their social relationships are mechanical, rationalist and impersonal and so less cohesive, intimate and enduring than those of societies of the *Gemeinschaft*-type. Such social relations are segmental and exclusive for they are with "a man under a particular description or acting from within a particular role." Persons so related encounter each other primarily as roles or functions, not as persons, and regard one another as means rather than ends. In the *Gesellschaft*, social bonds are nurtured for things other than themselves; they are selectively formed according to the criteria of efficiency and functionality. Human associations of the *Gesellschaft*-type are formed on the principles of the social contract and self-interest. Rader characterizes this social type as "an artifical social construction expressing some common function, law, intent, or contract,"[180] examples of which are bureaucracies, political parties, labor unions, corporations, and nations.

Edwards' and Tönnies' social typologies, then, are remarkably alike in the following respects: (1) In both schemes, the social bond is conceived of as being either essentially *affective* (as Edwards' cordial

130

consent *qua* love, or as Tönnies' natural will) or
rational (as Edwards' cordial consent *qua* choice and
natural consent, or as Tönnies' rational will) in
nature; and societies are classified according to which
of these types of social bond they principally
exemplify. (2) In each scheme, the affective social
bond is deemed the more primordial, integrative, and
permanent. (3) Finally, in Edwards' pious society or
Tönnies' *Gemeinschaft*, the person *qua* person has
primacy; whereas in Edwards' civil society or Tönnies'
Gesellschaft, abstractions, such as roles or functions,
have primacy.

The third element of Edwards' social theory,
namely, his conception of the indispensable social role
of language, is a presentiment of Weber's theory of
social or *symbolic interaction*. "Symbolic interaction"
is simply a more precise term for social interaction.
It identifies the symbol, or meaning, as what makes
interaction social. According to Weber, an agent acts
socially if, through his interpretation of his act, he
acts with reference to the actions of others: "Action
is social in so far as, by virtue of the subjective
meaning attached to it by the acting individual (or
individuals), it takes account of the behaviour of
others and is thereby oriented in its course."[181] When
agents exchange social actions they are *interacting*
socially. So "social interaction," as defined by
Nisbet,

> is interaction of human beings which is
> mediated by symbols, mutually and incessantly
> interpretative, and, on each side, literally
> responsive to the reactions of the other.
> Social interaction is inseparable from
> *meaning*, meaning endowed by the symbols
> through which the interaction takes place.[182]

Edwards prefigures modern sociological insights into
the nature of symbolic interaction as in the following:

> Social acts are mediated by symbols, symbols
> which we possess in common with others. The
> most obvious and important form of symbol is
> language. It is language, spoken and written,
> above any other symbolic element that makes
> human culture possible.[183]

And, in remarking that "the *moral* world, and the
conversible world, are the same thing," Edwards
recognizes the intimacy between human culture and
symbols. In this too, Edwards anticipates the modern
sociological insight that, as Nisbet expresses it, "at
bottom culture is rooted by and inseparable from what
we call symbolic interaction." Nisbet adopts Edward B.
Tylor's definition of "culture" as "that complex whole
which includes knowledge, belief, art, morals, law,
custom, and any other capabilities *acquired by man as a
member of society.*"[184] In brief, culture, as what is
specific to human beings in their sociality, is what
Edwards means by "moral world."

These four socio-theoretic elements we have
unearthed from *Humble Attempt* and collateral texts can
be synthesized into a social theory. The following
amounts to a *descriptive* theory of society: There are
fundamentally two types of social order--the pious and
the civil. The social bond distinctive and constitutive
of pious society is cordial consent *qua* love, and that
of civil society is cordial consent *qua* choice and
natural consent. Pious society is essentially an
affective and benevolent union of persons founded on
the disinterested love of its members wherein they, as
the objects of the bonding benevolent love, have
primacy as ends in themselves. By contrast, civil

society is essentially a rationalist and functionalist union of persons founded on the self-love of its members. Here, where the objects of cordial consent (*qua* choice) are means and ends, the *roles* of persons have primacy, and persons themselves are regarded as means. The social bond is mediated, i.e expressed and maintained, by conversation, the medium of the entire moral order. The end of pious society is communion with God, and that of civil society is the expeditious realization of political and economic ends.

The following amounts to a *normative* theory of society: Pious society, as primary beauty and both the means and the penultimate goal of redemption, is the ideal society. However, the social ideal represented by millennial society will not be ushered in until the millennium. The Christian utopia ever remains an eschatological hope, not to be fulfilled outside the eschaton. As such, it is the absolute standard against which to evaluate any historical society, and thereby serves as a principle of social criticism.

In addition, there seem to be some noteworthy elements of a political theory, coordinate with his social theory, latent in Edwards' discussion of the necessity of conversation to mediate the union between the governors and the governed in civil society. One is that the political order is essentially hierarchical and complex, its parts being involved in a dynamic and harmonious interplay: "Moral government . . . consists [in] the intercourse between superior and inferior constituents, between that which is original, and that which is dependent, directing and directed in the society."

A second element is the idea of the contract[185] as being foundational to the civil order; and a third, related element, is the doctrine that the consent of the governed is required for legitimating political authority. Allusions to both these elements appear to be made in Edwards' statement that the citizens' "opportunity to consent" is "necessary for the establishment and confirmation of the government."

A fourth element of political theory is the need of an ongoing political dialogue between people and their leaders, with its implication of the need of the citizenry's participating in the political process. This is evinced in Edwards' saying, "there should be conversation between the governors and governed." And, interestingly, a by-product of this political dialogue is a special kind of civic happiness. Edwards thinks that such dialogue gives the citizens the opportunity to "rejoice in the goodness, wisdom, and benefit of the administration."

A fifth element is the intriguing possibility of a visible "civic beauty,"[186] as it were, superadded to the social beauty of a well-ordered civil society, through the cordial consent of the people to "the goodness, wisdom and benefit of the administration."

Finally, a sixth element of political theory is that citizens are to be treated as persons, as dignified beings with minds, and that the art of *moral* politics is the art of persuasion by appeals to reason. Thus Edwards says, "moral government . . . consists in, an application to their [citizens'] understandings." This is the opposite of treating citizens as so many pawns to be manipulated and coerced by appeals to their fears or even their appetites. Edwards throughout

evinces a conception of an open political society of
the nature of a republic, or constitutional monarchy,
and potentially a thing of beauty and a source of joy.

CHAPTER III

NOTES

[1]Jonathan Edwards, *An Humble Attempt to Promote Explicit Agreement and Visible Union of God's People in Extraordinary Prayer for the Revival of Religion and the Advancement of Christ's Kingdom on Earth, pursuant to Scripture-Promises and Prophecies concerning the Last Time*, in *The Works of Jonathan Edwards*, ed. by Stephen J. Stein, V (New Haven, 1977), p. 325.

[2]Ibid., p. 326.

[3]Edwards, *Some Thoughts*, in *Works*, IV (New Haven, 1972), p. 520.

[4]Edwards, *Personal Narrative*, in Faust and Johnson, eds. *Jonathan Edwards*, p. 68.

[5]Edwards, *Some Thoughts*, in *Works*, IV (New Haven, 1972), p. 516.

[6]Edwards, *Personal Narrative*, pp. 61, 64.

[7]Edwards, *Humble Attempt*, pp. 357-358.

[8]Rutman, ed., *Great Awakening*, p. 99.

[9]Letter, Jonathan Edwards to Thomas Gillespie, July 1, 1751, printed in *Works*, IV (New Haven, 1972), p. 563.

[10]Miller, "Edwards' Sociology," p. 57.

[11]Letter, Edwards to Gillespie, July 1, 1751, printed in *Works*, IV (New Haven, 1972), 564.

[12]Edwards, *Humble Attempt*, p. 459.

[13]Ibid., pp. 358-359.

[14]Letter, Jonathan Edwards to Benjamin Colman, May 30, 1735, printed in *Works*, IV (New Haven, 1972), p. 103.

[15]Ibid., p. 104.

[16]Letter, Jonathan Edwards to Thomas Prince, Dec. 12, 1743, printed in *Works*, IV (New Haven, 1972), p. 557.

[17]Pfisterer, *Prism of Scripture*, p. 215.

136

[18]Heimert, *American Mind*, p. 100.

[19]Miller, "Edwards' Sociology," p. 57.

[20]Ibid., p. 60.

[21]Ibid., pp. 59-60.

[22]Ibid., p. 59.

[23]Ibid., p. 61.

[24] C. C. Goen, "Editor's Introduction," pp. 31-32.

[25]Edwards, *Some Thoughts*, in *Works*, IV (New Haven, 1972), p. 353.

[26]Ibid., p. 346.

[27]Ibid., p. 353.

[28]Letter, Jonathan Edwards to William McCulloch, March 5, 1743/4, printed in *Works*, IV (New Haven, 1972), pp. 559-560.

[29]Edwards, *Humble Attempt*, p. 354.

[30]Stephen J. Stein, "Editor's Introduction," in *Works*, V (New Haven, 1977), p. 38.

[31]Edwards, *Humble Attempt*, p. 357.

[32]Arthur Fawcett, *The Cambusland Revival: The Scottish Evangelical Revival of the Eighteenth Century* (London, 1971), pp. 20-21.

[33]Nathan Söderblom, Late Archbishop of Upsala, *The Living God: Basal Forms of Personal Religion*, The Gifford Lectures of 1931 (London, 1933), p. 232.

[34]Fawcett, *Cambusland Revival*, pp. 23, 26.

[35]Ibid., p. 17.

[36]Ibid., p. 11.

[37]Edwards, *Humble Attempt*, p. 320.

[38]Ibid., p. 313.

[39]Ibid., p. 314.

[40]Ibid., p. 315.

[41]Ibid., p. 317.

[42]Ibid., p. 318.

[43]Ibid., p. 320.

[44]Ibid., p. 364.

[45]Ibid., pp. 364-365.

[46]Ibid., p. 365.

[47]Ibid., p. 366.

[48]Ibid., p. 365.

[49]Ibid., p. 366.

[50]Ibid., p. 338.

[51]Ibid., p. 339.

[52]Ibid., p. 339.

[53]Ibid., p. 339.

[54]Ibid., p. 340.

[55]Ibid., p. 341.

[56]Ibid., p. 342.

[57]Ibid., p. 344.

[58]Ibid., p. 345.

[59]Ibid., p. 346.

[60]Ibid., p. 367.

[61]Ibid., p. 353.

[62]Ibid., p. 359.

[63]Ibid., p. 370.

[64]Ibid., p. 371.

[65]Ibid., p. 371.

138

66Ibid., p. 374.

67Ibid., p. 375.

68Ibid., p. 372.

69Ibid., pp. 376-377.

70Ibid., p. 377.

71Ibid., p. 378.

72Ibid., p. 377.

73Ibid., pp. 377-378.

74Ibid., p. 378.

75Ibid., p. 379.

76Ibid., p. 394.

77Allen, *Jonathan Edwards*, pp. 233-234.

78Alfred Owen Aldridge, *Jonathan Edwards* (New York, 1964), p. 34.

79Arthur Cushman McGiffert, *Jonathan Edwards* (New York, 1932), p. 102.

80Samuel Miller, *The Life of Jonathan Edwards, President of the College of New Jersey*, in *Library of American Biography*, ed. Jared Sparks, Vol. VIII (New York, 1837), p. 93.

81Miller, *Jonathan Edwards*, p. 198.

82Ibid., p. 320.

83Ibid., p. 321.

84Marcus Darrol Bryant, "America as God's Kingdom," *Religion and Political Society*, ed. and trans. in the Institute of Christian Thought (New York, 1974), p. 79.

85Jonathan Edwards, *An Humble Attempt to Promote Explicit Agreement and Visible Union of God's People in Extraordinary Prayer, For the Revival of Religion and the Advancement of Christ's Kingdom on Earth, pursuant to Scripture Promises and Prophecies Concerning the Last Time*, in *Works of Jonathan Edwards* (Worcester ed.)

(New York: Leavitt and Allen, 1844), III, 463, quoted ibid., p. 79.

[86]Bryant, "America as God's Kingdom," pp. 79-80.

[87]Edwards, *Humble Attempt*, p. 317.

[88]Ibid., p. 318.

[89]Ibid., p. 366.

[90]Jonathan Edwards, *A History of the Work of Redemption, containing the Outlines of a Body of Divinity, including a View of Church History, in a Method Entirely New*, in *The Works of President Edwards*, Burt Franklin: Research and Source Work Series, No. 271, ed. by E. Williams and E. Parsons, V (London, 1817), p. 254.

[91]Ibid., p. 251.

[92]Jonathan Edwards, "Miscellany No. 26," in *The Philosophy of Jonathan Edwards from his Private Notebooks*, ed. by Harvey Gates Townsend (Eugene, Oregon, 1955), p. 207.

[93]Edwards, *Humble Attempt*, p. 365.

[94]Edwards, "Miscellany No. 262," in *Private Notebooks*, p. 208.

[95]Westbrook, "Social Criticism," p. 403.

[96]Conkin, "Jonathan Edwards," p. 71.

[97]Heimert, *American Mind*, p. 100.

[98]Edwards, *Work of Redemption*, p. 253.

[99]Heimert, *American Mind*, p. 80.

[100]Ibid., p. 81.

[101]Ibid., p. 155.

[102]Edwards, *Humble Attempt* pp. 353- 354.

[103]Ibid., p. 359.

[104]Ibid., p. 320.

[105]Bryant, "History and Eschatology," p. 115.

140

[106]Ibid., p. 294.

[107]C. C. Goen, "Jonathan Edwards: A New Departure in Eschatology," *Church History*, XXVIII, No. 1 (1959), pp. 25-40.

[108]Ibid., p. 26.

[109]Heimert, *American Mind*, p. 64.

[110]Stein, "Editor's Introduction," p. 34.

[111]Robert A. Nisbet, *History of The Idea of Progress* (New York, 1980), pp. 195-196.

[112]Goen, "Jonathan Edwards," p. 38.

[113]Edwards, *Humble Attempt*, p. 394.

[114]Stein, "Editor's Introduction," p. 24.

[115]Edwards, *Humble Attempt*, p. 354.

[116]Jonathan Edwards, "The Mind," in *The Works of Jonathan Edwards*, ed. by Wallace Earl Anderson, VI (New Haven, 1980), p. 336.

[117]Jonathan Edwards, "Beauty of the World," in *Works*, VI (New Haven, 1980), p. 305.

[118]Edwards, "The Mind," p. 337.

[119]Nisbet, *Social Bond*, p. 50.

[120]Edwards, *Humble Attempt*, p. 339.

[121]Jonathan Edwards, *The Nature of True Virtue*, ed. by William K. Frankena (Ann Arbor, Michigan 1960), p. 35.

[122]Ibid., p. 28.

[123]Edwards, "The Mind," p. 380.

[124]Edwards, *True Virtue*, p. 28.

[125]A. Owen Aldridge, "Edwards and Hutcheson," *Harvard Theological Review*, XLIV, No. 1 (1951), p. 45.

[126]Edwards, *True Virtue*, p. 28.

127Ibid., p. 29.

128Edwards, "The Mind," p. 362.

129Edwards, *True Virtue*, p. 27.

130Ibid., p. 30.

131Ibid., pp. 30-31.

132Edwards, "The Mind," p. 382.

133Ibid., p. 380.

134Edwards, *True Virtue*, p. 30.

135Edwards, "The Mind," p. 336.

136Ibid., p. 362.

137Edwards, *True Virtue*, p. 31.

138Ibid., p. 31.

139Jonathan Edwards, "On the Medium of Moral Government--Particularly Conversation," *Miscellaneous Observations on Important Theological Subjects, Original and Collected*, in *The Works of President Edwards*, ed. by E. Hickman, II (London, 1834),p. 485,#1.

140Jonathan Edwards, "Concerning God's Moral Government, a Future State, and the Immortality of the Soul," *Remarks on Important Theological Controversies*, in *Works*, II (London, 1834)p. 513, #10.

141Jonathan Edwards, "Heaven," *Miscellaneous Observations* in *Works*, II (London, 1834),p. 624, #571.

142"Medium of Moral Government," p. 486, #8.

143Ibid., p. 487, #13.

144Ibid., p. 486, #7.

145Ibid., p. 486, #10.

146Ibid., p. 486, #8.

147Ibid., p. 486, #9.

148Ibid., p. 486, #7.

[149]Ibid., p. 486, #8.

[150]Ibid., p. 486, #7.

[151]Ibid., p. 486, #6.

[152]Ibid., p. 487, #13.

[153]Ibid., p. 485, #3.

[154]Ibid., p. 486, #7.

[155]Ibid., p. 487, #13.

[156]Ibid., p. 485, #3.

[157]Ibid., p. 485, #3.

[158]Ibid., p. 487, #11.

[159]Ibid., p. 485, #2.

[160]"God's Moral Government," pp. 513-14, #11.

[161]"Medium of Moral Government, p. 487, #11.

[162]Ibid., p. 487, #13.

[163]Ibid., p. 486, #9.

[164]Edwards, *Work of Redemption*, p. 254.

[165]Jonathan Edwards, *The Portion of the Righteous*, in *The Works of President Edwards*, in Works, II (London, 1834),p. 898, #4.

[166]Edwards, "Heaven," p. 624, #571.

[167]Edwards, "Heaven," pp. 623-624, #571.

[168]Edwards, "God's Moral Government," p. 513, #10.

[169]Ibid., p. 511, #3.

[170]Edwards, "Medium of Moral Government," p. 485, #5.

[171]Emile Durkheim, *The Elementary Forms of the Religious Life*, trans. by Joseph Ward Swain (London, 1915), p. 38.

[172]Nisbet, *Social Bond*, p. 236.

[173]Ferdinand Tönnies, *Community and Society (Gemeinschaft and Gesellschaft)*, ed. and trans. by Charles P. Loomis (East Lansing, Michigan, 1957), p. 33.

[174]Charles P. Loomis, "Tönnies, Ferdinand," *The Encyclopedia of Philosophy*, ed. by Paul Edwards, VIII (New York, 1967), p. 150

[175]Melvin Rader, *Ethics and the Human Community* (New York, 1964), p. 388.

[176]Nisbet, *Social Bond*, p. 105.

[177]Raymond Plant, *Community and Ideology: An Essay in Applied Social Philosophy* (London, 1974), p. 23.

[178]Rader, *Ethics*, p. 388.

[179]Loomis, "Tonnies, Ferdinand," p. 150.

[180]Rader, *Ethics*, p. 388.

[181]Max Weber, *The Theory of Social and Economic Organization*, trans. by A. M. Henderson and Talcott Parsons (New York, 1947), p. 88.

[182]Nisbet, *Social Bond*, p. 50.

[183]Ibid., p. 58.

[184]Ibid., p. 59.

[185]Though Edwards speaks quite plainly of political consent and alludes to something like a political contract, his social thought is not fundamentally contractarian, as will be shown in a subsequent chapter. Though he might think civil society is constituted by contract, he does not think pious society is so constituted. Pious society is constituted by the covenant, which is quite distinct from any kind of legal or political contract. Furthermore, Edwards denies the "social atomism" that is the presupposition of contractarian theories of society in the seventeenth and eighteenth centuries.

[186]For a discussion of this possibility see Delattre's, "Beauty and Politics."

CHAPTER IV

AUTHENTIC INDIVIDUALISM: DAVID BRAINERD AND EDWARDS' NORMATIVE THEORY OF CITIZENSHIP

Historical Background

David Brainerd came to Jonathan Edwards' attention
as a rather head-strong young man who had been sent
down from Yale College for impugning the piety of a
tutor, Chauncey Whittelsey, with the remark, "He has no
more grace than this chair."[1] Edwards interceded
(though to no avail) for Brainerd who subsequently
became an intimate of the Edwards family and eventually
the betrothed of Edwards' daughter, Jerusha.

Brainerd did become ordained, and was commissioned
by the Scottish Society for Propagating Christian
Knowledge as a missionary to the Indians. He
consequently spent the remainder of his short life
zealously spreading the gospel among the heathen of New
Jersey and New York. However, he contracted
tuberculosis, a condition exacerbated by the frenetic
pace of his missionizing, and lived out his last days
in the Edwards manse in Northampton. On October 9,
1747, he died in the arms of his nurse, Jerusha.
Shortly thereafter, she herself succumbed to the same
malady and was buried beside him in the town cemetery.

It was fitting, then, that Edwards should have
undertaken to collate, edit, and publish the memoirs of
his son-in-law, whose character and piety he so much
admired, together with commentaries and a brief
biography from his own pen. He regarded Brainerd's
piety or virtue as exemplary of his own ideal. What

146

could have been more appropriate than Edwards' making
public that piety, as documented in Brainerd's literary
remains and in his own glowing testimonials, for the
emulation of others, especially in the dark aftermath
of the Great Awakening? In Edwards' view, Brainerd's
pious example would serve the same purpose as quarterly
public prayer: it would tend to rekindle the embers of
piety in others.

Edward M. Griffin, in tribute to Edwards' talent
for characterization, writes:

> He did not try fiction as such, but his
> accounts in the *Faithful Narrative* of Phebe
> Bartlet and Abigail Hutchinson--prodigies of
> piety during the Northampton awakening--and
> his self-depiction in the *Personal Narrative*
> demonstrate his ability to create
> characters.[2]

Griffin might also have mentioned the *Life of Brainerd*
as similarly attesting Edwards' skill in the art of
creating characters, and Brainerd as a prodigy of piety
worthy of ranking with Phebe and Abigail. Indeed, Ola
E. Winslow has specifically commented on Edwards'
uncanny and graphic characterization of Brainerd:

> Jonathan Edwards . . . in the editorial
> remarks from page to page succeeds amazingly
> in bringing Brainerd to life, clad in all his
> depressing humilities, pieties, and
> unspeakable sufferings. If it is impossible
> to share his admiration for such a man, it is
> at least possible to honor him for the
> portraiture, which, one may suspect, is a
> picture to the life.[3]

Griffin's omitting the *Life of Brainerd* and its subject
is the more surprising since this work describes the
piety of a learned man; however it is indicative of the
obscurity into which this work has fallen, contrasting
with its enormous vogue in the last century as an

evangelical tract that "immortalized the young missionary in the sagas of evangelical Christendom."[4] According to Winslow, through Edwards' edition of his memoirs, Brainerd became "the saintly example of the ideal missionary,"[5] inspiring future generations of emulators:

> In fact, the influence of this *Life and Diary* toward a new era of missionary labor would be hard to measure. Surprisingly enough, it also made the name of David Brainerd better known to the average church-goer of the next generation than the name of Jonathan Edwards.[6]

In fact, one missionary, Hawley, carried a copy of the *Life of Brainerd* in his saddle bag for inspiration and comfort against the days of despair,[7] and another, Henry Martyn, was converted on the occasion of reading this book.[8] Edwards himself, though, would probably have disavowed any intention of having published the book as a manual for missionaries. There is nothing in the record of his own missionizing to suggest that he esteemed the vocation of missionary above all others for its saintliness.[9]

Throughout his life, Edwards was exercised by the perennial question as to the nature of true religion or virtue. He admits this is "a subject on which my mind has been peculiarly intent, ever since I first entered on the study of divinity," and that there is "no question whatsoever, that is of greater importance to mankind."[10] This is corroborated by Samuel Hopkins, Edwards' disciple and first biographer, who writes, "perhaps none has taken more pains, or labored more successfully"[11] over this question of true religion than Jonathan Edwards. And a later commentator, John E.

Smith, has even suggested that the whole of Edwards'
thought might be construed as "one magnificent
answer"[12] to this question.

If Smith is right, then the first sustained and
most systematic stage of Edwards' answer is in his
treatise, *Religious Affections* (1746), and the second
in his dissertation, *True Virtue* (published
posthumously in 1765). In the interim, Edwards changed
his mind as to the nature of piety or virtue. Edwards,
however, was not satisfied merely with theorizing about
it; he was anxious to have it actually lived by people.
Thus, in the preface to the *Life of Brainerd*, Edwards
allows that there are "two ways of representing and
recommending true religion and virtue to the world; the
one, by doctrine and precept; the other, by instance
and example."[13] There is a meticulous description in
the treatise of the characteristics of true piety, i.e.
"the distinguishing notes of that virtue and holiness,
that is acceptable in the sight of God."[14] And there
is in Brainerd's memoirs, as Edwards says, "an
opportunity, as I apprehend, in a very lively instance,
to see the nature of true religion; and the manner of
its operation when exemplified in a high degree and
powerful exercise."[15] Thus, if both *Religious
Affections* and *True Virtue* are about the nature of true
religion or virtue as "doctrine and precept," then the
Life of Brainerd is about it as "instance and example."

Religious Affections and *Life of Brainerd* thus
complement one another; both put, in Hopkins' words,
"the distinction between true and false religion in the
most clear and striking light."[16] More recently,
Winslow has commented that the Brainerd memoirs,
appearing but three years after the treatise,

"naturally furnishes occasional addenda in the same
line of thought" as it. In her view, the concluding
section of the *Life of Brainerd*, which is Edwards'
editorial commentary on the preceding memoirs,
"contains one of the clearest as well as one of the
most eloquent delineations of the Christian's
experience to be found in all his writings."[17]
Religious Affections anatomizes authentic religious
experience and establishes criteria for its
authenticity; the *Life of Brainerd*, on the other hand,
exemplifies it, thereby enriching and fleshing out the
theory of the former text. Edwards' avowed intention in
publishing the *Life of Brainerd* was to promulgate true
piety, as delineated doctrinally and prescriptively in
the treatise, by showing how it was dynamically and
strenuously lived by a particular person.

Edwards had good reasons for wanting to publish a
sterling instance of the vital piety represented and
recommended in *Religious Affections*. Religion in New
England at that time was, as we saw in our previous
chapter, at its nadir. Calvinism, in particular, had
become increasingly and successfully challenged by its
archrival Arminianism. The doctrines of Calvinism were
often presumed, in Edwards' words, "to undermine the
very foundations of all religion and morality, and to
enervate and vacate all reasonable motives to the
exercise and practice of them."[18] The determinism of
Calvinism did not sit well with those who nurtured the
hope of taking human affairs into their own hands and
inaugurating an era of infinite progress. Nor did
evangelicalism, of the sort advocated by Whitefield and
Wesley, escape the opprobrium of mainline churchmen and
rationalists who anathematized it as enthusiasm or

fanaticism. Consequently, the piety espoused by Edwards
in *Religious Affections*, which is thoroughly both
evangelical and Calvinistic, predictably raised the
hackles of Charles Chauncy, the rationalistic cleric of
Boston,[19] who condemned it outright as a defense of
enthusiasm. Even John Wesley, himself an admirer of and
fellow-traveller with Edwards, and who read *Religious
Affections* in the saddle, found it necessary to play
down the Calvinistic tone of the text in his own
expurgated edition of it.[20]

Edwards was quick to emphasize that Brainerd's
piety, though evangelical and from the heart, was far
from enthusiasm, for it was disciplined by the
understanding and based on an "experimental" knowledge,
or direct experience of God:

> His religion did apparently and greatly
> differ from that of many high pretenders to
> religion, who are frequently actuated by
> vehement emotions of mind, and are carried on
> in a course of sudden and strong impressions,
> and supposed high illuminations and immediate
> discoveries, and at the same time are persons
> of a virulent zeal, *not according to
> knowledge.*[21]

Edwards, in fact, abominated enthusiasm no less than
Chauncy, but unlike him considered that religion could
be experiential, vital, emotional and active--in a
word, "experimental"--without being irrational,
hysterical and fanatical. He believed that Brainerd's
example proved it:

> There is indeed such a thing as true
> experimental religion, arising from immediate
> divine influences, supernaturally
> enlightening and convincing the mind, and
> powerfully impressing, quickening,
> sanctifying and governing the heart; which
> religion is . . . of no hurtful consequence
> to human society; notwithstanding there

having been so many pretences and appearances
of what is called experimental vital
religion, that have proved to be nothing but
vain, pernicious enthusiasm.[22]

Edwards takes Brainerd's character and life after
conversion as positive proof that living the
experimental religion outlined in *Religious Affections*
is eminently practicable and beneficial.

Edwards, moreover, saw Brainerd's piety as
vindicating the Calvinist doctrines of grace
underpinning the model of experimental religion
constructed in *Religious Affections*.

So that it is very evident Mr. Brainerd's
religion was wholly correspondent to what is
called the Calvinistical scheme, and was the
effect of those doctrines applied to his
heart: and certainly it cannot be denied that
the effect was good, unless we turn Atheists
or Deists.[23]

According to Edwards, Brainerd underwent "the greatest
moral change that ever he passed under" at the time of
his conversion. Edwards believed that this radical
transformation, bringing with it a "remarkable new
habit and temper of mind, which he held all his life
after," proved the Calvinist principle "that the grace
or virtue of truly good men, not only differs from the
virtue of others in degree, but even in nature and
kind."[24] Edwards challenged the Arminians, who
confidently believed that man had the power within
himself to make such a moral change, to cite an
example, like Brainerd, of one radically changed in his
conversion but whose change is explicable on their
doctrines:

Can the Arminians produce an instance, within
this age, and so plainly within our reach and
view, of such a reformation, such a

transformation of a man, to scriptural
devotion, heavenly-mindedness, and true
Christian morality, in one that before lived
without these things, on the foot of their
principles, and through the influence of
their doctrines?[25]

Edwards thus intended the publication of
Brainerd's memoirs, in the words of Edward Davidson,
"to declare the power and the actuality of the workings
of divine providence in the lives of ordinary men."[26]
However, he seems to have intended something more,
though something not unrelated to his avowed intention
of "representing and recommending true religion." This
has been overlooked by Edwards commentators, which is
hardly surprising since his other purpose is allied to
the neglected Humble Attempt. It seems that Edwards
hoped the memoirs would spur its readers particularly
to emulate Brainerd's concern for the Kingdom of God:

> There is much in the preceding account [the
> memoirs] to excite and encourage God's people
> to earnest prayers and endeavors for the
> advancement and enlargement of the kingdom of
> Christ in the world. Mr. Brainerd gave us an
> excellent example in this respect. He sought
> the prosperity of Zion with all his might. He
> preferred Jerusalem above his chief joy. How
> did his soul long for it, and pant after
> it![27]

Edwards reports that Brainerd strongly advocated the
concert for prayer, and was surprised at people's
laxness in joining it:

> He several times expressed his wonder, that
> there appeared no more forwardness to comply
> with the proposal lately made, in a memorial
> from a number of ministers in Scotland, and
> sent over into America, for united,
> extraordinary prayer, among Christ's
> ministers and people, for the coming of
> Christ's kingdom: and sent it as his dying

advice to his own congregation that they
should practice agreeably to that proposal.[28]

Throughout his diary and journal, Brainerd often
confides his eschatological hope. The following entries
are representative: "This morning I was considerably
refreshed with the thought, yea, the hope and
expectation of the enlargement of Christ's kingdom";[29]
and "O that his kingdom might come in the world; that
they might all love and glorify him, for what he is in
himself."[30] And Edwards actually quotes Brainerd as
saying this to him about his concern for the Kingdom:

> My thoughts have been employed on the old
> dear theme, the prosperity of God's church on
> earth. As I waked out of sleep, I was led to
> cry for the pouring out of God's Spirit, and
> the advancement of Christ's kingdom, which
> the dear Redeemer did [sic] and suffered so
> much for.[31]

However, when Edwards comments that there was much
in Brainerd's memoirs to incite God's people to
"endeavors" for the Kingdom and that "Mr. Brainerd
gives us an excellent example in this respect," he has
more in mind than Brainerd's incessant ruminations and
expatiations upon God's Kingdom. As amply proved by
Edwards' testimony and the memoirs themselves, Brainerd
did more than speak or even pray on behalf of the
Kingdom; he actually acted upon it. Brainerd, writes
Edwards, "sought the prosperity of Zion with all his
might." It was Brainerd's own endeavors, as well as his
prayers, for the Kingdom that Edwards hoped would be
emulated. Among Brainerd's particular endeavors was
enlarging the Kingdom by missionizing to Indians.
Evidently Brainerd believed with Edwards that the elect
were to be found inhabiting even the uncivilized
regions of the world and that God had ordained that his

154

earthly Kingdom would be ushered in only as a response
to the prayers and labors of the faithful. Brainerd
thus understood his purpose as a missionary to be the
"ingathering of God's elect"[32] from among the native
populations of America. That Brainerd regarded this as
his task his memoirs amply attest. In one entry, for
instance, Brainerd typically expresses "some desires of
the enlargement of Christ's kingdom by the conversion
of the Heathen";[33] in another, he confides that he
"desired nothing so much as the conversion of the
Heathen to God, and that his kingdom might come in my
own heart, and the hearts of others";[34] and elsewhere
he relates how he spent a morning "in fervent prayer
for my Indians, that God would set up his kingdom among
them and bring them into his church,"[35] and had cried
"to God for the enlargement of his kingdom in the
world, and in particular among my dear people,"[36] and
praying that God would "set up his kingdom among the
poor Indians in the wilderness."[37] And Edwards himself
attests that this was Brainerd's hope: "He often
expresses great longings for the enlargement of
Christ's kingdom especially by the conversion of the
Heathen to God; and speaks of this hope as all his
delight and joy."[38]

Exposition

The *Life of Brainerd* is actually a five-part
compilation of several texts differing in genre,
authorship and aim--besides a biography, diary and
journal, it includes correspondence, a sermon, and
three short papers on theological topics.[39] Our
exposition of this work takes its form from the

principle laid down by Edwards in his preface that
there are "two ways of representing and recommending
true religion and virtue to the world; the one by
doctrine and precept; the other, by instance and
example." Edwards represents and recommends Brainerd as
an exemplar, not only of the precepts of the earlier
Religious Affections, but also of the quite different
ones of *True Virtue*. The following exposition, then, is
in three sections. The first concerns Brainerd's life
as being exemplary of true religion as defined in the
treatise on religious affections, the second concerns
its being exemplary of true virtue as defined in the
dissertation on virtue, and the third section
identifies the change in Edwards' moral thinking from
the writing of the treatise to that of the
dissertation.

Brainerd as an Exemplar of "True Religion"

Edwards defines true religion in *Religious
Affections* as essentially and summarily "holy love":
"The essence of all true religion lies in holy love;
and that in this divine affection, and an habitual
disposition to it, and that light which is the
foundation of it, and those things which are the fruits
of it, consists the whole of religion."[40] To be holy
and so qualify as the essence of true piety, according
to Edwards, love must be of a certain kind with respect
to its cause, motive and object. It must be the effect
of *saving* grace,[41] or the Holy Spirit's indwelling the
human heart and influencing it from within as "a
principle or spring of new nature and life."[42] As such,
this love is "altogether of a different kind from

anything that men find within themselves by nature, or
only in the exercise of natural principles."[43] Holy
love must be disinterested; that is, its primary motive
must not be a form of self-interest, such as gratitude
or the expectation of some future reward or punishment,
but rather the transcendental excellence of God's
nature: "The first objective ground of gracious
affections, is the transcendentally excellent and
amiable nature of divine things, as they are in
themselves; and not any conceived relation they bear to
self, or self-interest."[44] There is nothing holy about
self-interest for it is a "principle entirely natural,
and as much in the hearts of devils as angels."[45]
However, self-interest may serve as a *secondary* motive
of holy love: "The saint's affections [e.g. love]
begin with God; and self-love has a hand in these
affections consequentially, and secondarily only."[46]
Its disinterestedness is a sign that love is indeed the
effect of saving grace. Finally, holy love has as its
primary object the moral goodness of the beloved: "Holy
persons, . . . love divine things primarily for their
holiness: they love God, in the first place, for the
beauty of his holiness or moral perfection."[47]

Edwards believed Brainerd truly religious since he
thought him animated to a high degree by this holy
love. His love was the effect of saving grace for it
apparently sprang from "a change of nature, a change of
the abiding habit and temper of his mind." It was
disinterested for "his love to God was primarily and
principally for the supreme excellency of his own
nature, and not built on a preconceived notion that God
loved him, had received him into favor, and had done
great things for him, or promised great things to him."

Lastly, Brainerd's love had as its primary object God's
moral goodness or holiness: "That beauty, that sort of
good, which was the great object of the new sense of
his mind, the new relish and appetite given him in
conversion, and thenceforward maintained and increased
in his heart, was holiness."[48]

Brainerd as an Exemplar of "True Virtue"

Edwards defines "true virtue" in his dissertation
on the subject as *benevolence to being in general*," or
"that consent, propensity and union of heart to being
in general, which is immediately exercised in a general
good will."[49] By "being in general," says Edwards, "I
thereby mean intelligent being in general. Not
inanimate things, or beings that have no perception or
will."[50] Being in general, then, comprises all sentient
beings--men, angels and God--who are capable of acting
intentionally.

Now Edwards distinguishes *benevolence* from
complacence. Benevolence is "that affection or
propensity of the heart to any being, which causes it
to incline to its well-being, or disposes it to desire
and take pleasure in its happiness." In other words, it
is love, or the disposition thereto, of a person for
his own sake, and expressed in promoting and enjoying
his welfare. Complacence, on the other hand, is
"delight in beauty,"[51] and it is love, or the
disposition thereto, of a person for his moral beauty
or virtue, rather than for himself. Edwards'
distinction between these two kinds of love can be put
this way: The primary motive or object in benevolence
is the good of another (though it is effectually one's

own as well), whereas the primary motive or object in
complacence is one's own good, i.e. pleasure, *alone*.

Benevolence, in Edwards' analysis, has two
motives or objects: being as such and moral beauty. Its
primary motive or object is being *qua* being: "The first
object of a virtuous benevolence is being, simply
considered." From this Edwards derives two corollaries.
The first is that all being, or general being, is the
principal object of benevolence: "If being, simply
considered, be its object, then being in general is its
object."[52] And the second corollary is that the degree
of benevolence owed a being should be apportioned to
its degree of being, such that the greater the quantity
of being (other things being equal) the greater the
benevolence owed it: "Further, if *being*, simply
considered, be the first object of a truly virtuous
benevolence, then that object who [apparently] has most
of being [caeteris paribus]..., will have the
greatest share of the propensity and benevolent
affections of the heart." By "degree of being" Edwards
understands degree of mental capacity. He equates
intellectual and volitional capacity with being, such
that the more there is of mind the more existence.
Insofar as a being has "a greater capacity and power,
greater understanding, every faculty and every positive
quality in a higher degree" than another, it has
greater existence or being. Thus, "an archangel must be
supposed to have more existence," says Edwards, "than a
worm."[53] So in his second corollary, Edwards is
correlating desert of benevolence with (more precisely)
degree of mental power.

The secondary motive or object of benevolence is
moral beauty, which is benevolence itself, in the being

beloved for his own sake: "A secondary ground of pure
benevolence is virtuous benevolence itself in its
object."[54] But insofar as benevolence has moral beauty
as its object, it is complacence. In other words, love
motivated by the benevolence or virtue of the beloved
is complacence. However, Edwards makes it clear that in
the case of benevolence "being, simply considered" is
logically prior to "virtuous benevolence" as its motive
or object. He gives two reasons for this. First,
benevolence cannot be primarily from gratitude for or
gratification in a person for his benevolence; to
suppose so is to beg the question as to what that
benevolence is in the first place that is so beloved.
To answer that it too is love for benevolence, or
benevolence to benevolence, is to precipitate an
infinite regress:

> If virtue consists primarily in love to
> virtue, then virtue, the thing loved, is the
> love of virtue: so that virtue must consist
> in the love of the love of virtue--and so on
> in infinitum. It is absurd to say, that
> virtue is primarily and first of all the
> consequence of itself; which makes virtue
> primarily prior to itself.[55]

Second, complacence "necessarily arises from pure
benevolence to being in general, and comes to the same
thing."[56] Edwards explains that we naturally approve or
are pleased by dispositions in others like our own:

> For he that has a simple and pure good will
> to general existence, must love that temper
> in others, that agrees and conspires with
> itself. . . . That which truly and sincerely
> seeks the good of others, must approve of,
> and love that which joins with him in seeking
> the good of others.[57]

In the case of benevolence, we are complacent in
others' benevolence because we are benevolent ourselves

and so pleased by the agreement between theirs and
ours. Indeed, our own benevolence is prerequisite for
complacence in others' benevolence. It would be
psychologically inconsistent for those of us lacking a
"general good will" ourselves to enjoy another's. "For
how should one love and value a disposition to a thing,
or a tendency to promote it, and for that very reason,
when the thing itself is what he is regardless of, and
has no value for, nor desires to have promoted?"[58]

Since the objects of benevolence are, primarily,
being as such and, secondarily, benevolence itself in
the being beloved, then the degree of love owed a being
should be apportioned to its own degree of general good
will *in proportion* to its degree of mental capacity.
"One who loves being in general, will necessarily value
good will to being in general, wherever he sees it. But
if he sees the same benevolence in two beings, he will
value it more in two, than in one only." And the reason
is that the greater the quantity of being desiring and
promoting the general good the greater the benefit
accruing to being in general:

> So if one being be as great as two, has as
> much existence as both together, and has the
> same degree of general benevolence, it is
> more favourable to being in general, than if
> there were general benevolence in a being
> that had but half that share of existence. As
> a large quantity of gold, with the same
> quality, is more valuable than a small
> quantity of the same metal.[59]

As Edwards defines it, then, true virtue is
essentially the proportionality between love and the
beloved's worthiness of love or dignity, i.e. the
proportion of benevolence to being. Certain
consequences follow from this definition. One is the

highest degree of love is owed God who, as the very
ground of being, has perfect benevolence and infinite
being, or the greatest degree of dignity. "True virtue
must chiefly consist in *love to God*; the Being of
beings, infinitely the greatest and best."[60] However, a
degree of love is also owed finite beings in proportion
to their dignity, or of the degree of their benevolence
proportional to the degree of their being: "He who
loves being, simply considered, will naturally, other
things being equal, love particular beings in a
proportion compounded of the degree of being, and the
degree of virtue, or benevolence to being, which they
have."[61] Moreover, the individual good of each being
will be promoted "unless it be conceived as not
consistent with the highest good of being in
general."[62]

A second consequence of Edwards' definition of
virtue is the definition of vice, or sin, as
essentially the disproportionality between love and
the beloved's dignity or worthiness of love. This is
what Edwards means when he says, "All sin has its
source from selfishness, or from self-love *not
subordinate* to a regard to being in general."[63]
(Italics mine.) The turpitude of self-love consists not
in love for self *per se*. After all, in God, self-love
is identical with, and even the paradigm, of virtue,
according to Edwards. As we have seen, love is truly
virtuous (benevolent) if it is proportionate to the
worthiness of its object. As absolute being, God
encompasses being in general; and since he is
absolutely benevolent, God perfectly loves being in
general. So, in loving being in general, God

162

necessarily loves himself. In him, then, self-love and virtue are the same:

> That in God, the love of himself and the love
> of the public, are not to be distinguished,
> as in man: because God's being, as it were,
> comprehends all. His existence, being
> infinite, must be equivalent to universal
> existence. And for the same reason that
> public affection in the creature is fit and
> beautiful, God's regard to himself must be so
> likewise.[64]

The turpitude of self-love consists, rather, in the disproportion of love to the worthiness of the self, which is infinitely less than general being, or the inordinateness of self-love relative to a more inclusive love for being:

> If by selfishness be meant, a disposition in
> any being to regard himself; this is no
> otherwise vicious or unbecoming, than as one
> is less than a multitude; and so the public
> weal is of greater value than his particular
> interest. . . . But it is vicious on no other
> account, than as it is a disposition that
> does not agree with the nature of things; and
> that which is indeed the greatest good.[65]

However, if one's own self "were indeed all, and so more considerable than all the world besides, there would be no ill desert in a man regarding himself above all, and making all other interests give place to private interest."[66] A love in proportion to the worthiness or dignity of the self beloved, or a self-love subordinate or consonant to a general love to being, far from being vicious and contrary to virtue, is entirely compatible with it.

We shall now consider more closely Edwards' understanding of self-love, paying particular attention to his distinction between the ordinate (virtuous) and the inordinate (vicious) kinds. In *True Virtue*,

Edwards defines "self-love" as "a man's love of his own
happiness." He notes, though, that the phrase "his own"
is ambiguous. It can mean either "whatever is grateful
and pleasing to men" or "the pleasure a man takes in
his own proper, private, and separate good." This
ambiguity is the basis of Edwards' distinction between
two senses of self-love. Self-love in one sense
(hereinafter referred to as its "first" sense) is a
man's "loving whatsoever is pleasing to him,"[67] or "an
inclination to pleasure and averseness to pain,"[68] or,
most succinctly, "a capacity of enjoyment or
suffering."[69] Self-love, in this tautological and
somewhat trivial sense, is as fundamental to human
nature as the will. "That a man should love his own
happiness," writes Edwards, "is as necessary to his
nature as the faculty of the will is."[70] Self-love, in
the other sense (hereinafter referred to as its
"second" sense), is a man's "love to himself with
respect to his private interest." By "private interest"
Edwards means "that which most immediately consists in
those pleasures, or pains, that are personal." These
include "perceptions agreeable or contrary to certain
personal inclinations implanted in our nature; such as
the sensitive appetites and aversions." Further
examples would be the aesthetic pleasure we take in
secondary beauty, and the pleasure in our "being the
objects of the honour and love of others, and
displeased with others' hatred and contempt."[71] Edwards
explains our enjoyment of others' honor and esteem, or
misery over others' contempt and hatred, wholly in
terms of self-love. "It is easy to see that a man's
love to himself will make him love love to himself, and
hate hatred to himself."[72]

Now Edwards analyzes even apparently altruistic
love, such as filial and patriotic love, into self-
love: "that a man should love those who are of his
party, and who are warmly engaged on his side, and
promote his interest, is the natural consequence of a
private self-love." This follows, not with a
"metaphysical" (logical), but with a psychological
necessity "according to the common method and order
which is maintained in the laws of nature."[73] Hence,
"there is no more true virtue in a man thus loving his
friends merely from self-love, than there is in self-
love itself, the principle from whence it proceeds."[74]

In a "Miscellany," Edwards distinguishes between
simple and *compounded* self-love. Simple (egoistic)
self-love is "a man's love to his own proper, single,
and separate good, and is what arises simply and
necessarily from the nature of a perceiving, willing
being." Compounded self-love, on the other hand, is
"exercised in the delight that a man has in the good of
another--it is the value that he sets upon that
delight." Compounded self-love is so-called by Edwards
because it arises from the combination of two
principles of human nature. The one principle Edwards
associates with "the nature of a perceiving, willing
being,"[75] which is the principle of simple self-love.
The other is "a certain principle uniting this person
with another that causes the good of another to be its
good, and makes that to become delight which otherwise
cannot."[76] We might call this principle "empathy,"
which makes possible sympathetic affections. "For there
is a comfort, and a grief, that some have in others'
pleasures or pains; which are in others originally, but
are derived to them, or in some measure become theirs,

by virtue of a benevolent union of heart with others."[77]

In *True Virtue*, Edwards describes this "benevolent union of heart" as a kind of *self-enlargement*, as an "enlargement of the mind, whereby it so extends itself as to take others into a man's self: and therefore it implies a disposition to feel, to desire, and to act as though others were one with ourselves." Such an empathetic "enlargement of the mind" is what enters into a "pure love to others"[78] wherein the interest of those we love becomes our own:

> By love, a man's self is so extended and enlarged, that others, so far as they are beloved, do, as it were, become parts of himself, so that wherein their interest is promoted, he believes his own is promoted, and wherein theirs is injured, his also is injured.[79]

And an empathy or largeness of mind inclusive of being in general is the distinctive principle of benevolence:

> And those that are possessed of the spirit of Christian charity, are of a more enlarged spirit still, for they are concerned, not only for the thrift of the community, but for the welfare of the church of God, and of all the people of God individually.[80]

Benevolence, however, can be engendered in a person only supernaturally through the indwelling of the Holy Spirit (saving grace). "But as self-love is the offspring of natural principles, so divine love is the offspring of supernatural principles."[81] The sign that benevolence is of supernatural origin is "that it goes out even to enemies; and that it is its nature and tendency, to go out to the unthankful and evil, and to those that injure and hate us, which is directly contrary to the tendency of a selfish principle, and entirely above nature."[82]

The inordinateness of simple self-love, then, does not consist in an inordinate degree of self-love in its "first" sense *"in our love of our own happiness being, absolutely considered, too great in degree."*[83] It consists, rather, in placing our happiness, however great, more in our own private good than in the public good. Insofar as we make the good of others our own, we are not selfish:

> Some,...do not place ...[their] happiness in their own confined good, ..., but more in the common good; . . . A man's love of his own happiness, when it runs in this last channel, is not what is called selfishness, but is the very opposite of it. But there are others, who . . . , place . . . [their] happiness in good things that are confined or limited to themselves to the exclusion of others. And this is selfishness.[84]

Simple self-love cannot be inordinate absolutely, but only relatively to a compounded self-love.

Now just as simple self-love can be inordinate relative to compounded one, the latter can be so relative to benevolence to being in general. The inordinateness of compounded self-love consists in placing our happiness more in a *limited* public good instead of the most general public good, which is the good of being in general. In *True Virtue*, Edwards designates compounded self-love for a limited object, though altruistic, as "private affection" which is love to anything less than being in general such as any "society of beings that contains but a small part of the great system, comprehending the universality of existence."[85] Examples of finite societies are

families, tribes, nations, empires, races, and even the
whole of mankind. In Edwards' analysis, a private
affection is nothing more than aggrandized self-love.
For any finite society, "notwithstanding it extends to
a number of persons, which taken together are more than
a single person, yet the whole falls infinitely short
of the universality of existence; and if put in the
scales with it, has no greater proportion to it than a
single person."[86] Indeed, Edwards considers compounded
self-love, however extensive its object, to be as
pernicious as selfishness if it falls short of a love
for general being:

> If persons have a benevolent affection
> limited to a party, or to the nation in
> general of which they are a part, or the
> public community to which they belong, though
> it be as large as the Roman empire was of
> old; yea, if there could be a cause
> determining a person to benevolence towards
> the whole world of mankind, or even all
> created sensible natures throughout the
> universe, exclusive of union of heart to
> general existence and of love to God--not
> derived from that temper of mind which
> disposes to a supreme regard to him, not
> subordinate to such divine love--it cannot be
> of the nature of true virtue.[87]

But how is disproportionate self-love,
whether simple or compounded, pernicious? Edwards'
explanation is that an inordinate private affection
tends invariably to oppose a general affection. A
person of a disproportionately private disposition is
inclined to put his own interest ahead of and (when
they conflict) in opposition to the larger public
interest. Moreover, an inordinate private affection
itself, quite apart from its tendency or consequences,

is an affront to the universal society of general
being:

> For he that is influenced by private
> affection, . . . sets up its particular or
> limited object above being in general; and
> this most naturally tends to enmity against
> the latter, which is by right the great
> supreme, ruling, and absolutely sovereign
> object of our regard.[88]

Edwards sardonically cites, as an instance of the
turpitude of inordinate private affection masquerading
as virtuousness, the classical virtue of patriotism:
"Hence, among the Romans, love to their country was the
highest virtue; though this affection of theirs so much
extolled, was employed as it were for the destruction
of the rest of mankind."[89]

Compounded self-love, or private affection, is not
vicious, however, if it is subordinated to and derived
from an inclusive love, or general affection. It is
virtuous if its objects are "loved not because of their
relation to self [which is the case in a compounded
self-love of the vicious kind], but because of their
relation to God as his children."[90] Such a love
corresponds to God's own love for persons, and is one
that promotes their true happiness, consisting in a
palpable experience of God's holiness and a loving and
joyful communion with him:

> And so far as a virtuous mind exercises true
> virtue in benevolence to created beings, it
> chiefly seeks the good of the creature;
> consisting in its knowledge or view of God's
> glory and beauty, its union with God,
> conformity and love to him, and joy in him.[91]

Edwards believed Brainerd truly virtuous since he
thought him animated to a high degree by a
disinterested benevolence to being in general. This was

manifested in his "high degree of love to God" and
"placing the happiness of life in him,"[92] as well as in
his "great and universal benevolence to mankind."[93]
Brainerd's missionary endeavors were apparently
motivated by disinterested benevolence. "If the blessed
work might be accomplished to the honour of God," he
reports in his memoirs, "this was all my desire and
care."[94] Edwards editorially corroborates this by
declaring that Brainerd's missionizing on behalf of the
kingdom was "animated by a pure love to Christ, an
earnest desire of his glory, and a *disinterested*
affection to the souls of mankind." [95] (Italics mine.)

Interestingly, Brainerd more than exemplified
Edwards' later conception of true virtue in his
character and conduct; he also holds to it in his
thought, as revealed in some theological reflections
scattered throughout his memoirs. Brainerd shares
Edwards' conception of self-love. Like Edwards, he
distinguishes virtuous self-love from selfishness but
in terms of "regular" and "irregular" self-love. He
defines regular self-love as one wherein our own
interests and God's are one, but irregular self-love as
one wherein they are disjunct. Regular self-love,
therefore, is compatible with benevolence:

> [I] took pains to describe the difference
> between a *regular* and *irregular* SELF LOVE;
> the one consisting with a *supreme love to
> God*, but the other *not*; the former uniting
> God's glory, and the soul's happiness, that
> they become one common interest, but the
> latter disjoining and separating God's glory
> and man's happiness, seeking the latter with
> a neglect of the former.[96]

For Brainerd agrees with Edwards that in God self-love
and benevolence are identical, and that the highest

virtue for man is to love God as God loves himself,
thereby becoming like him in this respect:

> When a soul *loves* God with a supreme love, he
> therein acts *like* the blessed God himself,
> who most justly loves himself in that manner.
> So when God's interest and his are become
> one, and he longs that God should be
> *glorified*, and rejoices to think that he is
> unchangeably possessed of the highest glory
> and blessedness, herein also he acts in
> *conformity* to God.[97]

Apparently, Brainerd exhibited regular self-love
inasmuch as he identified God's interest as his own.
"God himself could not make me happy," Brainerd
confides, "unless I could be in a capacity to 'please
and glorify him forever.'"[98] And Edwards recalls
Brainerd's declaring, "*My heaven* is to *please* God, and
glorify him, and give all to him, and to be wholly
devoted to his glory: . . . I see nothing else in the
world, that can yield any satisfaction, besides *living
to God, pleasing him, and doing his whole will.*"[99]

From *Complacence* to *Benevolence*

As we saw in the previous section, Brainerd is
represented as having exemplified both of Edwards'
conceptions as to the nature of true piety or virtue:
the conception delineated in *Religious Affections*, and
the later one delineated in *True Virtue*. Brainerd
exemplified the first insofar as he exhibited the signs
of truly religious or holy affections enumerated in the
treatise, particularly the second and third signs: "his
love to God was primarily and principally for the
supreme *excellency* of his own nature"; specifically,
"that *beauty*, . . . , which was the great object of the

new sense of his mind, . . . , was *holiness*." (Italics
mine.) Brainerd exemplified the second insofar as he
was "animated by a pure love to Christ, and earnest
desire of his glory"; in such declarations as, "My
heaven is to *please God*, and to *glorify him*, and give
all to him, and to be *wholly devoted to his glory*";
and in his exercising a "*great* and *universal
benevolence* to mankind" or a "*disinterested* affection
to the souls of mankind." (Italics mine.) How, then, do
these conceptions of true piety or virtue differ, and
how is this difference reflected in Edwards'
representation of Brainerd's character?

    With respect to their nature, the piety or virtue
prescribed in *Religious Affections* and that prescribed
in *True Virtue* are the same: both are a kind of *love*.
Edwards states in the treatise, "the essence of all
true religion lies in holy love" and in True Virtue,
"virtue most essentially consists in love."[100] However,
with respect to the kind of love, as determined by its
object or motive, they differ fundamentally. The
primary object or motive of pious love, according to
the treatise, is moral virtue or holiness: "Holy
persons,...do love divine things primarily for
their holiness: they love God, in the *first* place, for
the *beauty* of his holiness or moral perfection."
(Italics mine.) The primary motive of virtuous love,
according to the dissertation, is God's being as such:
"The *first* object of a virtuous benevolence is *being*,
simply considered." (Italics mine.) The kind of love
that is truly pious described in the earlier work is
what Edwards would call "love of complacence," i.e.
"delight . . . in the person or being beloved for his
[moral] beauty."[101] The kind of love that is virtuous

described in the later work is what Edwards there calls "love of benevolence." This distinction between "complacence" and "benevolence" is not drawn in *Religious Affections*.

Insofar as Brainerd's love to "divine things" was primarily for their moral excellency or holiness, it was complacence. Insofar as it was a "pure love to Christ [presumably for his own sake]" manifested in an "earnest desire of his glory," it was benevolence. That it was the benevolence described in *True Virtue* is evident from two things: First, a benevolent person, according to that dissertation, is wholly oriented towards the glory of God: "a truly virtuous mind, . . . above all things, seeks the glory of God, and makes this his supreme, governing, and ultimate end."[102] Second, Edwards characterizes Brainerd's love in terms of the ethical idiom of *True Virtue*, i.e. as a "great and universal *benevolence* [Italics mine]." Moreover, it was a "great and universal benevolence to *mankind* [italics mine]" no less. Edwards explicitly mentions in *True Virtue* such benevolence to man as being the necessary effect of true virtue: "virtue, in its most essential nature, consists in benevolent affection or propensity of heart towards being in general; and *so flowing out to particular beings in a greater or lesser degree*, according to the measure of existence and beauty which they are possessed of [italics mine]."[103] But nowhere in *Religious Affections* does he either explicitly mention or enjoin it.

What is the most likely explanation of this ambiguity in Edwards' description of Brainerd's piety or virtue: on the one hand, his description of it in terms of "love of benevolence," the essence of true

virtue according to the dissertation; on the other, his
description of it in terms of "love of complacence,"
the essence of true religion according to the treatise?
His description certainly seems to reflect the conflict
between the two conceptions of piety or virtue.

This conflict has long been noted, and so long as
it is assumed that Edwards' thought never changed in
its essentials it remains as an inexplicable and
irresolvable contradiction. Nancy Manspeaker has noted
that one of the many "distinctions" accorded Edwards is
that he "presents an almost unparalleled example of a
major thinker whose thought never developed."[104] That
Edwards "altered little from his adolescence at Yale to
his death in Princeton," or that his "works are
statement and restatement of an essentially static
conception"[105] is the canonical opinion as expressed by
Perry Miller. Manspeaker, however, has challenged this
assumption, and in a recent extensive study has
demonstrated that "Edwards' thought had developed
substantially from his adolescence at Yale to his death
at Princeton,"[106] as evidence of which she cites the
change in his conception of piety or virtue.

On this developmental view of Edwards' thought,
the ambiguity in the *Life of Brainerd* becomes
explicable: it is not unlikely that at the time of his
preparing this text Edwards was in the process of
changing his mind as to the nature of true piety or
virtue. Hence, his early conception of it as primarily
and essentially complacence and his later conception of
it as essentially and primarily benevolence represent
not a contradiction, but simply the supersession of the
one by the other. On this explanation, the *Life of
Brainerd* would be a significant text in Edwards'

oeuvres, if for no other reason than that it is the
first to signal this shift in Edwards' moral philosophy
and thereby mediates his positions in *Religious
Affections* and *True Virtue*.

Evaluations & Interpretations

This work has had its detractors and admirers.
Among the former is Henry Bamford Parkes who thinks,
"Brainerd's diary belongs to the pathology of the
religious life,"[107] as far as I know the only author to
damn it so. One should note, however, that his remark
concerns only the diary itself and not Edwards' own
editorial comments on it. Had he considered these,
Parkes perhaps would have been more judicious in his
estimate of the work. For Edwards anticipated just such
a reaction as Parkes' and, far from trying to disguise
the pathological dross in the diary, sympathetically
exposes, explains, and repudiates it while admonishing
the reader not to throw out the genuine spiritual gold
because of it:

> Besides the imperfections already mentioned,
> it is readily allowed that there were some
> imperfections that ran through his whole
> life, and were mixed with all his religious
> affections and exercises, some mixture of
> what was natural with that which was
> spiritual; as it evermore is in the best
> saints in this world. . . . There was
> undoubtedly very often some influence of his
> natural disposition to dejection in his
> religious mourning, some mixture of
> melancholy with truly godly sorrow and real
> Christian humility, and some mixture of the
> natural fire of youth with his holy zeal for
> God, and some influence of natural principles
> mixed with grace in various other respects,
> as it ever was and ever will be with the
> saints while on this side of heaven. . . .

> 'Tis easy for the judicious reader to oberve,
> that his graces ripened, and the religious
> exercises of his heart became more and more
> pure, and he more and more distinguishing in
> his judgment, the longer he lived.[108]

For Perry Miller, however, the *Life of Brainerd* is
"a minor masterpiece of psychological confession,"[109]
thereby locating it in the tradition of Augustine's and
Rousseau's *Confessions*. And for Edward H. Davidson the
book belongs to the literature of the psychology of
religion as "an affirmation of the depths and vividness
of the emotional content of life in the coming of
salvation," as well as reflecting Edwards' own
psychological state when he edited it inasmuch as it is
"fraught with a recognition of the flagging power and
loss of feeling which Edwards was knowing in his own
life and person."[110]

Samuel Miller commends the *Life of Brainerd* to
clergy as an invaluable tool for assessing one's
spiritual estate, thereby linking it to *Religious
Affections* as a manual of piety: "the whole work is one
of those, which ought to be *studied* by every minister
of the Gospel, ... Few uninspired books are better
adapted to expose enthusiasm and every kind of spurious
religion."[111]

Charles H. Spurgeon esteems Brainerd as a paragon
of prayer and Edwards' hagiography of him as still
inspiring, and convicting, aspirants to the devout
life: "Could we read Jonathan Edwards' description of
David Brainerd and not blush?"[112]

Aldridge regards the *Life of Brainerd* as being for
Edwards virtually as important as his treatise on the
will since it diverted him for a while from "publishing
something against some of the Arminian tenets."[113]

Nevertheless, the anti-Arminian polemic is by no means absent from the Brainerd book. "Edwards was moved by a desire to furnish irresistable evidence against the Arminians or deists, who denied the validity of religious experiences."[114] And that evidence, Edwards thought, was Brainerd's religious life.

Scholars treat the *Life of Brainerd*, if at all, only in passing and in a larger context. Thus, Ola Winslow mentions it in the course of her biography of Edwards, and Heimert discusses it in his massive study of American religion. Their treatments, however, fall far short of being in-depth and systematic interpretations of this problematic text--and are fundamentally flawed as interpretations.

Winslow errs by overlooking Brainerd's overarching eschatological concern. According to her, Brainerd was principally motivated in his missionary endeavors by the propect of personal sanctification through soul-winning. She remarks that "he failed to see that he had been pursuing sainthood, and to that end glorying in the very hardships and sufferings which hastened his death." And she claims that Brainerd, and others of his ilk, "had little interest in Indians except as souls to be saved," and "believed them as a race to be of a low order of creation."[115] However, the *Life of Brainerd* suggests otherwise. Certainly sanctification was an important consideration for Brainerd, as is evident from his remarking, "Sanctification in myself, and the ingathering of God's elect, was all my desire; and the hope of its accomplishment, all my joy."[116] However, as this remark also makes clear, sanctification is an end distinct from that of enlarging the Kingdom, and both personal holiness and the salvation of souls are subordinate to the more ultimate end of God's Kingdom, as is made quite clear in the following excerpt from the diary: "My soul was concerned, not so much for souls as such, but rather for Christ's kingdom, that it might appear in the world, that God might be known to be God, in the whole earth."[117]

Furthermore, Brainerd's diary and journal suggest that he had a considerable interest in Indians other than as souls to be saved. This is evident from the nature of Brainerd's piety, as exhibited and confessed by him and described by Edwards. Edwards considered Brainerd to have exhibited all twelve signs of truly gracious affections as laid down in the treatise, evidence of the genuineness of his piety. In particular, Brainerd manifested a beneficent and merciful (i.e. Christ-like) spirit, the eighth sign of religious affections.[118] An aspect of such a spirit, according to Edwards, is a charitable regard to the physical needs of men. In *Religious Affections*, Edwards maintains, on the authority of Scripture, "that none are true saints, but those whose true character it is, that they are of a disposition to pity and relieve their fellow creatures, that are poor, indigent and afflicted."[119] In *Christian Love*, he describes this disposition as "*a sympathizing and merciful spirit*," which "disposes persons to consider not only their own difficulties, but also the burdens and afflictions of others, and the difficulties of their circumstances, and to esteem the case of those who are in straits and necessities, as their own."[120] Moreover, Brainerd exhibited a symmetry or proportion in his affections, the tenth sign of their genuineness. One way affections are proportionate, according to Edwards, is that in

their exercise a charitable regard is paid equally to
the spiritual and the material well-being of others:

> [Some] pretend a great love to men's souls,
> that are not compassionate and charitable
> towards their bodies. The making a great shew
> of love, pity, and distress for souls, costs
> 'em nothing; but in order to shew mercy to
> men's bodies, they must part with money out
> of their pockets. But a true Christian love
> to our brethren, extends both to their souls
> and bodies.[121]

Consequently, inasmuch as Edwards considered Brainerd
to have exhibited the eighth and the tenth signs of
holy affections, Brainerd must have had more than a
little interest in the "bodies" of Indians. Brainerd
himself attests to that interest in the following entry
from his journal:

> The concern I have had for the settling of
> these Indians in New-Jersey in a compact
> form, in order to their being a Christian
> congregation, in a capacity of enjoying the
> means of grace; the care of managing their
> worldly business in order to this end, and to
> their having a comfortable livelihood, have
> been more pressing to my mind, and cost me
> more labour and fatigue, for several months
> past, than all my other work among them.[122]

Indeed, such was his solicitude for the temporal well-
being of Indians, and such their ineptness in the
pursuit of it, that Brainerd personally undertook its
supervision: "Visited the Indians, and took care of
their *secular* business, which they are not able to
manage themselves, without the constant care and advice
of others."[123] Brainerd was mindful that the Indians'
material prosperity was important, if for no other
reason than that it could contribute significantly to
their spiritual estate. Thus, in another entry he
writes:

> Visited my people again, and took care of
> their *worldly* concerns, giving them
> directions relating to their business.--I
> daily discover more and more of what
> importance it is like to be to their
> *religious* interests, that they become
> laborious and industrious, acquainted with
> the affairs of *husbandry*, and able, in a good
> measure, to raise the necessaries and
> comforts of life *within themselves*; for their
> present method of living greatly exposes them
> to temptations of various kinds.[124]

Brainerd's concern for the worldly weal of his
Indians extended even to the realm of social justice,
making him something of an eighteeth-century advocate
of native rights. He was hard pressed to understand the
antipathy of certain white settlers towards him,

> unless it was my attempting sometimes to
> vindicate the rights of the Indians, and
> complaining of the horrid practice of making
> the Indians drunk, and then cheating them out
> of their lands and other properties: and
> once, I remembered, I had done this with too
> much warmth of spirit."[125]

In the following entry from his journal, we read that
Brainerd, anxious lest a group of Indians might lose
title to their lands in the remission of debts incurred
by heavy drinking, persuaded the authorities to use
some of the funds being collected for proselytical
purposes to pay them:

> The Indians in these parts have in times
> past, run themselves in debt by their
> excessive drinking; and some have taken the
> advantage of them, and put them to trouble
> and charge by arresting sundry of them;
> whereby it was supposed their hunting lands,
> in great part, were much endangered, and
> might speedily be taken from them. Being
> sensible, that they could not subsist
> together in these parts, in order to their
> being a Christian congregation, if these
> lands should be taken, which was thought very

180

> likely, I thought it my duty to use my utmost
> endeavours to prevent so unhappy an event.
> And having acquainted the gentlemen concerned
> with this *mission* of the affair, according to
> the best information I could get of it, they
> thought it proper to expend the money they
> had been, and still were collecting for the
> *religious* interest of the Indians, (at least
> a part of it), for discharging their debts,
> and securing these lands, that there might be
> no entanglement lying upon them to hinder the
> settlement and hopeful enlargement of a
> *Christian congregation* of Indians in these
> parts.[126]

Ultimately, though, Brainerd regarded Indians as
neither disembodied souls to be saved nor soulless
bodies to be nurtured, but rather as composite persons
who, like him, would take their rightful place as
subjects of God's Kingdom. And though, according to
Winslow, Brainerd and Edwards believed Indians "as a
race to be of a low order of creation," yet certainly
Edwards, and presumably Brainerd too who shared
Edwards' postmillennialism, dignified them with the
hope that in the millennium even "many of the Negroes
and Indians will be divines." For Edwards and Brainerd,
improving the social lot of Indians, like saving their
souls, was only ancillary to the wider establishment of
God's Kingdom.

Heimert correctly asserts that "Edwards used
Brainerd's recorded experience as both substantiation
and illustration of his analysis of regeneration"[127] in
Religious Affections. Heimert, however, seriously
distorts the purport of that treatise, a distortion
that consequently colors his interpretation of the *Life
of Brainerd*.

Heimert erroneously supposes that Edwards defines
true religion as the doing of good works: "In both

works [viz. *Religious Affections* and *Life of Brainerd*]
the 'enthusiast' or 'evangelical hypocrite' was advised
that true religion consisted . . . in some 'act,
exercise, or exertion' whereby the saint served to
forward the Work of Redemption."[128] However, in the
treatise, Edwards unambiguously defines true religion
as the undergoing of religious affections: "True
religion, in great part, consists in holy
affections,"[129] of which the chief is love. Now good
works are singularly important for him in the religious
life, but only as the fruits or effects of true
religion--specifically, the result of undergoing
religious affections--not as its essence. Good works
are but an aspect of true religion, albeit a supremely
important one, which also includes the quite as
important affections and the illumination of the
understanding:

> But it is doubtless true,...that the
> essence of all true religion lies in holy
> love; and that in this divine affection, and
> an habitual disposition to it, and that light
> which is the foundation of it, and those
> things which are the fruits of it [e.g. good
> works], consists the whole of religion.

Moreover, it is not merely some "act, exercise, or
exertion," or even a series of such acts, that for
Edwards constitutes the fruit of true religion, but
rather a steady *disposition* or inclination so to act.
Thus, in *Religious Affections*, Edwards states, "Indeed
it cannot be supposed, when this affection of love is
here, and in other Scriptures, spoken of as the sum of
all religion, that hereby is meant the act, *exclusive
of the habit*."[130] (Italics mine.)

Elsewhere in the same vein Heimert states, "The
Religious Affections was far more than a mere

exposition of the Calvinist doctrine of sanctification.
It was an exhortation to Edwards' readers to be up and
doing, and to the ministers of the colonies to urge
their people on their way." Curiously, Heimert's
reading of this text as a manifesto for social activism
contrasts markedly with Mead's and others' reading of
it as a mandate for quietism. Evidently, the
inspiration for Heimert's interpretation is the
undeniable importance Edwards attaches to the twelfth
sign,[131] i.e. Christian practice or behavior. Heimert
seems to have read the entire treatise exclusively in
terms of this last sign. This, however, is a profound
misreading.

The question is why is the sign of practice so
supremely important for Edwards. It is important solely
because it is the best evidence by far for the
genuineness of one's piety, and the vindication of all
the other signs:

> Christian practice is the most proper
> evidence of the gracious sincerity of
> professors, to themselves and others; and the
> chief of all the marks of grace, the sign of
> signs, and evidence of evidences, that which
> seals and crowns all other signs. . . . There
> may be several good evidences that a tree is
> a fig tree; but the highest and most proper
> evidence of it, is that it actually bears
> figs.[132]

And Christian behavior qualifies as such evidence and
vindication because, according to Edwards' conception
of an integral mind, it is the necessary and natural
concomitant of the new habit or disposition implanted
in the mind at regeneration. Nowhere, though, does
Edwards extoll good works for their own sake, or as the
substance of piety, but only as a good *sign* or *test* of
piety.[133] Nowhere does he specifically exhort his

readers "to be up and doing." But everywhere in
Religious Affections Edwards exhorts them to be
scrupulous in the examination of their faith. For
Edwards, if one's faith is authentic, the good works
will take care of themselves.

It is little wonder, therefore, that Heimert
should have interpreted Brainerd as the exemplar of one
who was "up and doing," i.e. the social activist *par
excellence*. This is what he says:

> The exemplary Christian, Brainerd, was a
> creature neither of meditation nor of
> introspection, but of endeavor-- . . . . It
> was not by a probing of the inner self, but
> through out-reaching extensions of the will,
> that the would-be saint was provided the data
> whereby he tested his pretensions.[134]

That Brainerd was a creature of endeavor is
indisputable. As we have seen, he manfully missionized
for the sake of the Kingdom, and diligently labored
along the way to promote the prosperity and rights of
Indians. But that he was a creature of neither
meditation nor introspection does not at all comport
with the texts of his diary and journal, and Edwards'
editorial remarks. We only have to open the diary at
any place to realize that Brainerd was a creature of
obsessive introspection and virtuosic meditation.
Indeed, the assaying of one's spirituality with the
signs established by Edwards (something Brainerd
evidently did) would require an uncommon degree of
introspection. The following passages from Brainerd's
diary (to which numberless others could be added) amply
attest to his introspective and meditative turn:

> I think, my soul scarce even penetrated so
> far into the immaterial world, in any one
> prayer that ever I made, nor were my
> devotions ever so free from gross conceptions

> and imaginations framed from beholding
> material objects.[135]

> God enabled me to pray with as much
> spirituality and sweetness as I have done for
> some time: my mind seemed to be unclothed of
> sense and imagination, and was in a measure
> let into the immaterial world of spirits.[136]

> I viewed the infinite excellency of God, and
> my soul even broke with longings, that God
> should be *glorified*.[137]

Furthermore, Edwards himself testifies that Brainerd,
through loving Christian fellowship, especially
relished his private meditations:

> Though he was of a very sociable temper, and
> loved the company of saints, and delighted
> very much in religious conversation, and in
> social worship; yet his warmest affections,
> and their greatest effects on animal nature,
> and his sweetest joys, were in his closet
> devotions, and solitary transactions between
> God and his own soul: . . . . He delighted
> greatly in sacred retirements; and loved to
> get quite away from all the world, to
> converse with God alone, in secret duties.[138]

In a comment on both *Religious Affections* and
Life of Brainerd, Heimert remarks that "it was not by a
probing of the inner self, but through out-reaching
extensions of the will, that the would-be saint was
provided the data whereby he tested his pretensions."
However, as is abundantly clear from both texts, the
data provided to the would-be saint are the affections,
which are to be tested as much through introspection as
action. How else, for example, but through a regimen of
painstaking self-examination could the sixth sign[139] of
gracious affections, i.e. evangelical humility, be
discerned?

Implications for Social and Political Theory

The significance of the *Life of Brainerd* for
social and political philosophy lies in (a) its
apparent signalling of the shift in Edwards' thinking
as to the nature of true piety or virtue, and (b) in
Brainerd's exemplification of Edwards' later conception
of true virtue. The shift in Edwards' thinking on piety
or virtue is socio-philosophically significant inasmuch
as it marks the development in Edwards' thought from a
fundamentally individualistic ethic to a genuinely
social one. Brainerd's exemplification of Edwards'
later conception of virtue is socio-philosophically
significant in three ways: First, it further clarifies
the nature of the social bond constitutive of Edwards'
pious or ideal society. It does so by specifying that
the cordial consent, or love, making for a pious social
union is *primarily* a "love of benevolence" and
secondarily a "love of complacence." Thus, the social
bonding in a pious union makes for a "double" unity
grounded in the loves of benevolence and complacence:
what we shall term a "benevolent union" and a
"complacent union" respectively. Second, it makes
explicit Edwards' conception of individualism. This
further enriches our understanding of Edwards' social
theory by enabling us to see that his conception of the
pious or ideal society is actually a conception of
authentic community. And third, it suggests that
Edwards has a conception of citizenship in the
benevolent community, revealing thereby the political
dimension of his thought.

From an Individualistic to a Social Ethic

The change in Edwards' conception as to the nature
of true piety or virtue--from his conceiving it as
being essentially complacence to conceiving it as
essentially benevolence--marks the development in his
thought from a fundamentally individualistic ethic,
founded on a still self-interested and personal relish
of holiness, to a profoundly social ethic, founded on a
radically disinterested allegiance, or loyalty, to the
universal system or society of beings "comprehending
the universality of existence." Alternatively, it marks
the transition from an essentially anthropocentric to a
wholly theocentric ethic.

Complacence, as the "delight in beauty," is
essentially a self-interested love, for it is "the
pleasure a man takes in his own proper, private, and
separate good." In complacence, the appreciation of an
object, according to Joseph Haroutunian, "is determined
by its significance for the person who does the
appreciating. The center of reference is the self, as
if it were the point around which all creation
moves."[140] Benevolence, by contrast, as the "propensity
of the heart to any being, which . . . disposes it to
desire and take pleasure in its happiness," is a wholly
other- or dis-interested love insofar as it involves
the pleasure a man takes, not in his own private good,
but in that of another. And benevolence to general
being is the pleasure he takes in the greatest possible
public good, which is the glory of God.

It is surely noteworthy that commentators who have
argued that Edwards' thought is socially irrelevant
have in mind Edwards' conception of true piety qua

complacence in *Religious Affections*, and cite that treatise in support of their contention. This is the text, for example, that Mead cites in contending that Edwards' theology "obviously legitimated the privatization of religion," and "gave the convert the possibility of disengagement with honor from active participation in the political and social life of his society"; and one that DeJong had in mind when he maintains that "in his various treatises he [Edwards] conceived of religion too much in terms of the individual's relation to God." It is to this conception of true piety *qua* complacence that Bates is referring in claiming that Edwards' "facilitated the withdrawal of religion into the limited field of individual conduct to concern itself above all with the subjective consciousness."

Edwards' conception of true virtue *qua* benevolence in *True Virtue*, and the *Life of Brainerd*, is in explicit contrast to the above readings of Edwards as a theological individualist. Edwards conceived of virtue *qua* benevolence in terms of the individual's relation to being in general which includes *created* as well as uncreated being. And he explicitly allows that God's deserves of the greatest share of our esteem in virtue of his absolute dignity by no means precludes finite being, or groups thereof, being esteemed *in proportion* to their relative degrees of dignity: "He who loves being, simply considered, will naturally, other things being equal, love particular beings in a proportion compounded of the degree of being, and the degree of virtue, or benevolence to being, which they have." Edwards in *True Virtue* certainly does conceive of religion *fundamentally* in terms of the individual's

relation to God--but not "too much," or exclusively
of others. For being in the right relation to God,
according to Edwards, entails being in the right
relation to all his creatures: "virtue, . . . consists
in benevolent affection or propensity of heart towards
being in general; and so flowing out to particular
beings in a greater or lesser degree, according to the
measure of existence and beauty which they are
possessed of." Furthermore, Brainerd's religion, in
Edwards' account, far from being a private affair
limited to a personal relationship to God, was a fully
public one with humanity as its object, as evidenced in
his "great and universal benevolence to *mankind*" and
his "disinterested affection to the souls of *mankind*."
(Italics mine.) Edwards regarded Brainerd as the very
type of the splendidly magnanimous soul who was all the
richer and freer for his benevolence. In Carse's
words,

> The vast differences between heaven and hell
> point to the vast differences between the
> kinds of lives people currently are living.
> The one is dark and self-enclosed, turned in
> upon itself, feeding on its own emotions and
> organizing all values around its own needs
> and tastes. The other is brilliantly life-
> affirming, it is open and free, seeing in the
> darkness not the estuary of its self-
> destruction but the possibility of new and
> surprising caring for the world. Jonathan
> Edwards thought that Brainerd had lived the
> latter kind of life.[141]

The Pious or Virtuous Individual

The *Life of Brainerd* is about the pious or
virtuous individual in much the same way that *Humble
Attempt* is about the pious or virtuous society. These
two works thus complement one another: If in the latter

work we have Edwards' picture of the ideal society, in
the former we have his portrait of its ideal member.
How, though, is Brainerd the type of the member of the
virtuous society as conceived by Edwards? He is the
type insofar as he was truly virtuous or benevolent.
This means that he had, in Edwards' words, a "consent,
propensity and union of heart" to general being; that
is, Brainerd *cordially consented qua* love to the great
society of intelligent beings, particularly to the
Being of beings, or God. And cordial consent *qua* love,
as we saw, is the social bond making for a pious or
virtuous society. Hence, inasmuch as Brainerd cordially
consented to, or benevolently loved, being as such, he
is the type of the member of Edwards' virtuous society.

Benevolence and Complacence as the Bonds of Pious Society

Brainerd is, in Edwards' conception, the typical
member of the benevolent society because he loved
benevolently. His example, then, makes explicit the
kind of love that makes for a benevolent or virtuous
society. It is a "love of benevolence," or a cordial
consent to the infinite society of general being.
Benevolence, moreover, entails complacence. A virtuous
society, then, has a complex or "double" unity: a unity
based on the "love of benevolence" (a *benevolent union*)
and a unity based on the "love of complacence" (a
complacent union). First, there is the radically
extensive union constituted by benevolence, or the
cordial consent to being *per se*. Second, there is the
derivative and more intensive union constituted by
disinterested complacence, or the cordial consent to
benevolence itself in being. A complacent union, as

consent to consent to being, is "a union with union,"
or a kind of "meta-union" that serves to deepen and
strengthen the benevolent union. In a sermon wherein he
extolls the felicities of heavenly society, Edwards
provides a paradigm of a complacent union ordered
according to a moral hierarchy based on the degree of
dignity:

> There will be a perfect harmony in that
> society; those that are most happy will also
> be most holy, and all will be both perfectly
> holy and perfectly happy. But yet there will
> be different degrees of both holiness and
> happiness, according to the measure of each
> one's capacity; and, therefore, those that
> are lowest in glory will have the greatest
> love to those that are highest in happiness,
> because they will see most of the image of
> God in them; and having the greatest love to
> them, they will rejoice to see them the most
> happy and the highest in glory. And so, on
> the other hand, those that are highest in
> glory, as they will be the most lovely, so
> they will be fullest of love; as they will
> excel in happiness, they will proportionately
> excel in divine benevolence and love to
> others, and will have more love to God and to
> the saints than these that are lower in
> holiness and happiness. And besides, those
> that will excel in glory will also excel in
> humility.[142]

Pious Society as *Communitas*

As the typical member of Edwards' pious society,
Brainerd makes explicit by his example the conception
of individualism latent in Edwards' ethics. To see how
this is so, let us consider what Edwards' conception
is.

An aspect of individualism is one's pursuing what
he perceives to be in his own best interest.
Individualism, then, is necessarily self-interested.

Now Edwards, we have seen, distinguishes two kinds of
self-interest (or self-love): the selfish kind that is
"*not subordinate* to a regard to being in general," and
the unselfish kind that is. Therefore, two kinds of
individualism are implicit in this distinction: a
selfish kind, consisting in one's pursuit of his own
private interest; and a "disinterested" kind,
consisting in his pursuit of the highest public
interest as his own. This disinterested individualism
is given succinct expression in Edwards' dictum, "that
not to seek your own [interest], in the selfish sense,
is the best way of seeking your own in a better sense.
It is the directest course you can take to secure your
highest happiness."[143]

Brainerd's individualism was evidently of the
disinterested kind for his self-love was unselfish, or
"regular," and consisted of "uniting God's glory, and
the soul's happiness, that they become one common
interest." Brainerd's unselfish self-love is
illustrated in the following remark of his: "to *please*
God, and *glorify* him, and to give all to him, and to be
wholly devoted to his glory: . . . that is my
happiness." And such a union of "God's glory, and the
soul's happiness" is, for Edwards, nothing other than
the union of the highest public happiness with the
soul's own. To seek the glory of God is thereby to seek
the greatest common good of his creatures. For seeking
God's glory as one's "ultimate end," according to
Edwards, consists in "the manifestation of God's glory
to created understandings." The "good of the creature"
ultimately consists in "its knowledge or view of God's
glory and beauty, its union with God, conformity and
love to him, and joy in him."[144]

Edwards' disinterested individualism is a socio-philosophically significant idea for it suggests a solution to the problem of reconciling the individual with the group, a perennial concern in social philosophy. Nagy has observed that at the imaginative center of Edwards' vision is an Emersonian "each and all" doctrine, and that constituting the warp and woof of his metaphysics is "a dynamic and ever-continuing reconciliation of opposites" whose dialectic is cordial consent to being. "Reconciliation" means that neither of the things reconciled is thereby nullified, which is the Emersonian social ideal wherein the "uniters are isolated,"[145] i.e. they are not thereby dissolved in a monolithic union, but retain their individual identities.

Nagy identifies Edwards' category of cordial consent to being, or benevolence, as the "standpoint for achieving reconciliation when the reconcilers are isolated."[146] How, precisely, is that reconciliation achieved through the "love of benevolence"? According to Edwards, benevolence is the disposition to "desire and take pleasure in" the highest happiness or good of general being--specifically, the happiness or glory of God and of all his intelligent creatures. Thus, the most public happiness becomes the individual's own happiness through a principle of divinely bestowed empathy. Moreover, disinterested love or benevolence presupposes self-love, in the "first" sense defined above (i.e. a man's "loving whatsoever is pleasing to him"). Self-love in this sense is a man's love for his own good or happiness considered *absolutely*, wherever he places it. However, any good--whether private or public--can be appropriated as one's own only so far as he actually delights or takes pleasure in it:

> Any good whatsoever that a man any way
> enjoys, or anything that he takes delight in-
> -he makes it thereby his own good whether it
> be a man's own proper and separate pleasure
> or honor, or the pleasure or honor of
> another. Our delight in it renders it our own
> good in proportion as we delight in it. 'Tis
> impossible that a man should delight in any
> good that is not his own, for to say that
> would be to say that he delights in that in
> which he does not delight.[147]

An individual, then, can appropriate the public weal as his own--desiring and seeking it--only if he can take pleasure in it, thereby exercising his innate capacity for self-love.

To the extent that the individual appropriates the public interest as his own, his disinterested love becomes a function of his self-love in the "second" sense defined above (i.e. a man's "love to himself with respect to his private interest"; or "the pleasure a man takes in his own proper, private, and separate good"). That is, the public interest becomes to a degree his "private" interest; the individual takes pleasure in the public good as if it were "his own proper, private, and separate good." To the extent that his private interest and the public coincide, he approaches the benevolent disposition of God in whom there is a perfect coincidence of private and public interest.

Edwards' conception of a disinterested individualism, in which the individual comes to regard the highest public interest as his own, is socio-theoretically significant insofar as it further defines his conception of the nature of a truly pious or

virtuous society. One attribute of such a society as
conceived by Edwards is, as we have seen, unity. A
second attribute, as we now see, is the primacy of the
individual. It is this that distinguishes Edwards'
ideal social order from collectivism; just as its unity
distinguishes it from ordinary individualism. Pure
individualism, while allowing for individuality, is
anarchic; whereas pure collectivism, while making for
unity, is totalitarian. Community, however, avoids both
these extremes. It is, says Martin Buber, the
"essential human reality" which is "neither one of
individual nor of collective existence, but lies in the
relation of man to man, and is a matter between you and
me."[148] Authentic individualism is an essential trait
of community. Thus, according to Josiah Royce, as
paraphrased by John E. Smith,

> Community never meant a blending of selves, a
> merging into one another in mystical fashion.
> There can be no community without distinct
> selves because it is a living unity of
> diverse individuals and not a mass in which
> all are swallowed up.[149]

And, according to Melvin Rader, community actually
fosters the individuality of its constituents:

> Concrete individuality is enhanced, not
> emasculated and repressed, by fraternal
> bonds. Each person steps forth in his
> singleness to join the other single ones in
> giving and receiving. The members of a
> community are able to bridge their
> differences in virtue of the things they have
> in common, but they are able to enrich one
> another by the rich ferment of their
> contrasting individualities. The mark of a
> community is not likeness but free
> mutuality.[150]

Inasmuch as disinterested self-love coincides with a
disinterested "love of benevolence" it is constitutive

of a pious or virtuous society. As Nagy has observed,
the coincidence in the individual of public and private
affection "strongly suggests authentic individualism,
rooted in self-love, to be the cornerstone of
society."[151] And inasmuch as such individualism is
intrinsic to Edwards' conception of the ideal social
order, that conception is one of true community.

Citizenship in the Benevolent Community

The implicit civic character of Brainerd's public
mindedness becomes clear in comparison with the
explicit civic mindedness of Col. John Stoddard,
Edwards' magistrate uncle, whom Edwards eulogized in
God's Awful Judgment, his most explicitly political
text. Interestingly, the virtues of statesmanship
delineated therein are ones exemplified by Brainerd.
Thus we might say that Stoddard's merits of
statesmanship are mirrored in Brainerd as the
complementary merits of citizenship. Brainerd
represents the model citizen of Edwards' ideal society
as Stoddard represents the model statesman.[152] To see
this, let us compare Stoddard's civic virtues with
Brainerd's, as enumerated by Edwards.

In the exposition of *God's Awful Judgment*, Edwards
sets forth the virtues of statesmanship. Preeminent
among them is *benevolence* or, as he there expresses it,
"largeness of heart, and a greatness and nobleness of
disposition."[153] Ideally, a statesman is "one that is
of a public spirit, and not of a private, narrow
disposition; a man of honour, and not of mean artifice
and clandestine management, for filthy lucre." Indeed,

> it is peculiarly unbecoming them [statesmen]
> to be of a mean spirit, a disposition that
> will admit of their doing those things that
> are sordid and vile; as when they are persons
> of a narrow, private spirit, that may be
> found in little tricks and intrigues to
> promote their private interest.[154]

A second virtue is *piety*, expressed as faithfulness to
God and the good of man: "He is one of inflexible
fidelity, who will be faithful to God, whose minister
he is, to his people for good, and who is immoveable in
his regard to his supreme authority, his commands, and
his glory." A third is *personal rectitude*. A statesman
ought to be "a man of strict integrity and
righteousness, firm and immoveable in the execution of
justice and judgment. . . . He is well principled, and
firm in acting agreeably to his principles, and will
not be prevailed with to do otherwise through fear or
favour."[155] Finally, the fourth virtue of statesmanship
is *social decorum*, or "decency of behaviour, becoming
one in authority."[156]

Such statesmen, according to Edwards, are public
benefactors in two ways: First, they contribute to the
public's material well-being: "Their influence has a
tendency to promote wealth, and cause temporal
possessions and blessings to abound." Second, they
foster the public's moral well-being and cultivate good
citizenship among their people. Thus, the influence of
good rulers tends "to promote virtue amongst them, and
so to unite them one to another in peace and mutual
benevolence, and make them happy in society, each one
the instrument of his neigbour's quietness, comfort,
and prosperity."[157] Edwards conceives of politicians as
"eminently the ministers of God" and, like Christ, the
"vehicles of good to mankind."[158]

In the "application" of the sermon, Edwards holds
up Stoddard as an exemplar of these political virtues.
Thus Stoddard was benevolent, as "a man of a remarkably
public spirit" and "who greatly abhorred sacrificing
the public welfare to private interest."[159] The
"greatness and honourableness of his disposition" was
such, according to Edwards, that he "greatly abhorred
things which were mean and sordid, and seemed to be
incapable of a compliance with them."[160] Moreover, he
was pious. Stoddard believed in the correctness of the
"vital" piety, or "experimental" religion, delineated
and extolled by Edwards in *Religions Affections*: "He
was thoroughly established in those religious
principles and doctrines,...usually called the
doctrines of grace, . . . he was a friend to vital
piety and the power of godliness."[161] And Stoddard
could speak of such piety as one who was personally
conversant with it: "And as he was able . . . to
discourse very understandingly of experimental
religion,...he gave intimations sufficiently
plain, while conversing of these things, that they were
matters of his own experience."[162] In addition,
Stoddard was a man of surpassing rectitude:

> He was strictly conscientious in his conduct,
> both in public and private. I never knew the
> man that seemed more steadfastly and
> immoveably to act by principle, and according
> to rules and maxims, established and settled
> in his mind by the dictates of his judgment
> and conscience. He was a man of strict
> justice and fidelity.[163]

Finally, he was socially decorous and sedate, as "a
person of a serious and decent spirit." This, according
to Edwards, was exhibited by Stoddard in three social
graces: In temperance, i.e.

> He was a noted instance of the virtue of
> temperance, unalterable in it, in all places,
> in all companies, and in the midst of all
> temptations. Though he was a man of a great
> spirit, yet he had a remarkable government of
> his spirit; and excelled in the government of
> his tongue.[164]

In discretion, i.e. "He was exceeding far from a disposition and forwardness to intermeddle with other people's business."[165] And in good conversation, i.e. "How far was he from trifling and impertinence in his conversation,"[166] with "no profane language, no vain, rash, unseemly, and unchristian speeches."[167] In Edwards' estimation, Stoddard was an exemplary public benefactor:

> He took care of the country as a father of a
> family of children, not neglecting men's
> lives,...but with great diligence,
> vigilance, and prudence, applying himself
> continually to the proper means of our safety
> and welfare. And especially has this his
> native town, where he has dwelt from his
> infancy, reaped the benefit of his happy
> influence.[168]

Significantly, the very virtues that Edwards commends specifically as civic virtues in Stoddard he commends in Brainerd. Thus, Brainerd was *benevolent*, exercising a "great and universal benevolence to mankind, reaching all sorts of persons without distinction, manifested in sweetness of speech and behaviour, kind treatment, mercy, liberality, and earnest seeking the good of the souls and bodies of men." He was eminently *pious*: "Mr. Brainerd's religion was wholly correspondent to what is called the Calvinistical scheme, and was the effect of those doctrines applied to his heart." Brainerd had considerable *personal rectitude*, or "a great degree of

honesty and simplicity, sincere and earnest desires and
endeavours to know and do whatever is right, and to
avoid every thing that is wrong."[169] And he exhibited
social decorum, or "a modest, discreet, and decent
deportment, among superiors, inferiors, and equals."[170]
These were the virtues that Edwards extolled as the
political virtues of statesmanship in *God's Awful
Judgment*. Furthermore, Brainerd, like Stoddard, was a
public benefactor *par excellence*, both materially and
spiritually, as a "vehicle of good" to the Indian
nations where he effected a remarkable and thorough-
going social reformation:

> And this [Brainerd's] example and these
> endeavours we see attended with most happy
> fruits, and blessed effects on *others*, in
> humanizing, civilizing, and wonderfully
> reforming and transforming some of the most
> brutish savages; idle, immoral, drunkards,
> murderers, gross idolators [sic], and
> wizards; bringing them to permanent sobriety,
> diligence, devotion, honesty,
> conscientiousness, and charity.[171]

Among these "happy fruits" of Brainerd's ministry was
the establishment of a stable Indian community, replete
with church, school, and homes and farms:

> They [the Indians] . . . were formed into a
> church, . . . and had a school set up and
> established, in good order, among them. . . .
> were collected in a town by themselves, on a
> good piece of land of their own; were
> introduced into the way of living by
> husbandry, and begun to experience the
> benefits of it, &c.[172]

Brainerd's benevolent solicitude evidently extended to
the total welfare of his charges. Brainerd, moreover,
had turned many of the Indians into model citizens.
Thus Job Strong, in a laudatory account of Brainerd's
missionary enterprise, writes, "It is surprising to see

this people, . . . now living soberly and regularly,
and not seeking every man his own, but every man, in
some sense, his neighbour's good."[173]

Now if these virtues exemplified by Stoddard and
Brainerd alike are preeminently civic ones, being the
virtues of statesmanship in the one case, can they not
be considered the virtues of citizenship in the other?
And as Stoddard is the type of the statesman in
Edwards' benevolent community, cannot Brainerd be
similarly regarded as the type of the citizen? The
complementary merits of Stoddard's statesmanship and
Brainerd's citizenship make explicit the socio-
political thrust of Edwards' later conception of true
virtue which can be summed up as a principle of radical
public-mindedness:

> A man of a right spirit, is not a man of
> narrow and private views, but is greatly
> interested and concerned for the good of the
> community to which he belongs, and
> particularly of the city or village in which
> he resides, and for the true welfare of the
> society of which he is a member.[174]

CHAPTER IV

NOTES

[1]Faust and Johnson, eds., *Jonathan Edwards*, p. 424.

[2]Edwards M. Griffin, *Jonathan Edwards*, University of Minnesota Pamphlets on American Writers, No. 97 (Minneapolis, 1971), p. 39.

[3]Ola Elizabeth Winslow, *Jonathan Edwards, 1703-1758: A Biography* (New York, 1940), p. 239.

[4]Goen, "Editor's Introduction," p. 57.

[5]Winslow, *Jonathan Edwards*, p. 273.

[6]Ibid., p. 240.

[7]Ibid., p. 274.

[8]Allen, *Jonathan Edwards*, p. 247.

[9]Ibid., pp. 275-276.

[10]Jonathan Edwards, *A Treatise concerning Religious Affections*, in *The works of Jonathan Edwards*, ed. by John E. Smith, II (New Haven, 1959), p. 84.

[11]Samuel Hopkins, *The Life and Character of the Late Reverend Mr. Jonathan Edwards* (Boston, 1765), reprinted in *Jonathan Edwards: A Profile*, American Profiles, ed. by David Levin (New York, 1969), p. 2.

[12]John E. Smith, "Editor's Introduction," *Religious Affections*, in *Works*, II (New Haven, 1959), p. 2.

[13]Jonathan Edwards, *The Life and Diary of The Rev. David Brainerd: with Notes and Reflections*, in *The Works of President Edwards*, Burt Franklin: Research and Source Work Series, No. 271, ed. by E. Williams and E. Parsons, III (London, 1817), p. 75.

[14]Edwards, *Religious Affections*, p. 84.

[15]Jonathan Edwards, *An Account of the Life of the Rev. David Brainerd*, in *The Works of President Edwards*, 8th ed., I (New York, 1851), p. 656.

[16]Hopkins, *Life of Edwards*, p. 52.

202

[17]Winslow, *Jonathan Edwards*, p. 239.

[18]Edwards, *Life of Brainerd*, p. 665.

[19]Charles Chauncy (1705-87) co-pastor of Boston's First Church, was the intellectual leader of the anti-revival forces in eighteenth-century New England. He dismissed the religiosity resulting from the revivals as "the effect of enthusiastic heat." *Seasonable Thoughts on the State of Religion in New England, a Treatise in Five Parts* (Boston, 1743) is Chauncy's rejoinder to Edwards' *Some Thoughts concerning the Present Revival of Religion in New-England* (Boston, 1742), whose position he mistook for enthusiasm. See Goen's "Editor's Introduction," pp. 61-64, 80-83.

[20]Smith, "Editor's Introduction," in *Works*, II (New Haven, 1959), pp. 79-80.

[21]Edwards, *Life of Brainerd* (New York, 1851), p. 658.

[22]Ibid., p. 662.

[23]Ibid., p. 665.

[24]Ibid., p. 664.

[25]Ibid., p. 665.

[26]Edward Hutchins Davidson, *Jonathan Edwards; the Narrative of a Puritan Mind* (Cambridge, Mass., 1968), p. 107.

[27]Edwards, *Life of Brainerd* (New York, 1851), p. 669.

[28]Ibid., p. 647.

[29]Ibid., p. 648.

[30]Ibid., p. 655.

[31]Ibid., p. 653.

[32]Edwards, *Diary of Brainerd*, in *Works*, III (London, 1817), p. 170.

[33]Ibid., p. 197.

[34]Ibid., p. 194.

[35]Ibid., p. 187.

[36]Ibid., p. 231.

[37]Ibid., p. 264.

[38]Ibid., p. 195.

[39]The first part, "The life and Diary of the Rev. David Brainerd; with Notes and Reflections," contains Brainerd's private diary, together with Edwards' brief biography and editorial comments, and a preface by the correspondents of the Society in Scotland for Propagating Christian Knowledge which comissioned Brainerd. The second, "Mr. Brainerd's Journal in Two Parts" and originally included in his diary, contains the journal recording his missionary progress kept for the society and a set of three appendices. The third part, "Mr. Brainerd's Remains" contains Brainerd's letters and his theological papers. The fourth is the sermon delivered by Ebenezer Pemberton at Brainerd's ordination. The fifth and last part, "Some Reflections and Observations on the Preceding Memoirs, &c. of the Rev. David Brainerd," is Edwards' own assessment of Brainerd's life, character and piety.

[40]Edwards, *Religious Affections*, p. 107.

[41]For an explanation of saving grace and its distinction from common grace see p. 92 below.

[42]Edwards, *Religious Affections*, p. 200.

[43]Ibid., p. 205.

[44]Ibid., p. 240.

[45]Ibid., p. 242.

[46]Ibid., p. 246.

[47]Ibid., p. 256.

[48]Edwards, *Life of Brainerd*, p. 659.

[49]Edwards, *True Virtue*, p. 3.

[50]Ibid., p. 5.

[51]Ibid., p. 6.

[52]Ibid., p. 8.

[53] Ibid., p. 9.

[54] Ibid., p. 9.

[55] Ibid., p. 7.

[56] Ibid., p. 10.

[57] Ibid., pp. 10-11.

[58] Ibid., p. 13.

[59] Ibid., p. 12.

[60] Ibid., p. 14.

[61] Ibid., p. 38.

[62] Ibid., p. 8.

[63] Ibid., p. 92.

[64] Jonathan Edwards, *A Dissertation concerning the End for Which God Created the World*, in *The Works of President Edwards*, Burt Franklin: Research and Source Work Series, No. 271, ed. by E. Williams and E. Parsons, I (London, 1817), p. 475.

[65] Ibid., pp. 471-72.

[66] Edwards, *True Virtue*, p. 92.

[67] Ibid., p. 42.

[68] Edwards, "The Mind," p. 337.

[69] Jonathan Edwards, "Miscellany No. 530," in *Private Notebooks*, p. 202.

[70] Jonathan Edwards, *Christian Love, as Manifested in the Heart and Life*, ed. by Tryon Edwards, 6th American ed. (Philadelphia, 1874), p. 229.

[71] Edwards, *True Virtue*, p. 45.

[72] Ibid., p. 46.

[73] Ibid., p. 47.

[74] Ibid., p. 48.

[75] Edwards, "Miscellany No. 530," p. 203.

[76]Ibid., p. 204.

[77]Edwards, *True Virtue*, p. 45.

[78]Ibid., p. 61.

[79]Edwards, *Christian Love*, p. 248.

[80]Ibid., p. 245.

[81]Ibid., p. 251.

[82]Ibid., p. 252.

[83]Ibid., p. 231.

[84]Ibid., pp. 236-237.

[85]Edwards, *True Virtue*, p. 18.

[86]Ibid., p. 19.

[87]Ibid., pp. 78-79.

[88]Ibid., pp. 20-21.

[89]Ibid., p. 88.

[90]Edwards, *Christian Love*, p. 251.

[91]Edwards, *True Virtue*, p. 25.

[92]Edwards, *Diary of Brainerd*, pp. 552-553.

[93]Ibid., p. 553.

[94]Ibid., p. 229.

[95]Ibid., p. 564.

[96]Ibid., p. 169.

[97]Ibid., p. 291.

[98]Ibid., p. 297.

[99]Ibid., p. 303.

[100]Edwards, *True Virtue*, p. 4.

[101]Ibid., p. 6.

[102]Ibid., p. 25.

[103]Ibid., p. 23.

[104]Nancy Manspeaker, "Did Jonathan Edwards' Thought Develop? A Comparison of the Doctrine of Love Expressed in His First and Last Writings" (unpublished Ph.D. dissertation, Institute of Christian Thought, University of St. Michael's College, Toronto, 1983), p. 2.

[105]Miller, *Jonathan Edwards*, pp. 44-45.

[106]Manspeaker, "Did Edwards' Thought Develop?," p. 60.

[107]Henry Bamford Parkes, *Jonathan Edwards: The Fiery Puritan* (New York, 1930), p. 174.

[108]Jonathan Edwards, "Author's Preface," *The Life of David Brainerd*, in *The Works of Jonathan Edwards*, ed. by Norman Pettit, VII (New Haven, 1985), pp. 95-96.

[109]Miller, *Jonathan Edwards*, p. 246.

[110]Davidson, *Jonathan Edwards*, p. 109.

[111]Samuel Miller, *The Life of Jonathan Edwards, President of the College of New Jersey*, in *Library of American Biography*, ed. Jared Sparks, Vol. VIII (New York, 1837), p. 97.

[112]Charles Haddon Spurgeon, *Lectures to My Students: A Selection From Addresses Delivered to the Students of the Pastors' College, Metropolitan Tabernacle*, First Series (London, 1875), p. 48.

[113]As quoted in Aldridge, *Jonathan Edwards*, p. 44.

[114]Allen, *Jonathan Edwards*, p. 248.

[115]Winslow, *Jonathan Edwards*, p. 274.

[116]Edwards, *Diary of Brainerd*, p. 170.

[117]Ibid., p. 150.

[118]The eighth sign reads: "Truly gracious affections . . . naturally beget and promote such a spirit of love, meekness, quietness, forgiveness and mercy, as appeared in Christ." See Edwards, *Religious Affections*, pp. 344-345.

119Edwards, *Religious Affections*, p. 355.

120Edwards, *Christian Love*, p. 242.

121Edwards, *Religious Affections*, p. 369.

122Edwards, *Diary of Brainerd*, pp. 460-461.

123Ibid., p. 408.

124Ibid., p. 403.

125Ibid., p. 241.

126Ibid., p. 379.

127Heimert, *American Mind*, p. 42.

128Ibid., p. 133.

129Edwards, *Religious Affections*, p. 95.

130Ibid., p. 107.

131The twelfth sign reads: "Gracious and holy affections have their exercise and fruit in Christian practice." See Edwards, *Religious Affections*, p. 383.

132Edwards, *Religious Affections*, p. 443.

133Norman Fiering, *Jonathan Edwards's Moral Thought and Its British Context*, The Institute of Early American History and Culture (Chapel Hill, North Carolina, 1981), p. 349.

134Heimert, *American Mind*, p. 314.

135Edwards, *Diary of Brainerd*, p. 129.

136Ibid., p. 131.

137Ibid., p. 302.

138Ibid., p. 542.

139The sixth sign reads: "Gracious affections are attended with evangelical humiliation . . . a sense that a Christian has of his own utter insufficiency, despicableness, and odiousness, with an answerable frame of heart." See Edwards, *Religious Affections*, p.311.

[140] Joseph G. Haroutunian, *Piety versus Moralism: The Passing of the New England Theology*, Studies in Religion and Culture: American Religion Series IV (Hamden, Connecticut, 1932), p. 73.

[141] James Pearce Carse, *Jonathan Edwards and the Visibility of God* (New York, 1967), p. 160.

[142] Edwards, *The Portion of the Righteous*, p. 349.

[143] Edwards, *Christian Love*, pp. 265-266.

[144] Edwards, *True Virtue*, p. 25.

[145] Nagy, "Beloved Community," p. 94.

[146] Ibid., p. 95.

[147] Edwards, "Miscellany No. 530," p. 203.

[148] Erwin Anton Gutkind, *Community and Environment: A Discourse on Social Ecology*, with a foreword by Martin Buber (London, 1953), p. viii.

[149] John E. Smith, *The Spirit of American Philosophy* (New York, 1963), p. 93.

[150] Rader, *Ethics*, p. 391.

[151] Nagy, "Beloved Community," p. 100.

[152] It might be objected that no comparison can be made here between Brainerd and Stoddard since Edwards extolls Brainerd as a pious individual and Stoddard as a civil magistrate. That is, Brainerd's virtues are suitable to a member of a pious society, whereas Stoddard's are suitable to a leader of civil society. Thus, Brainerd's religious virtues cannot be seen as mirroring and complementing Stoddard's civic virtues. However, though distinct, Edwards' pious and civil societies are analogous. The pious society represents the ideal to which the civil aspires, though ever falling short.

[153] Jonathan Edwards, *God's Awful Judgment in the Breaking and Withering of the Strong Rods of a Community*, in *The Works of President Edwards*, Burt Franklin: Research and Source Work Series, No. 271, ed. by E. Williams and E. Parsons, VIII (London, 1817), 83.

[154] Ibid., p. 84.

[155]Ibid., p. 85.

[156]Ibid., p. 86.

[157]Ibid., p. 86.

[158]Ibid., p. 87.

[159]Ibid., p. 92.

[160]Ibid., p. 91.

[161]Ibid., p. 93.

[162]Ibid., pp. 93-94.

[163]Ibid., p. 92.

[164]Ibid., p. 93.

[165]Ibid., pp. 90-91.

[166]Ibid., p. 91.

[167]Ibid., p. 93.

[168]Ibid., p. 94.

[169]Edwards, *Diary of Brainerd*, p. 552.

[170]Ibid., p. 553.

[171]Ibid., p. 553.

[172]Ibid., pp. 566-567.

[173]Letter, Job Strong to his parents, January 14, 1748, printed in *Works*, III (London, 1817), pp. 560-561.

[174]Edwards, *Christian Love*, pp. 243-244.

CHAPTER V

THE IMPLEMENTATION OF EDWARDS' IDEAL SOCIETY: THE CHURCH AS THE HISTORICAL EMBODIMENT OF ESCHATOLOGICAL COMMUNITY

Historical Background

Edwards states in the preface to *Humble Inquiry*
that he originally went along with the policy on church
admission of Stoddard, his grandfather and predecessor
in the Northampton church, though not without scruples:
"I have formerly been of *his opinion*, . . . and have in
my proceedings conformed to *his practice*; though never
without some difficulties in my view, which I could not
solve."[1] However, since these difficulties were
exacerbated with further experience and study, Edwards
at last formulated the position defended in this
treatise. Edwards' own policy on church Communion is a
reversal of Stoddard's, and represents a reversion to
much earlier Puritan conceptions of the Church and its
sacraments. To see this, we need to sketch the
development of Puritan thinking on the qualifications
for Communion up to the time of Edwards' break with
Stoddard.

In the beginning, New England Puritans regarded
the sacraments as "professing ordinances," or as
expressions and ratifications of sanctifying grace
already bestowed. In the words of the *Westminster
Symbols*, adopted in the New World by the Cambridge

Synod of 1646, "sacraments are holy signs and seals of
the covenant of grace."[2] As such, they are diplomatical
rites, attesting to the regeneracy or piety of either
the communicants themselves or, in the case of infant
baptism, their parents. Therefore, the manifestly
regenerate alone were qualified to receive the
sacraments, and only their children were qualified for
baptism. This policy of regarding the sacraments as
"diplomas" of proven grace was designed to ensure the
emergence of a "pure" church, separate from the world
and composed exclusively of pious communicants.
According to Thomas Hooker, "Visible saints are the
only true and meet matter, whereof a visible church
shall be gathered"[3]--a *visible* saint being one whose
faith was evident. Puritans inherited this conception
of the church from Anabaptists.

Later in the seventeenth century, however,
Puritans came to regard only the sacrament of the
Lord's Supper as a professing ordinance or a seal of
grace, regarding baptism instead as a "converting
ordinance"--that is, a rite that would help convert the
unconverted. The Synod of 1662 ruled that the children
of even visibly unregenerate, though baptized, parents
who declared at least an "interest" in the covenant of
grace, i.e. expressed a desire for conversion, were
eligible for baptism. This ruling was an expedient for
reversing a drastic decline in church membership.[4] It
was thus a concession to the theocratic ideal of a Holy
Commonwealth, a more inclusive conception of the church
that Puritans inherited from Calvinists. The Lord's
Table, though, still remained sacrosanct, a seat at
which depended on visible holiness.

Stoddard, however, changed this by declaring even
the Lord's Supper a "converting ordinance."[5] In his *An
Appeal to the Learned* (hereinafter cited as *An Appeal*),
he maintains that the Lord's Supper is a "means" to
grace through its graphic representation of Christ's
atonement and man's salvation:

> This Ordinance has a proper tendency in its
> own nature to Convert men. Herein men may
> learn the necessity and sufficiency of the
> Death of Christ in order to Pardon. Here is
> an affecting offer of Christ crucifyed; here
> is a Sealing of the Covenant, that if men
> come to Christ, they shall be Saved, which is
> a great means to convince of safety in coming
> to Christ.[6]

Thus, in Stoddard's view, "Sanctifying Grace is not
necessary in order to a lawful partaking of the Lord's
Supper."[7] His justification for this is the authority
of Christ, who "requires men to observe . . . all such
Religious Worship & Ordinances as God requireth in his
word,"[8] and the precedent set by the analogous rite of
the Passover in which the unsanctified are commanded to
participate. What is necessary for lawful attendance at
the Lord's Supper, according to Stoddard, is baptism
(i.e., membership in the so-called "external
convenant"), conventionally moral behavior, "historical
faith" (i.e., an intellectual assent to the truth of
Christian doctrine), repentance, and an *interest* in
"saving faith" (i.e., a desire for conversion).[9]
Moreover, since the Lord's Supper is a converting
ordinance, those fulfilling these conditions are
obligated, no less, to attend it thereby putting
themselves in the way of saving grace. People, in
Stoddard's words,

> may and ought to come, tho' they know
> themselves to be in a natural condition; this
> ordinance is instituted for all adult members
> of the church who are not scandalous and
> therefore must be attended by them; as no man
> may neglect prayer, or hearing the Word,
> because he cannot do it in faith, so he may
> not neglect the Lord's Supper.[10]

By thus waiving visible grace as a necessary
qualification for Communion, Stoddard hoped to realize
the theocratic ideal of Puritanism by enfranchising
more citizens as communicants in the church and
subjecting them to its discipline and control.

Edwards' earliest formulation (an entry from his
Miscellanies) of his changed position on church
Communion that would be formally defended in *Humble
Inquiry* dates from the winter or spring of 1741.[11] And
this position was already implicit in a series of
sermons (later published as *Religious Affections*) that
he gave in 1744.[12] Yet it was not until December 1748
that Edwards made his change of mind public, for nobody
applied for church membership in the intervening years.
On that date an applicant, though competent and
directed by Edwards to do so, declined to make a formal
profession of his faith on the grounds that it was not
the official policy of the Northampton church.[13] In the
spring of the following year, a young girl was
pressured out of making her profession, and the church
voted to suspend the administration of the Lord's
Supper.[14] And, since his request to defend his
position from the pulpit was denied, Edwards commenced
work on *Humble Inquiry*, which was published in August
1749.

Why, then, did Edwards rescind Stoddard's policy
on Church admissions? After all, did it not bear the

authority of tradition, having been instituted in the Northampton church in 1677 and implemented by Edwards for twenty years; did not both Edwards and his congregation have a vast esteem for Stoddard, whom Edwards himself called "so great and eminent a divine";[15] and did not Edwards adamantly pursue this course, in his own words, "with the fullest expectation of being driven from my ministerial office, and stripped of a maintenance for my numerous family"?[16] "Without any doubt," writes Carse, "the most significant event in Edwards' life was his brave decision to contravene his grandfather on the question of visible sainthood."[17] There are three probable reasons: One resulting from the Great Awakening, another from Edwards' having systematically thought through the nature of true piety in *Religious Affections*, and the third from Stoddard's policy of open Communion.

A result of the Great Awakening was an increase in the number of converts, many of whom, undoubtedly, sought admission to the church. The piety of some of them, moreover, would have been suspect. For one of the revivals' baneful effects, condemned by Edwards and Chauncy alike, was a virulent outbreak of "enthusiasm"--that strain of religiosity whose symptoms are emotionalism, anti-intellectualism, fanaticism and bigotry in individuals, and schisms within the church. It is hardly surprising, then, that the position Edwards would systematically defend in *Humble Inquiry* should have been formulated in 1741, a year in which the Awakening was in full swing. Perhaps Edwards felt that he had, under the circumstances, to be especially

vigilant about keeping hypocrites and other false
converts out of the church.

In the post-Awakening period of 1744, Edwards
delivered the sermon-series--to be published as
Religious Affections in 1746--that is a critical
response to the sort of religious experience engendered
by the great revivals. In the published treatise,
Edwards provides a set of "signs," or criteria, whereby
the genuineness of such experiences could be assayed.
As we remarked in the previous chapter, a life-long
project of Edwards was determining the exact nature of
true piety. Now having been concerned that the
individual should distinguish true from false piety
with regard to himself, it is natural that Edwards
should also have been concerned that the church should
do the same with regard to its members. Hence, Edwards'
rethinking the qualifications for Communion can be
understood as a logical extension of his thinking
through the nature of piety; *Humble Inquiry*, then, can
be regarded as a corollary of sorts of *Religious
Affections*.

By 1748, the Northampton church was in a steep
spiritual decline, as will be recalled from our second
chapter. For one thing, a lifeless and man-made
morality had usurped a vital and God-created piety in
the hearts of many church members. Various forms of
Neonominianism and Arminianism increasingly held sway
against the traditional principles of evangelical
Calvinism, not only in the Northampton church but also
in other churches where Stoddardeanism was the rule. In
Walker's words, "increasing weight was laid upon the
cultivation of morality as a means to a Christian
life, rather than upon an insistence on the prime

necessity of a divinely wrought change in man's nature,
a change of which morality should not be the means, but
the fruit."[18] Carse comments,

> Edwards knew that because the church had
> capitulated to the world, it could do nothing
> more than apply the stamp of its vapid, pious
> approval to whatever the world wanted to do.
> The church had ceased to act as a moral
> influence in the very society which its moral
> courage had created.[19]

And for another thing, even immorality itself was being
covertly practiced by some members of Edwards'
congregation: "men and women who had been recognized as
visible saints in Northampton still wallowed in
clandestine immorality and flagrant pride."[20] An
explanation in part for this decline in spirituality in
the Northampton church and elsewhere was the lack of an
institutional incentive for becoming regenerate; one
could enjoy all the privileges, and prestige, of church
membership in complete standing without ever being
converted. Thus, both the revivals--those of 1734-35
and those of the Great Awakening of 1741-42--and
Stoddard's policy on open Communion had failed
conspicuously to live up to the spiritual promise of
the Great Awakening and to create a genuinely pious
community, a visible society of the elect.

Thus, Edwards' change of mind over the
qualifications for Communion can be explained as a
response to the false religion spawned by revivalism,
an extension of the precepts in *Religious Affections* to
the problem of church membership, and a reaction to the
spiritual deadness of the Northampton church.

Exposition

The *Humble Inquiry* is in three parts: in the
first, Edwards states and clarifies his position on the
qualifications for Communion; in the second, he defends
it; and in the third part, he anticipates and meets
possible objections. We shall be mainly concerned with
the first part and sections in the second, and shall
sometimes cite *Misrepresentations Corrected*, Edwards'
reply to Solomon Williams' animadversions of *Humble
Inquiry*, to illuminate further his position.

Edwards avers that only those who, by word and
deed, give evidence to the congregation of being truly
Christian are qualified for full membership in the
church and admission to the Lord's Supper. "*None ought
to be admitted to the communion and privileges of
members of the visible church of Christ in complete
standing*," asseverates Edwards, "*but such as are in
profession, and in the eye of the church's christian
judgment, godly or gracious persons.*"[21] Edwards
distinguishes church members "in complete standing"
from church members "in general,"[22] or those not
apparently godly who either are incompetent to make a
credible profession of faith because of immaturity (as
in the case of children), ignorance of Christian
doctrine, plain lack of grace, or "scandalous" conduct.

Now Edwards makes clear that the qualification for
Communion is not a person's actual faith, but only the
"visibility," or appearance and evidence, thereof:

> The question is not, whether Christ has made
> converting grace or piety *itself* the
> condition or rule of his people's admitting
> any to the privileges of members in full
> communion with them. . . . It is the credible

profession and *visibility* of these things,
that is the church's rule in this case.[23]

It is to be made visible to *all* members of the
congregation in complete standing, for it is they as a
group, and not a privileged individual or select
company of them, who should openly determine whether
the candidate is qualified: "It is properly a
visibility to the eye of the public charity [i.e.
judgment], and not of a private judgment, that gives a
person a right to be received as a visible saint by the
public." Certainly the minister should not so determine
on his own. Edwards notes that the minister has no
adjudicative prerogative whatsoever; his role is simply
that of the congregation's representative: "The
minister . . . is to act as a public officer, and in
behalf of the public society, and not merely for
himself, and therefore is to be governed, in acting, by
a proper visibility of godliness in the eye of the
public."[24]

The reasons Edwards adduces for his policy on
church admissions most relevant to our purposes are
derived from the authority of Scripture and the
prevailing theological consensus, his interpretation of
the Lord's Supper as a "professing" ordinance that
"seals" the covenant of grace, and his conception of
the church as a pious society. We shall now consider
each of them in turn.

"It is both evident by the word of God, and also
granted on all hands," declares Edwards, "that none
ought to be admitted as members of the visible church
of Christ but *visible* and *professing saints*."[25] This
principle is not in dispute. Even Stoddard, notes
Edwards, adhered to it, albeit inconsistently given his

interpretation of the Lord's Supper as a "converting"
ordinance. The problem, in Edwards' diagnosis, and the
source of the disagreement between him and Stoddard *et
alia* over qualifications for Communion, is a
misunderstanding of the phrase "visible saint." Some
speak, says Edwards, "as though by visible saints were
not meant those who to appearance are real saints or
disciples indeed, but properly a distinct sort of
saints, which is an absurdity." "Visibility," explains
Edwards, "has relation to an eye that views"; moreover,
"the thing which must be visible and probable, in order
to *visible saintship*, must be saintship *itself*, or real
grace and true holiness"; therefore, "to be a visible
saint is the same as to appear to be a real saint in
the eye that beholds."[26]

A person's faith or holiness is made visible or
public, according to Edwards, by the observable means
of its "*profession*, and outward *behaviour* agreeable to
that profession." Edwards defines "profession" as an
"exhibiting, uttering, or declaring, either by
intelligible words, or by other established signs [e.g.
sacramental actions] that are equivalent." And he
stipulates that the thing to be professed is "piety of
heart,"[27] the essence of Christianity, which issues
from so called "saving grace" in contradistinction to
"common grace." This piety of heart is nothing other
than the true religion Edwards expounds in *Religious
Affections*:

> The *saintship, godliness*, and *holiness*, of
> which, according to Scripture, professing
> Christians and visible saints do make a
> profession and have a visibility, is not any
> religion and virtue that is the result of
> common grace, or moral sincerity, (as it is
> called,) but saving grace.[28]

Edwards explains this distinction between the two
kinds of grace in his *Treatise on Grace*. "Grace" can
refer to either the Holy Spirit's actual operation on a
person or its moral effect.[29] Common grace operates
superficially upon the "natural principles" of the
mind, without imbuing it with a "new spiritual
principle"[30] or disposition, thereby producing "those
religious or moral attainments that are common to both
saints and sinners," such as concern for neighbor,
patriotism, moral conscience, the scrupulous
performance of religious duties, and the enactment of
other articles in the conventional moral and religious
codes. By contrast, saving grace does not merely
operate tangentially upon the mind's natural principles
but imbues it with an entirely new or spiritual
principle. As such, saving grace *indwells* the human
heart as the principle of a new or sanctified nature
thereby producing the unique and distinctive moral
character, the "distinguishing saving virtue"[31] or
disinterested benevolence to being, which belongs to
the regenerate alone:

> But the Spirit of God in his spiritual
> influences on the hearts of his saints
> [saving grace], operates by infusing or
> exercising new, divine and supernatural
> principles; principles which are indeed a new
> and spiritual nature, and principles vastly
> more noble and excellent than all that is in
> natural men.[32]

Edwards further stipulates that the person making the
profession must be sincere about it, not merely
morally, but *graciously*; that is, the professor must
believe according to his best lights that the grace he
professes is of the *saving* rather than the *common* kind,
and thus authentic faith:

> There is but one sort of sincerity in loving
> God as God, and setting our hearts on him as
> our highest happiness, loving him above the
> world, and loving holiness above all the
> objects of our lusts. He that does not these
> things with a gracious sincerity, never
> really doth them at all.[33]

Edwards' second reason for restricting Communion
to "visible" or apparent Christians follows from his
doctrine of the Eucharist. "The Lord's supper," writes
Edwards, "is most evidently a *professing* ordinance."[34]
Through its elements and symbolic actions, Christ (by
proxy) and man--both parties in the covenant of grace--
make professions to one another:

> There is in the Lord's supper a mutual solemn
> profession of the two parties transacting the
> covenant of grace, and visibly united in that
> covenant; the Lord Christ by his minister, on
> the one hand, and the communicants (who are
> professing believers) on the other.[35]

Each professes his willingness to fulfill his part in
the covenant. Christ professes his willingness "to be
theirs who truly receive him" in faith, whereas the
communicants profess their willingness "to receive him,
which they declare by significant actions."[36] Edwards
equates the profession of faith with the public owning
of the covenant of grace: "For a person explicitly or
professedly to enter into the union or relation of the
covenant of grace with Christ, is the same as
professedly to do that which on our part is the uniting
act, and that is the act of faith." And he equates
faith itself (piety of heart) with the actual act of
convenanting: "To own this covenant, is to profess the
consent of our hearts to it; and that is the sum and
substance of true piety."[37] Owning the covenant is
equivalent to declaring that God is "our chief good and

last end, the supreme object of our esteem and regard."[38]

Now in Edwards' view, by partaking of the Lord's Supper, the communicants, with Christ, ratify their accedence to the covenant:

> Thus the Lord's supper is plainly a *mutual* renovation, confirmation, and seal of the covenant of grace: both the covenanting parties *profess* their consent to their respective parts in the covenant, and each affixes his *seal* to his profession.

The Lord's Supper represents a virtual or implicit profession of faith. Indeed, Edwards regards the eucharistic elements and actions as symbols equivalent in meaning to the language of a profession of faith or the owning of the covenant:

> The established signs in the Lord's supper are fully equivalent to words; they are a renewing and reiterating the same thing which was done *before*; only with this difference, that now it is done by *speaking signs*, whereas before it was by *speaking sounds*.

Thus, since the Lord's Supper confirms or seals a profession of faith with signs, it presupposes a prior profession with words. So for one to sit at the Lord's Table without first making a verbal profession of faith is absurd, since it is to ratify what one has not explicitly professed before, "to profess that which he *does not* profess" with "his *actions* being no established *signs* of the *thing* supposed to be professed."[39]

A third reason of Edwards' for restricting church membership in complete standing to the visibly or probably pious follows from his conception of the visible church as "a *society having its several members united by the bond of christian brotherly love*."

Saints, though unconditionally loving all mankind,
reserve a special esteem for each other, which is the
foundation of their deeper union:

> Besides that general benevolence or charity
> which the saints have to mankind,...
> there is a *peculiar* and very *distinguishing*
> kind of affection, that every true Christian
> *experiences* towards those whom he looks upon
> as truly *gracious* persons. The soul, at least
> at times, is very sensibly and sweetly knit
> to such persons, and there is an ineffable
> *oneness of heart* with them.[40]

However, this "distinguishing kind of affection"
towards another can be elicited only if his piety of
heart is perceived: "In order to a real and fervent
affection to another, on account of some amiableness of
qualification or relation, the mind must first judge
there is that amiableness in the object."[41]
Consequently, the sort of ecclesial society envisioned
by Edwards could emerge only if the piety of its
members were made visible through their profession and
practice.

Evaluations and Interpretations

Of any commentator, Perry Miller gives the
shortest shrift to *Humble Inquiry*, which is surprising
given that his student, Heimert, gives considerable
attention to it. Miller says of this book, and its
companion piece *Misrepresentations Corrected*, "Today,
the two books are the least rewarding of Edwards' works
since the issue is utterly forgotten." Though he does
allow that they have some dialectical merit, since "for
sheer destructive argumentation, they are a joy to
those who like that sort of thing,"[42] and that they

have considerable historical interest for what they
have to say about how the degeneration of the covenant
idea in New England produced a native form of
Arminianism:

> For students of American institutions, the
> books [*Humble Inquiry* and *Misrepresentations
> Corrected*] are useful for their astute
> tracing of the effects of the Half-Way
> Covenant, of the multiplication of covenants
> and the degeneration of the ceremonial owning
> of the covenant into formality, and of the
> historical logic of Stoddard's abandonment of
> all covenants, showing these to be a single
> process which produced, by imperceptible
> stages, the indigenous form of Arminianism
> that Edwards first attacked in 1734. For the
> social historian they are invaluable though
> neglected works.[43]

Edward H. Davidson sees nothing more in the treatise
than the dialectical skill noted by Perry Miller: "To a
modern reader *An Humble Inquiry* is painstaking in its
logic and tedious in the unrelenting proofs of its
argument."[44]

Miller's and Davidson's dismissal of these texts
is somewhat surprising considering others' high
estimate of it, including Edwards' own, in the
eighteenth and nineteenth centuries. The earlier
commentators on *Humble Inquiry* are unanimous in their
praise of it. Thus, in an advertisement dated May 15,
1790, for the Edinburgh edition of the work, we find
this encomium:

> And nothing will prevent Christians from
> considering the present Treatise as one of
> the most able and interesting parts of his
> [Edwards'] work, but prejudice and
> indifference about the subject of it. His own
> opinion of it may be seen in his preface.[45]

Sereno Edwards Dwight, who published his remarks in
1830, considers it "a discussion so thorough and
conclusive, that it has been the standard work with
evangelical divines from that time to the present."[46]
And nine years later, Samuel Miller declares, "This
work is generally considered, both by friends and foes,
as one of the ablest, perhaps the most complete and
powerful, ever written in support of the doctrine which
it advocates."[47] However, Edwards' own opinion of his
text, which it behooves us to take seriously, is that
it is perhaps the most important of his output since at
stake here are nothing less than the interest of true
religion, which also prompted the publication of
Religious Affections and all his other revivalistic
books, together with his reputation and livelihood.
Thus Edwards writes in the preface to *Humble Inquiry*,

> I am conscious, not only is the interest of
> religion concerned in this affair, but my own
> reputation, future usefulness, and my very
> subsistence, all seem to depend on my freely
> opening and defending myself, as to my
> principles, and agreeable conduct in my
> pastoral charge; and on my doing it from the
> press.[48]

These contrasting evaluations of *Humble Inquiry*
should be considered in light of the cultural impact it
has supposedly had. It has been supposed the principal
cause of an ecclesiological revolution in
Congregationalism which saw the eventual vindication
and victory of Edwards' policy on church admissions in
the evangelical churches of New England. Thus Samuel
Miller in 1839 writes:

> In a few years after the appearance of this
> treatise, an entire revolution was effected
> in almost all the evangelical churches of New
> England, so that,...it is now as rare

> to find an orthodox church in that part of
> the United States, which does not adopt and
> act upon it, as it once was to find one, that
> regarded it with any degree of approbation.
> That the work of Edwards had a principal
> instrumentality in effecting this change,
> there can be no doubt.[49]

And Bamford Parkes, writing in 1930, agrees with
Miller's historical assessment:

> His [Edwards'] attack on Stoddardeanism and
> the Half-Way Covenant made as great a
> revolution in the ecclesiastical theory of
> Puritanism as the "Treatise on the Religious
> Affections" had made in its ethics. . . . By
> the triumph of his doctrine the true church
> became once more a minority in the devil's
> world.[50]

Humble Inquiry has been variously interpreted as
about the nature of faith (Cherry); as a theocratic
defense of an absolutist ecclesiastical authority
(Tracy); as sounding a democratic note in making an
equalizing piety the sole qualification for membership
in the church (Wetzel); as a latter-day expression of
Donatist quietism (Allen and Gaustad); as a prophetic
call for a morally and socially active faith (Carse);
and as containing an eschatological conception of the
local church as a type of millennial society and an
instrument of redemption (Bryant, Heimert, and
Westbrook). It is noteworthy that the same text has
yielded the opposed interpretations of Tracy and
Wetzel, and of Allen and Carse, whereas those of Bryant
et alia are in essential harmony and form something of
a continuum. All these commentators, though, with the
exceptions of Tracy and Allen, see social significance
in *Humble Inquiry*. We shall now give fuller
expositions and, wherever necessary, critiques of these
interpretations in their above order.

Conrad Cherry recognizes that in *Humble Inquiry* Edwards is addressing nothing less than the following momentous issues: the nature of the Church, particularly whether it should be inclusive or exclusive in its membership; the nature of the sacraments, whether they are a converting means to grace or the seals thereof; and the locus of ecclesiastical authority, whether the congregation, the church council, or the clergy. But more profoundly, according to Cherry, Edwards is here addressing the perennial issue of the nature of faith itself, and it is his stand on that issue that informs his positions on all the rest. Cherry correctly sees that in this treatise Edwards is anxiously steering a perilous middle-course between the extremes of neonomianism and antinomianism. Cherry's thesis is that Edwards' conception of faith is a central category of his philosophical theology and thus relevant to all his major works such as *Religious Affections* and *Freedom of the Will*.[51] Hence, Cherry discloses some of the larger, theological significance of *Humble Inquiry* by identifying the nature of faith as its deepest theme, thereby locating it at the very heart of Edwards' intellectual enterprise and integrating it with the acknowledged central texts of his oeuvre.

The most recent interpretation of the purport of *Humble Inquiry* has been advanced by Patricia Tracy. She has argued that behind Edwards' dispute with his congregation and Williams on the qualifications for Communion lay the deeper issue of the status and extent of clerical authority in an increasingly secular and mercantile age. Edmund S. Morgan, in a review of her

book, comments as follows on her sociological
assessment of Northampton during the 1740's:

> What she shows us is a community in the
> throes of transition from a pious, agrarian
> past to a secular, commercial future,
> confronting a minister who assumed an
> authority that belonged to the past....
> What defeated Edwards was . . . the
> disintegration of the old agrarian community,
> the rise of secularism, the cash nexus taking
> the place of "Puritan communalism."
> Northampton gone secular was unwilling to let
> any minister of God turn back the clock.[52]

This echoes Perry Miller who writes, "Social
distinctions,...growing out of increasing
differences in wealth, were transforming the Valley
from the pioneer simplicity of Stoddard's time, and
Edwards,...was a victim of it."[53]

Tracy's thesis is that Edwards tried, but failed,
to impose on his congregation and community an
ecclesiastical and a moral authority of the sort
successfully exerted by Stoddard, but rendered obsolete
in Edwards' day by socio-economic changes:

> He tried so hard to achieve the evangelistic
> and disciplinary success of his grandfather.
> He tried too hard--it was his image of
> Stoddard that kept him trying to use old-
> fashioned methods to deal with a community
> that was rapidly changing.[54]

By the mid-eighteenth century, Northampton was, in
Tracy's words, "well on its way toward commercial
development and popular acceptance of an ideology of
individualism," thereby departing significantly from
the traditional paths of Puritan agrarianism and
communalism. In such an incipiently modern society,
Edwards hoped to realize both the old theocratic ideal
of Calvinism and the "pure church" ideal of Anabaptism,

incompatible ideals under the best circumstances: "What
Edwards wanted, clearly, was a church with an intensity
of voluntary commitment like the Separatists' but also
with a community inclusiveness like the Presbyterians'-
-a 'come-outer' spirit in an establishment
institution." However, Edwards' ecclesiastical project,
especially regarding church admissions, foundered
because of the economic and social pluralism of the
town:

> There was no way to persuade the community to
> go back to the "city on the hill," to stake
> their souls on the approval of their
> neighbors when the community was so rapidly
> becoming the arena of honest differences and
> necessary competition.[55]

At the same time came a shift in the locus of moral
authority in the community. The moral authority that
had traditionally redounded on patriarchal ministers
now was being increasingly arrogated by secular agents
such as lawyers. As evidence of this secularization of
morality, Tracy cites the relinquishing of theology for
law by Joseph Hawley, Edwards' cousin, and the case of
the more famous John Adams.[56] Lawyers were replacing
ministers as the significant and influential
intellectuals.

Aside from the question of authority, there was,
according to Tracy, the question of who would judge a
candidate's qualification for full church membership,
one that, she claims, Edwards neglected to answer in
Humble Inquiry:

> What was missing in Edwards's proposals, most
> importantly, was an answer to the obvious and
> most critical question--who would judge?. . .
> When a prospective church member made his
> profession, who would point out brazen
> hypocrisy?[57]

In relation to this, Tracy explains Northampton's controversy with Edwards over church admissions as their reluctance "to stake their souls on the approval of their neighbors." Tracy further claims that what would be judged in the case was the religious experience or "felt" faith of a candidate: "In Misrepresentations Corrected,...Edwards insisted . . . that the experience he intended to examine was simply the quality of living faith in an applicant."[58]

It was the Great Awakening itself, ironically, that helped foment the social changes spelling Edwards' professional demise. According to Tracy, the evangelicals privatized piety, making it a wholly subjective affair divorced from ethical and social concerns. However, when intensified by the revivals, that inner piety expressed itself socially, though not ecclesially:

> On the other hand, the evangelists had emphasized the *inner* reality of true piety, and its distinction from mere outward morality: the effect was to make spirituality private. During the revivals, piety also became so emotionally intense that it could not be maintained for long without being translated into some social form. And that form would not be the church, although Edwards could never imagine any alternative.

Edwards, then, in Tracy's view, "wanted to renew the effectiveness of the church as a centralizing institution."[59]

According to Tracy, "Edwards never escaped the anachronistic grip of the Patriarchal model."[60] She, as some other commentators, cannot resist regarding Edwards as a tragic figure, but not, as for them, because he was by nature a philosopher of the Enlightenment who chose instead the role of a Calvinist

pastor, but because he was by nature more a political
revolutionary who cast himself in the role of a
reactionary:

> The tragedy of Jonathan Edwards was that he
> was so clearly a product of the changing
> patterns of authority and community life in
> eighteenth-century New England. He was more
> like a revolutionary than a Patriarch, but he
> thought of himself as a Patriarch.[61]

Like Miller, Tracy concedes that Edwards' "ideas were
potentially far in advance of their time," though she
does not specify which ones and why. Unlike Miller and
Heimert, however, she claims that Edwards "kept all his
best insights chained to the service of an antiquated
social ideal that few other men shared by 1750."[62]
Consistently with what is becoming something of a
tradition in Edwards scholarship, Tracy portrays
Edwards as, in Smith's evocative phrase, "an imposing
enigma,"[63] conspicuous by the manifold contradictions
of his thought and character.

There is much in Tracy's interpretation that is
correct. She correctly supposes that Edwards strove to
exert his moral authority on a recalcitrant community,
that he opposed the increasing secularization of
morality and society, that his ecclesiology contained
both Calvinist and Anabaptist elements, and that he
nurtured a social ideal which, we are arguing, he
attempted to realize by reestablishing the sacraments
as professing ordinances. There are some things,
however, that are disputable, such as whether Edwards
was in fact an authoritarian and patriarchal figure who
envied his grandfather and emulated his hold on the
people, considering Edwards' condemnation of and his
perspicacity regarding the sin of pride, and his

esteeming the authority of reason, experience and revelation above that of men. A maxim of Edwards', remember, was "that we ought to *call no man on earth Master*, or make the authority of the greatest and holiest of mere men the ground of our belief of any doctrine in religion."[64] And there are still other things in Tracy's account which are simply wrong, which cast doubt on her thesis that Edwards' dispute with his congregation over qualifications for Communion was really a dispute over authority.

To begin with, consider her claim that the evangelists had privatized piety and sundered it from public morality. Tracy does not say whether she considers Edwards one of them. One assumes she does not for, contra the opinion of Mead, Edwards most emphatically did not privatize piety and divorce it from morality. That he did not is, as we have seen, clear from his own comments and the commentaries of others. In *Religious Affections*, Edwards argues that a person's public behavior is not only the surest sign but also the necessary concomitant of his being genuinely pious:

> Gracious and holy affections have their exercise and fruit in Christian practice. I mean, they have that influence and power upon him who is the subject of 'em, that they cause that a practice, which is universally conformed to, and directed by Christian rules, should be the practice and business of his life.[65]

Elsewhere he states that holiness, or piety, consists "not only in contemplation, and a mere passive enjoyment, but consists very much in action."[66]

Let us now consider Tracy's more explicit claim that piety was not translated into the social form of the church. Piety did not, perhaps, become translated, despite Edwards' efforts, into the form of the establishment church represented by Edwards and Chauncy. But did not some of it, however dubious on Edwards' exacting criteria, issue in schismatic and separatist movements? In the wake of the Great Awakening, did not some congregations, assured of their purer faith, and led by such as James Davenport,[67] separate from what they judged a corrupt establishment church to form their own churches? As will be remembered from the first chapter, Edwards and his Scottish colleagues particularly lamented the schisms afflicting their church, and pledged to help heal them through concerted prayer. Was not the separatists' forming new churches this way a translation of evangelical piety into the form of a church, albeit not the establishment one?

Consider also Tracy's claim that Edwards could never imagine that piety might be translatable into a social form other than the church. Certainly he hoped that it would be locally translated into ecclesial form; this is why he made full admission to the church depend on visible piety. However, was he unable to imagine a social form for piety as an alternative to the church? To answer, we need to be clear about what Tracy means by saying that Edwards never imagined a social form for piety other than the church, for the term "church" is ambiguous. It can refer, most inclusively, to the society of all Christians, both in heaven and on earth, or, more exclusively, to a particular denomination of Christians, such as Congregationalists and Presbyterians, or even to a particular congregation within a denomination. Now, if the question is whether Edwards was unable to imagine a social form of piety other than the church in the denominational sense, then the answer is obviously negative. You will recall that Edwards' appeal in Humble Attempt for regular public prayer is explicitly ecumenical. Or, if the question is whether Edwards was unable to imagine a social form of piety other than the church in the sense of the total society of Christians, the answer is still negative, and for the following reasons: First, individual piety, for Edwards, translates into a pious social union, an example of which is millennial society. True, that society is preeminently the society of all earthly Christians, the church in its inclusive sense. However, as is evident from Edwards' discussion in Humble Attempt, the piety of that union suffuses every conceivable aspect of social life in the millennium--politics, the arts and sciences, and even technology and commerce. As we have seen, Edwards' conception of a pious union was more inclusive than even the ecumenically broad, but essentially ecclesiastical conception of his Scottish correspondents. Edwards' comparison of the two kinds of social union in Humble Attempt is a comparison of two kinds of society generally, not a comparison of an ecclesiastical union with some other kind. In Edwards' conception, a pious social union, insofar as it is distinguished from a civil one, is logically more inclusive than an ecclesiastical union, which is the paradigm of the former. Second, according to his discussion in True Virtue, the social manifestation of an individual's true virtue, being the ethical equivalent of true piety, is his cordial union with the universal system of sentient beings, whom he loves

benevolently for their own sakes, regardless of their
ecclesiastical affiliation if any. And third, as we
have seen, true piety for Edwards necessarily
translates into a broadly social rather than a narrowly
ecclesial form. As Smith remarks, "the *entire* social
order must ultimately be affected" according to the
tenor of Edwards' conception of piety. And Carse notes-
-correctly I think--"he [Edwards] judged men's actions
according to their effectiveness in bringing us to the
ultimate society."[68]

Against Tracy's claim that Edwards neglected to
answer the question as to who would judge a candidate's
qualification for Communion, Edwards himself provides a
decisive reply. On Edwards' policy as described in
Humble Inquiry it would be the church, consisting of
the full members in the congregation and their
minister, that would judge and indicate hypocrisy.
Edwards states quite clearly, "It is properly a
visibility to the eye of the *public* charity [i.e.
judgment], and not of a private judgment, that gives a
person a right to be received as a visible saint by the
public [italics mine]." Furthermore, "The minister is
*to act as a public officer, and in behalf of the public
society* [italics mine] and not merely for himself, and
therefore is to be governed, in acting, by a proper
visibility of godliness in the eye of the public."
Edwards evinces a similar awareness of the fallibility
of private judgment in *Religious Affections* where he
says, "But yet the best of men may be deceived, when
the appearances [of piety] seem to them exceeding fair
and bright, even so as entirely to gain their charity,
and conquer their hearts."[69] "The story of Edwards'
life," writes Carse, "is the story of his refusal to

accede to the principle of private judgment in matters
of religious and ethical importance."[70]

Tracy seems also to have misunderstood Edwards in
claiming that what would be judged is the "experience"
or "quality of living faith" in a candidate. However,
he most assuredly did not intend that the interior
experience or the quality of faith in an applicant
would be examined, either by him or others in the
church, but only the *visibility* of the applicant's
faith:

> The question is not, whether Christ has made
> converting grace or piety *itself* the
> condition or rule of his people's admitting
> any to the privileges of members in full
> communion with them. It is the credible
> *profession* and *visibility* of these things,
> that is the church's rule in this case.

Furthermore, Edwards is insistent that in matters of
faith actions speak much louder than words, even if
they are about religious experience: "And in general a
manifestation of the sincerity of a Christian
profession *in practice* [italics mine], is far better
than a relation of experiences."[71] Lastly, Edwards did
not regard faith, or piety, as a vague "quality," but
more specifically as a new principle or nature that
animates the whole being of a saint:

> But the Spirit of God in his spiritual
> influences on the hearts of his saints
> [saving grace], operates by infusing or
> exercising new, divine and supernatural
> principles; principles which are indeed a new
> and spiritual nature, and principles vastly
> more noble and excellent than all that is in
> natural men.

Edwards' caveat that the church ought not
adjudicate a "candidate's real state towards *God*" is
especially significant given Tracy's claim that

Edwards' congregation were reluctant "to stake their
souls on the approval of their neighbors." Edwards makes
it quite clear that church membership in complete
standing only, and not personal salvation, depends on
the approval of one's neighbors in the church.
Salvation depends on actual piety, whereas
ecclesiastical membership depends only on visible
piety. In an extended footnote in *Misrepresentations
Corrected*, Edwards iterates the same point:

> A person may be qualified for the society of
> heaven, while not qualified for full
> communion in a Christian church; because the
> natures of the two societies are different,
> and consequently the scriptural ends of their
> admission into each.[72]

Finally, as to Tracy's characterization of
Edwards' social ideal as antiquated and as stultifying
his best and, presumably, most innovative ideas. But
how is his social ideal of a pious society antiquated?
If we consider it, it might be seen as one of his most
advanced insights. As we know, Edwards conceives of a
pious union as a cordial union *qua* love, or a union of
wills, through the sharing of a common interest, namely
God's and man's best interest. For Edwards, a pious
society, like true piety itself, involves the heart and
the affections. By conceiving of a pious society as a
voluntaristic union forged in the hearts of the
uniters, Edwards is fully abreast of the moral
philosophy of his day. One of the innovative insights
of such as Hutcheson and Hume was that morality or
virtue was rooted in sentiment or feeling. Edwards'
analogous insight that religion and community were
similarly rooted in sentiment or feeling was no less
innovative. Edwards, as much as these representatives

of the Scottish renaissance in philosophy, exemplified
the modern trend in the eighteenth century stressing
the psychological and philosophical significance of the
emotions. Furthermore, Edwards' social philosophy,
given the importance it attached to human feeling and
affections, not only was as modern as any other in his
time, but also anticipated some nineteenth-century
trends. For example, a unifying factor in a pious
society, for Edwards, is being's disinterested
complacence in being's benevolence, which is remarkably
like Royce's principle of loyalty to loyalty.[73]
Generally speaking, the whole tenor of Edwards'
voluntarism seems to be an harbinger of some
intellectual developments in the next century.

In contrast with Tracy, Charles Wetzel detects a
leveling or democratizing element in *Humble Inquiry*. In
Edwards' view, according to Wetzel, qualification for
communion has nothing to do with one's social status or
economic class or even secular achievements, but has
everything to do with one's moral and spiritual estate.
Moreover, the elect, or the members of the invisible
church, are socially and economically indistinguishable
from natural men and women.[74]

Perhaps the earliest interpretation of *Humble
Inquiry* comes from Alexander Allen, the important
nineteenth-century biographer of Edwards. The dispute
between Edwards and Williams over the qualifications
for Communion reminds him of the fifth-century dispute
between the Donatists and St. Augustine over the nature
of the Church. According to Allen, "Edwards had
something of the Donatist spirit, which was seeking the
purity of the church."[75] Allen considers that Edwards'
attempt to purify the church by restoring the Eucharist

as a professing ordinance would likely have had the effect of emasculating the church as an organ of social change. In a theocracy, such a purification of the church would undoubtedly have had a social effect by serving to morally reinvigorate the state and society at large since only saints would have had the franchise. However, outside a theocracy, such a spiritual renovation might well lead to a retrenchment by the saints to quietism and a distancing of the world from the church:

> When this [theocratic] opportunity and privilege were withdrawn, there was danger of an unhealthy pietism invading the religious circle, which would not only destroy its attractiveness for the outer world, but might rob the church itself of a rebust manliness, if it did not empty religion of its positive significance. There are not wanting signs of a certain hollowness and unreality in the speculative thought of Edwards, which may owe their origin in some part to this defect.[76]

Edwin Scott Gaustad agrees that Edwards principally sought to purify the church: "To purify the parish church and to alter its status from an established church for all society to a holy community for saints alone was the aim of the *Humble Inquiry.*"[77]

However, Edwards' goal in revoking Stoddard's Half-Way covenant was not a purified church. Edwards realized that such a goal is unattainable in history, as he declares in *Religious Affections*:

> There never will, in this world, be an entire purity, . . . in the church of God, without any mixture of hypocrites with saints, and counterfeit religion, and false appearances of grace, with true religion and real holiness.[78]

Moreover, Edwards points out in Humble Inquiry that
restricting Church membership in complete standing only
to the visibly pious "by no means implies a pretense of
any scheme, that shall be effectual to keep all
hypocrites out of the church, and for the establishing
in that sense a pure church."[79] Edwards argues that the
apparent piety of each church member does not entail
the actual piety of all because of the fallibility of
our judgments as to the piety of others:

> It is not my design,...to affirm, that
> all who are regularly admitted as members of
> the visible church in complete standing,
> ought to be believed to be godly or gracious
> persons, when taken collectively, or
> considered in the gross, by the judgement of
> any person or society. This may not be, and
> yet each person taken singly may visibly be a
> gracious person to the eye of the judgment of
> Christians in general.[80]

And in the preface of Humble Inquiry, Edwards expressly
disavows all enthusiasts and separatists seeking to
establish a pure church. He hesitated to publish this
text, he informs us, because he was afraid it might be
misconstrued and enlisted in the separatists' cause:

> One thing among others that caused to me to
> go about this business with so much
> backwardness, was the fear of a bad
> improvement, some ill-minded people might be
> ready, at this day, to make of the doctrine
> here defended; particularly that wild
> enthusiastical sort of people, who have of
> late gone into unjustifiable separations,
> even renouncing the ministers and churches of
> the land in general, under pretence of
> setting up a pure church. It is well known,
> that I have heretofore publicly remonstrated,
> both from the pulpit and press, against very
> many of the notions and practices of this
> kind of people: and shall be very sorry if
> what I now offer to the public, should be any
> occasion of their encouraging or

242

strengthening themselves in those notions and practices.[81]

James Carse latches onto the theme of visibility in *Humble Inquiry*. Visibility, as it respects sainthood or the church, is a conspicuous theme, not only in *Humble Inquiry*, but also in *Humble Attempt, Life of Brainerd* and *Farewel-Sermon*, as is evident from some of their full titles. Indeed, visibility runs as a leitmotif through all these texts that we are considering, suggesting some deeper connection among them. For Carse, moreover, "the heart of his [Edwards'] thought from its very beginning required that the inward regeneration of the believer be attended with a corresponding visibility of it."[82] The requirement that faith be visible, i.e. bear the fruit of good works, had always been a prominent theme in Puritanism. Carse, in contrast with Allen and Gaustad, interprets *Humble Inquiry* as a prophetic work which repudiates quietism, the character of the religiosity regnant in Edwards' day, and affronts materialism and complacency with the world:

> It was in the year 1749 that Jonathan Edwards rose to take upon himself the mantle of prophet. . . . He published a short book, *An Humble Inquiry*, the sober and unembellished language of which struck a position that cut deeply across the almost universal inclinations of America society. Thanks partly to the gathering abundance of wealth and comfort, and thanks partly also to the humane accommodations to it on the part of his grandfather, it had become an implicit principle for most Americans of the age of Jonathan Edwards that religion was a private affair. The church's business in a world whose style of living is informed chiefly by the profit motive and the possession of property is to encourage the growth of personal piety. It is distinctly not the

church's office to point to the discrepancies
between the verbal expressions of a man's
religious beliefs and the ethical conduct of
his life. It is not the role of the religious
man *really to understand* the world. With this
"humble" book Edwards stood above his age...
as a prophet who challenged his contemporaries
to look at the world they had made, and to see
that their journey was still unfinished.[83]

James Carse has also recognized the social-
philosophical import of Edwards' stand on the
requirements for church membership in full standing. He
recognizes that for Edwards the church is to act as a
leaven of the good society:

But when he asked that visibility be joined
to a *profession of Christian faith* . . .
Edwards was asking that the church be a
community of men who clearly understand their
office in the world to be the vanguard, the
first legion, in the long journey toward the
ultimate society...they must make so
visible in their present life together the
nature of that ultimate society that the
world would eagerly follow them. . . . The
church,...must become the most apparent
good for the world. [84]

It has been suggested that by instituting the public
owning of the covenant in his church Edwards sought to
reform the moral behavior of those merchants who were
members of his congregation. Through this institution
Edwards was making full membership in the church depend
on one's public behavior, which would mean that
businessmen seeking to become church members in
complete standing would need to be very scrupulous
about their commercial dealings. Owning the covenant,
then, was more than an old-fashioned ecclesiastical
ritual; it was a mechanism of moral and social
amelioration.[85]

244

For Bryant, the heart of Edwards' *Humble Inquiry*
"was his notion of communion as 'the Christian church's
great feast of love.'" Therefore,the sacrament of Holy
Communion, for Edwards, is "an anticipation of the End,
an eschatological event."[86] Specifically, according to
Bryant, Edwards in *Humble Inquiry*, "sought a Holy
Communion which anticipated in time the Messianic
banquet of eternity and reminded the human family of
its ultimate ends."[87] Thus, "Edwards' understanding of
the church is profoundly eschatological: a witness to
and token of the Work of Redemption."[88] Against Allen,
Bryant maintains that in *Humble Inquiry* "Edwards'
concern is not a company of true Christians," i.e. a
pure church, "but a community of disciples who witness
to the eschatological objects of Christian faith."[89]

Heimert's interpretation of *Humble Inquiry* is a
curious mixture of truth and error. Heimert errs by
claiming that Edwards did not consider the Eucharist a
professing ordinance, or the seal of the covenant of
grace. But he correctly asserts that Edwards did
consider this sacrament a sign of the cordial bond
(i.e. disinterested complacence) uniting the members in
a pious society: "The sacrament he took to be not a
seal of the covenant nor even, in any seventeenth-
century sense, a remembrance of Christ, but rather an
expression of the '*peculiar* affection which gracious
persons have one to another.'"[90] Edwards, however,
states quite unambiguously in *Humble Inquiry* that the
Eucharist *is* the seal of the covenant:

> Thus the Lord's supper is plainly a *mutual*
> renovation, confirmation, and seal of the
> covenant of grace: Both the covenanting
> parties *profess* their consent to their
> respective parts in the covenant, and each
> affixes his *seal* to his profession.

Heimert's misunderstanding of Edwards on this point is
quite understandable; it is entirely consistent with
his humanistic reading of Edwards, which requires that
he "demythologize" such texts as *Humble Inquiry*, *Life
of Brainerd* and *Religious Affections*.

Heimert, though, is perceptive regarding the
larger social significance of *Humble Inquiry*. He
correctly perceives that Edwards' ideal congregation,
the constitution of which is defended in this text, is
the semblance of a pious society:

> A restricted church membership was a 'type'
> as it were, of Edwards' ideal particular
> church, one in which a whole congregation was
> 'happily united' in 'mutual sympathy with
> each other' and had 'a communion in each
> other's prosperity and joy.'

More than that, according to Heimert, such a
congregation, like the concert for prayer, would
prefigure millennial society and help precipitate the
advent of the millennium. Heimert thus sees a
connection between *Humble Inquiry* and *Humble Attempt*
with respect to eschatological society:

> In sum, the church polity into which Edwards
> inquired and which he sought to impose on
> Northampton was an image, however dim, 'a
> faint resemblance,' of the millennium and,
> like the Concert of Prayer, 'a forerunner of
> that future joy' and an instrument for
> bringing it into being.[91]

Like Heimert, Westbrook construes Edwards'
ecclesial polity in *Humble Inquiry* as a prelibation of
millennial society: "The church polity that Edwards
sought was to be an anticipation and harbinger of the
millennium, a rough and imperfect microcosm of the Great
Community." Specifically, "the communion table would be
a place where the saints could get a taste of the

community of true virtue." That polity represents
Edwards'

> efforts to take part in the work of
> redemption by fashioning in his own church a
> prototype of the millenial community. . . .
> It was to this end that he undertook to build
> his model of the Great Community by reversing
> the policy of his revered grandfather Solomon
> Stoddard and reinstituting the profession of
> faith as a requirement for full church
> membership.[92]

Now the interpretations of Carse, Bryant, Heimert
and Westbrook cohere and complement one another. Thus,
Carse interprets *Humble Inquiry* as a plea for a more
than nominal Christianity, but one expressing itself
socially in moral conduct and having an impact on the
world. Bryant sees in it a conception of the church as
"a community of disciples who witness to the
eschatological objects of Christian faith." Heimert
specifies that the millennium is among those objects,
and that this community will help usher it in, by
stating that "the church polity into which Edwards
inquired and which he sought to impose on Northampton
was an image, . . . of the millennium . . . and an
instrument for bringing it into being." And Westbrook,
in turn, not only specifies further that Edwards'
church polity was the image of millennial *society*, but
generalizes by characterizing it as no less than the
"Great Community" itself: "The church polity that
Edwards sought was to be . . . , a rough and imperfect
microcosm of the Great Community," and it represented
his "efforts to take part in the work of redemption by
fashioning in his own church a prototype of the
millennial community."

These interpretations make clear that *Humble Inquiry* is fundamentally about Edwards' eschatological conception of the church as both the harbinger of millennial society and the necessary means to its realization, and represents Edwards attempt to precipitate that society thereby contributing to the work of redemption. However, as we shall show, this text has more than the ecclesiological and eschatological significance found by Bryant and Heimert. In addition, it has philosophical significance. For millennial society is nothing less, as Westbrook suggests, than Edwards' paradigm of society, an eschatological vision of his social ideal; and that his church polity represents a blueprint for its implementation, however imperfect. Moreover, we shall demonstrate, contra Allen and Gaustad, that his restricting church membership by making the Lord's Supper a professing ordinance does not necessarily imply a reversion to Donatist quietism.

Implications for Social & Political Theory

In this section we shall demonstrate that Edwards set out to implement his social ideal envisioned eschatologically in *Humble Attempt*, an undertaking justified in *Humble Inquiry*. He thus conceived the church as a pious union, his social ideal, and sought to turn his congregation into a microcosm of pious society by restricting its membership in complete standing to the visibly pious. All but the visibly *benevolent* would be excluded from Communion. By the expedient of making the local church an *exclusive* society, Edwards would, in effect, establish a clear

248

boundary between the pious society of the church and
the environing civil society. This demarcation would
serve to unify the church and sharpen its profile as a
pious society. The church, as a *visibly* benevolent
union, would thereby be clearly distinguishable from
the larger civil order.

Ecclesia as Pious Society

That Edwards conceived of the church as a pious
social union is implied by Heimert's and Westbrook's
interpretation of Edwards' idea of the church as a
"type" of millennial society. And it is made explicit
in *Humble Inquiry* in Edwards' subscription to the
biblical representation of the church as "a *society
having its several members united by the bond of
christian brotherly love*," which iterates his
description of a pious union in *Humble Attempt* as that
"sweet agreement in . . . the business of religion; the
life and soul of which is love." The scriptural
representation of the church as a pious society is a
reason adduced by Edwards for restricting its
membership to the visibly pious, or those exhibiting a
"christian brotherly love." But of what kind is this
love whose visibleness Edwards requires for Communion
and which he conceives of as the bond of ecclesial
society?

Edwards does not make explicit in *Humble Inquiry*
the nature of this love or true piety as he does, for
example, in *Religious Affections*. He writes, "It does
not belong to the present question [i.e. whether any
but the visibly pious are qualified for Communion], to
consider and determine what the nature of Christian

piety is."[93] However, the text does suggest that
Edwards conceived of the nature of the piety or love to
be made visible as the "love of benevolence," his later
conception in *True Virtue*. Thus in connection with the
profession of faith, Edwards writes, "there is but one
sort of sincerity in loving God as God, and setting our
hearts on him as our highest happiness"; and, with
respect to owning the covenant, Edwards states that we
thereby choose God "to be our chief good and last end,
the supreme object of our esteem and regard, to whom we
devote ourselves." Now "loving God as God" (i.e. for
his own sake) translates into the ethical idiom of *True
Virtue* as benevolence to being "simply considered." And
choosing God "to be our chief good and last end, the
supreme object of our esteem and regard, to whom we
devote ourselves" corresponds to the virtue thus
described in the dissertation: "A truly virtuous mind,
being as it were under the sovereign dominion of love
to God, above all things, seeks the glory of God, and
makes this his supreme, governing, and ultimate end."[94]
Furthermore, in the following passage from *Humble
Inquiry*, Edwards anticipates his later distinction in
True Virtue between benevolence and complacence, which
suggests that he conceived of true piety in this work
as the former instead of the latter:

> Besides that general benevolence or charity
> which the saints have to mankind,...
> there is a *peculiar* and very *distinguishing*
> kind of affection, that every true Christian
> *experiences* towards those whom he looks upon
> as truly *gracious* persons. The soul, at least
> at times, is very sensibly and sweetly knit
> to such persons, and there is an ineffable
> *oneness of heart* with them.

250

The "general benevolence" exercised by the saints to
mankind is nothing other than "that affection or
propensity of the heart to any being" which is "love of
benevolence." Whereas the "*peculiar* and very
distinguishing kind of affection" they experience
towards those whom they regard as being truly gracious
is nothing other than that "complacence in the person
or being beloved for his beauty" which is "love of
complacence."[95] These observations, incidentally,
suggest that *Humble Inquiry* is another transitional
text (published in the same year as *Life of Brainerd*)
mediating Edwards' position in *Religious Affections* and
True Virtue.

Ecclesia as Exclusive Society

By restricting the church membership in complete
standing to the visibly benevolent, Edwards would have
made his congregation an exclusive society. He would
thereby have drawn a distinct boundary between it and
civil society, which would serve to strengthen its
unity and identity. The local church would thus be
conspicuous as a distinctively benevolent society, or a
truly moral community. Now these functions of social
exclusivism have been discussed at length by Georg
Simmel, the German philosopher-sociologist. In order,
then, to illuminate the socio-theoretic import of
Edwards' restrictive policy on church admissions, let
us consider it in light of Simmel's theory of group
formation.

Simmel distinguishes two fundamental principles of
human association, one a principle of inclusion and the
other a principle of exclusion: "On the one hand, there

is the principle of including everybody who is not
explicitly excluded; and, on the other, there is the
principle of excluding everybody who is not explicitly
included."[96] Social groups are more or less exclusive
depending on which of these principles they embody.
However, to have a distinct identity as such, a group
must be minimally exclusive and thus differentiated
from the larger social milieu; it must establish, as it
were, a "boundary" between itself and the general
society. Talcott Parsons describes such a boundary
thus:

> A boundary means simply that a theoretically
> and empirically significant difference
> between structures and processes internal to
> the system and those external to it exists
> and tends to be maintained. In so far as
> boundaries in this sense do not exist, it is
> not possible to identify a set of
> interdependent phenomena as a system; it is
> merged in some other, more extensive
> system.[97]

The principle of exclusion is a prerequisite for group
identity and solidarity. It fosters in the members of
the in-group a "distinct and emphatic consciousness
that they form a *society*." Social exclusivism is an
expression of a shared ethic: "people separate from
others because they do not want to make common cause
with them."[98] Furthermore, it is correlated with the
unity of the group, such that the more socially
exclusive the group--the clearer its boundary--the more
cohesive it is. Thus, in Simmel's words, "the
intensified seclusion against the outside is associated
with the intensification of cohesion internally: we
have here two sides, or external forms, of the same
sociological attitude."[99] Indeed, the "tie of
solidarity," for Simmel, "consists to a large degree

precisely in the position of being singled out of
larger groups and being in contrast with them."[100]

Simmel explains this correlation between the
exclusiveness and integrity of a group as follows:
Within the larger, more inclusive and open society, an
individual belongs simultaneously to several
subsocieties, each of which makes a claim on his
allegiance. Consequently, this divided loyalty can
cause him to come into conflict with any of these
groups. However, the further removed an individual is
from the open society where the conflicts of interests
occur, and the more monolithic the interest of the
relatively closed group to which he belongs, the less
likely is he to come into conflict with others: Thus,
the "secret society," which is the paradigm of the
exclusive group, "exercises over its members a sort of
absolute dominion, which gives them little opportunity
to engage in conflicts such as result from the
coordination of the plurality of spheres that represent
open groups."[101] The harmony of exclusive groups is
expressed and maintained through the "de-
individualization" or equality of its members. Again
with reference to the most exclusive kind of group,
Simmel writes, "Within the secret society, there often
is a brotherly equality among the members, which
constitutes a sharp and tendentious contrast to their
differences in their other life situations."[102]

We shall now relate Edwards' policy on church
admission to Simmel's theory of group formation.
Edwards' policy clearly represents an enactment of what
Simmel identifies as a principle of exclusion:
According to it, none but the manifestly benevolent are
explicitly included as communicants in the church. This

is the very opposite of Stoddard's policy on church
admissions which represents an enactment of Simmel's
principle of inclusion: According to it, only infidels,
heathens, and miscreants are explicitly excluded as
communicants. As Stoddard says, "the Lord's Supper may
be looked on as a Converting Ordinance, for church
Members that carry orderly [i.e. behave decently] yet
not for prophane Persons";[103] it was instituted "not
for the Conversion of Heathens to the Christian
Religion, but for the Saving Conversion of Professing
men."[104]

Visible benevolence functions as a principle of
exclusion for Edwards, doing so in the following four
ways: First, it marks the "boundary" between a pious
society and the surrounding civil society. Members of
the former would be clearly distinguishable from
nonmembers by their benevolent behavior. Second,
particularly through its manifestation of the rite of
the Lord's Supper, visible benevolence fosters in the
membership of a pious society a lively and intimate
sense of group-identity or, as Simmel expresses it, a
"distinct and emphatic consciousness that they form a
society." The Supper is thus "the christian church's
great feast of love; wherein Christ's people sit
together as brethren, ...to feast on the love of
their Redeemer, ...and sealing their love to him
and one another!" A purpose of this sacrament is,
according to Edwards, that the saints "might have the
comfort of uniting with such as their hearts are united
with."[105] Third, visible benevolence strengthens and
deepens the mutuality among the members of a pious
society by being the foundation of that "peculiar and
very distinguishing kind of affection" they experience

towards one another. This experience makes for what
Edwards calls "an ineffable *oneness of heart* with
them," or what Simmel would call a "tie of solidarity."
And fourth, visible benevolence in the membership of
pious society is the expression of an ethos
fundamentally opposed to that of civil society--an
ethos of public mindedness, or "general affection," in
contradistinction to private mindedness, or "private
affection."

Edwards' stand on qualifications for Communion,
therefore, has considerably more than just
ecclesiastical significance as a policy on church
admissions. It has socio-theoretic significance as
well, inasmuch as it represents a strategy for
facilitating the emergence on the local level of a
truly moral community, recognizably distinct from the
civil society and approximating the social ideal of the
millennium. This would be the community of the visibly
public-minded, evincing in their behavior a devotion to
the "highest good of being in general" as their own.
Its beauty is primary beauty, consisting in cordial
consent to or union of heart with general being.
Moreover, the public mindedness or "love of
benevolence" constitutive of pious society in Edwards'
conception throws in relief the essential character of
civil society. By contrast, it is private mindedness or
"love of complacence," as evinced in a devotion to the
good of some "private system of being" before that of
general being, that is constitutive of civil society in
Edwards' conception. This is evident from the beauty or
value of civil society which, according to Edwards, is
the secondary beauty of good order and utility. Hence,
if pious society belongs to the order of benevolence,

civil society belongs to the order of complacence.
Alternatively, pious society, being essentially a
benevolent social union (though derivatively a
complacent one) based ultimately on the public
interest, is theocentric in orientation. On the other
hand, civil society, being essentially a complacent
social union based ultimately on private interest, is
anthropocentric in orientation.

Finally, from our consideration of Edwards'
restrictive policy on church admissions in light of
Simmel's theory of group formation, it should be clear
that his policy does not imply the reversion to
Donatist quietism inferred by Allen and Gaustad.
Rather, it makes for a more cohesive and committed
community; and, far from encouraging its retreat from
the world, Edwards' exclusive stand on Communion
empowers the church to regenerate the larger society.
As Carse has remarked, "when he asked that visibility
be joined to a *profession of Christian faith* . . .
Edwards was asking that the church be a community of
men who clearly understand their office in the world to
be the vanguard, the first legion, in the long journey
toward the ultimate society."

CHAPTER V

NOTES

[1]Jonathan Edwards, *An Humble Inquiry into the Rules of the Word of God, concerning the Qualifications Requisite to a Compleat Standing and Full Communion in the Visible Christian Church*, in *The Works of President Edwards*, ed. by E. Hickman, I (London, 1834), p. 432.

[2]DeJong, *Covenant Idea*, p. 45.

[3]Ibid., p. 102.

[4]Ibid., pp. 110-111.

[5]Ibid., p. 132.

[6]Solomon Stoddard, *An Appeal to the Learned, being a Vindication of the Rights of Visible Saints to the Lord's Supper, though They be Destitute of a Saving Work of God's Spirit on Their Hearts: Against the Exceptions of Mr. Increase Mather* (Boston, 1709), p. 25.

[7]Ibid., p. 50.

[8]Ibid., p. 20.

[9]Ibid., pp. 128-129.

[10]Solomon Stoddard, *The Doctrine of the Instituted Churches* (London, 1700), p. 21, quoted in DeJong, *Covenant Idea*, pp. 130-131.

[11]Tracy, *Jonathan Edwards*, p. 259.

[12]Edwards, *Religious Affections*, pp. 413-420.

[13]Tracy, *Jonathan Edwards*, p.171-172.

[14]Miller, *Jonathan Edwards*, p. 220.

[15]Edwards, *Humble Inquiry*, p. 431.

[16]Jonathan Edwards, *Journal*, quoted in Tracy, *Jonathan Edwards*, p. 180.

[17]Carse, *Jonathan Edwards*, p. 26.

[18]Williston Walker, *The Creeds and Platforms of Congregationalism* (New York, 1893), p. 284, quoted in DeJong, *Covenant Idea*, p. 238.

[19]Carse, *Jonathan Edwards*, p. 27.

[20]Tracy, *Jonathan Edwards*, pp. 171-72.

[21]Edwards, *Humble Inquiry*, p. 436.

[22]Ibid., p. 434.

[23]Ibid., pp. 434-435.

[24]Ibid., p. 435.

[25]Ibid., p. 436.

[26]Ibid., p. 437.

[27]Ibid., p. 438.

[28]Ibid., p. 441.

[29]Jonathan Edwards, *Treatise on Grace and Other Posthumously Published Writings*, ed. by Paul Helm (Cambridge, England, 1971), p. 25.

[30]Edwards, *Religious Affections*, p. 206.

[31]Edwards, *Treatise on Grace*, p. 25.

[32]Edwards, *Religious Affections*, p. 207.

[33]Edwards, *Misrepresentations Corrected, and Truth Vindicated, in a Reply to the Rev. Mr. Solomon Williams's Book*, in *Works*, I (London, 1834), p. 503.

[34]Edwards, *Humble Inquiry*, p. 459.

[35]Ibid., p. 458.

[36]Ibid., p. 459.

[37]Ibid., p. 443.

[38]Ibid., p. 445.

[39]Ibid., p. 459.

[40]Ibid., p. 457.

[41]Ibid., p. 458.

[42]Miller, *Jonathan Edwards*, p. 222.

[43]Ibid., p. 223.

[44]Davidson, *Jonathan Edwards*, p. 128.

[45]Edwards, *Humble Inquiry*, p. 433.

[46]Sereno Edwards Dwight, *The Life of President Edwards* (New York, 1830), p. 308.

[47]Samuel Miller, *Jonathan Edwards*, pp. 108-109.

[48]Edwards, *Humble Inquiry*, p. 432.

[49]Samuel Miller, *Jonathan Edwards*, p. 241.

[50]Parkes, *Jonathan Edwards*, p. 211.

[51]Cherry, *Jonathan Edwards*, p. 203.

[52]Edmund S. Morgan, "The Great Awakener," review of *Jonathan Edwards, Pastor*, by Patricia Tracy, in *The New York Times Book Review*, July 13, 1980, p. 13.

[53]Miller, *Jonathan Edwards*, p. 218.

[54]Tracy, *Jonathan Edwards*, p. 188.

[55]Ibid., p. 189.

[56]Ibid., pp. 191-192.

[57]Ibid., p. 176.

[58]Ibid., p. 177.

[59]Ibid., p. 190.

[60]Ibid., p. 192.

[61]Ibid., pp. 193-194.

[62]Ibid., p. 194.

[63]John E. Smith, "Jonathan Edwards as Philosophical Theologian," *The Review of Metaphysics*, XXX, No. 2 (1976), p. 306.

[64]Edwards, *Humble Inquiry*, p. 431.

[65]Edwards, *Religious Affections*, p. 383.

[66]Jonathan Edwards, *True Saints, When Absent from the Body, are Present with the Lord*, in *The Works of President Edwards*, ed. by E. Hickman, II (London, 1834), p. 31.

[67]James Davenport (1716-57) was an especially virulent enthusiast. He was a text-book example of the religious vices that Edwards and Chauncy concurred in deploring. Davenport was censorious. In the summer of 1741, he went about Connecticut summoning ministers to give an account to him of their conversion experiences. Those that refused, being the majority, he denounced publicly as apostate. Davenport was a separatist. He urged congregations to abandon or dismiss "unconverted" pastors. And, Davenport was a fanatic. On March 6, 1743, he led his followers to the wharf at New London and exhorted them to renounce their "idolatrous love of worldly things." As a result, they stripped themselves of finery, wigs, and jewels and burned them. Thereafter, Davenport was arraigned and declared *non compos mentis*. See Goen, "Editor's Introduction," pp. 51-52, 60-61.

[68]Carse, *Jonathan Edwards*, p. 184.

[69]Edwards, *Religious Affections*, p. 182.

[70]Carse, *Jonathan Edwards*, pp. 27-28.

[71]Edwards, *Religious Affections*, p. 420.

[72]Edwards, *Misrepresentations Corrected*, p. 529.

[73]The historically significant intellectual kinship between Edwards and Royce has been noted as follows by Nagy: "More obvious are the significant parallels, too numerous to mention, between Edwards and Royce. The similarity between the idea of benevolence and Royce's notion of loyalty almost suggests itself because of their common origin in the Pauline doctrine of love as the foundation of the beloved community." See Nagy, "Beloved Community," p. 102.

[74] Angoff, ed., *Jonathan Edwards*, p. 58.

[75]Allen, *Jonathan Edwards*, pp. 268-269.

[76]Ibid., pp. 269-270.

[77]Edwin Scott Gaustad, *The Great Awakening in New England* (New York, 1957), p. 106.

[78]Edwards, *Religious Affections*, p. 86.

[79]Edwards, *Humble Inquiry*, p. 436.

[80]Ibid., p. 435.

[81]Ibid., p. 432.

[82]Carse, *Jonathan Edwards*, p. 131.

[83]Ibid.,pp. 130-131.

[84]Carse, *Jonathan Edwards*, p. 149.

[85]Aldridge, *Jonathan Edwards*, p. 39.

[86]Bryant, "History and Eschatology," p. 289.

[87]Ibid., p. 294.

[88]Ibid., p. 281.

[89]Ibid., p. 292.

[90]Heimert, *American Mind*, p. 125.

[91]Ibid., p. 125. Quotations from Jonathan Edwards, *Church's Marriage*, in *Works*, II (London, 1834), pp. 18-26.

[92]Westbrook, "Social Criticism," p. 408.

[93]Edwards, *Humble Inquiry*, p. 436.

[94]Edwards, *True Virtue*, p. 25.

[95]Ibid., p. 6.

[96]Georg Simmel, "Secrecy and Group Communication," in *Theories of Society: Foundations of Modern Sociological Theory*, ed. by Talcott Parsons (New York, 1961), p. 327.

[97]Talcott Parsons, "An Outline of the Social System," in *Theories of Society*, p. 36.

[98]Simmel, "Group Communications," p. 325.

[99]Ibid., p. 327.

[100]Kurt H. Wolff, ed. and trans., *The Sociology of Georg Simmel* (London, 1950), p. 90.

[101]Simmel, "Group Communication," p. 328.

[102]Ibid., p. 329.

[103]Stoddard, *An Appeal*, p. 28.

[104]Ibid., p. 71.

[105]Edwards, *Humble Inquiry*, p. 458.

CHAPTER VI

JUSTICE AS THE NORMATIVE FORM OF SOCIETY

Historical Background

Edwards' rescinding of Stoddard's policy of open
Communion was the catalyst among the events leading to
his expulsion from the Northampton pulpit; the others
were a quarrel over salary and a case of church
discipline. Exacerbating these events were Edwards'
increasing alienation from his parishioners, the
Williams' clan entrenched opposition to him, the
townspeople's blaming him for the troubles spawned by
the Great Awakening, and even some neighboring clergy's
dissatisfaction with him. The events themselves,
moreover, were symptomatic of a wide-spread crisis in
clerical authority that afflicted New England towards
the middle of the eighteenth century. This was the time
of an emergent power struggle in municipal politics
between clergy, gentry, and a rising middle class, and
of a laical challenge to traditional pastoral authority
in an increasingly secular age. According to Tracy,

> The issues that precipitated the ultimate
> confrontation were Edwards's perennial
> concerns--discipline of young people and
> piety in the church--and they exposed the
> most fundamental problem faced by ministers
> and congregations in eighteenth-century New
> England, the unresolved ambiguities of the
> authority of the minister within the
> Congregational system.[1]

"Mr. Edwards" writes Sereno E. Dwight, "was for
many years unusually happy in the esteem and love of
his people; and there was during that period the

264

greatest prospect of his living and dying in the same state of harmony." Beginning towards the end of 1742, however, in the aftermath of the Great Awakening, Edwards' moral authority and prestige were gradually eroded within a community in the throes of secularization. And in 1744 there occurred the first event that put him in disfavor with the town, the so-called "bad books" scandal which quickly entered the local folklore. In the spring of that year, Edwards was informed by a parishioner that a group of young adults, all members of the church, had certain "licentious books in their possession"[2] over which they had been pruriently gloating and joking. Actually, they possessed a single book which was a manual on midwifery. Church discipline was clearly called for and Edwards, with the full consent of his congregation, routinely instituted the required procedure for its implementation. After service one Sunday, he made an announcement and appointed an investigating committee. But then he publicly named the culprits in the affair, and without distinguishing the actual participants from witnesses; it happened that some of them either belonged, or were nearly related, to "the considerable families in the town." Consequently, according to Dwight, "the town was suddenly all in a blaze," and Edwards' actions "seemed in a great measure to put an end to his usefulness at Northampton, and doubtless laid a foundation for his removal."[3]

Now there was hardly anything unusual about Edwards' initiating formal proceedings against some youths for their lewdness. This had long been the custom in New England churches. The problem was that the times had changed, and clerical authority was increasingly being called into question. People had become unwilling that a minister, though within his rights, should arrogate to himself the paternal prerogative of disciplining their offspring. Winslow writes:

> Publicity given to private offense had been normal procedure in New England meetinghouses since the beginning. The pastor was doing exactly what his father and grandfather before him had done, but the hour had changed. In the late 1740's congregations were in no mood to be publicly rebuked with culprits brought before the membership for confession and public forgiveness. . . . This was a private affair for the parents to settle, and none of the minister's business.[4]

On Tracy's recent and exceptionally well-documented interpretation of the incident, "Edwards's mistake in this case was . . . in pointing out to the whole community that their young people were completely out of control."[5] The congregation's response to Edwards' discipline, however, was by no means an isolated incident. "The records of nearly every parish in New England," according to Winslow, "could show some critical case that offered a parallel involving the limits of pastoral authority in a sensitive time."[6]

Another perennial and typical bone of contention between pastor and congregation in mid-eighteenth-century New England was the former's salary.[7] And the bitter "salary dispute" between Edwards and his parish was the second critical event contributing to his demise in Northampton. In a letter of November 1744 addressed to the municipal agency for ecclesiastical affairs, Edwards made the first of several petitions to "settle a certain salary upon me" so that

> the affair of your minister's support, and
> the consideration of his families
> circumstances, won't come over every year, to
> exercise your minds, & to occasion various
> opinions & speeches, & to be a constant
> temptation to persons to look into the way in
> which the minister spends his money.[8]

Edwards also had become impatient with the delays in payment, quite apart from the unseemly haggling over the amount to be paid and the embarrassing prying into his expenditures which annually accompanied the grants. However, the local taxpayers, who suspected "lavish expenditure" on Edwards' part, did not grant his request until 1748, and only after rancorous debate.

Thus it was that, after Edwards formally announced in December of 1748 his decision to revoke Stoddard's liberal policy on church admission, the townspeople's long-smouldering animus against him finally flared up in public outrage. "When Mr. Edwards's sentiments [on church Communion] were known," records Samuel Hopkins, Edwards' first biographer, "it gave great offense, and the town was put into a great ferment."[9] And Edwards himself, in a letter written a few years later to Major Joseph Hawley (who had led the anti-Edwards faction in the town at the time), recalls that "the Town and Ch[urc]h were at once put into the greatest Flame: the Town was soon filled with Talk of dismissing & expelling me, and with Contrivances how to do it speedily & effectually."[10] Edwards' revocation of the "Stoddardean" way in church polity did not, understandably, sit well with his congregation, some of whom had known Stoddard personally and most of whom regarded him with a "vast veneration . . . almost as a sort of deity" such that "my [Edwards'] teaching and insisting on the doctrine, which Mr. Stoddard opposed, appears to them a sort of horrid profaneness."[11] Solomon Williams, Edwards' cousin and antagonist in the affair, even insinuated that Edwards had libelled Stoddard, a charge he was anxious to refute in the preface to *Humble Inquiry*. Furthermore, Stoddard's way had been the rule for forty-eight years, becoming a venerable Northampton tradition for which the town was widely known,[12] and for a long time it had also been Edwards' way.

What particularly rankled the people, however, was their suspicion that Edwards was arrogating a prerogative, which even Stoddard and most of Edwards' colleagues disclaimed, of sitting in judgment on another's spiritual estate and deciding whether he was qualified for Communion—though in *Humble Inquiry* Edwards explicitly disowned any such ministerial privilege, either for himself or for others, of perhaps exposing a candidate's spiritual shallowness, hypocrisy, or religiosity for the world to see. Even the ministers Solomon Williams and Peter Clark, who were asked to reply to Edwards' treatise, believed that he was claiming the right to pass judgment on a candidate's acceptability as a church member in complete standing. "The anger against Edwards had little to do with fine points of theology," reports Tracy. "It was based on hearsay and on the *expectation* that, whatever he wrote or preached, he would take an unacceptably authoritarian stance in the church."[13]

Perry Miller sees an economic side to the dispute between Edwards and the townspeople over the qualifications for communion: "The clash between Edwards and his people . . . was, among other things, a clash between America's great spokesman for absolute

Christian morality and representatives of the American
business ethic."[14] Miller bases his interpretation on a
draft of the profession of faith Edwards proposed be
administered to candidates for Communion. According to
that draft, the candidate would "promise to walk in a
way of obedience to all the commandments of God"[15]
which, in Miller's view, meant a promise of
scrupulosity in one's commercial transactions and other
business dealings. Presumably this did not sit well
with the entrepreneurs and merchants in the church who
would want to take advantage of an expanding economy
and would undoubtedly resent the congregation's, much
less the minister's, surveillance of their practices
that Edwards' ecclesiastical polity implied.[16]

Others have seen a political side to the
townspeople's dispute with Edwards over church polity.
According to them, Edwards' dismissal on a deeper level
was the result of a populist uprising against
aristocrats, among whom Edwards was placed. Harriet
Beecher Stowe, from an extraordinary reading of True
Virtue, portrayed Edwards as a Tory who even supported
the divine right of kings:

> President Edwards had constructed a
> marvellous piece of logic to show that, while
> true virtue in man consisted in supreme
> devotion to the general good of all, true
> virtue in God consisted in supreme regard for
> himself. This "Treatise on True Virtue" was
> one of the strongest attempts to back up by
> reasoning the old monarchical and
> aristocratic ideas of the supreme right of
> the king and upper classes.[17]

Miller rejects this interpretation, however. He claims
that it was the mercantile interests that conspired to
oust Edwards: "In so far as there is an economic or
class angle to the expulsion, Edwards was hustled out

of Northampton, not by the populace, but by the
entrepreneurs."[18] Contrary to expectation, Edwards,
according to Miller, though theologically conservative
was politically liberal, unlike Charles Chauncy and
Jonathan Mayhew who, while theologically liberal were
politically conservative: "while Edwards wore a wig,
his theology contains a democratic implication that was
an affront to men like Chauncy."[19] Charles Wetzel notes
that the combination of conservative theology and
radical politics in Edwards is a precedent for a
similar situation today: "in terms of politics or the
social fervor of Edwards, I can see the parallel
between his conservative theology and conservative
theology today, and his radical politics."[20]

Edwards' petition to the church committee, in
February of 1749, for permission to explain from the
pulpit his stand on qualifications for full Communion,
that the truth might be known and calm restored, was
refused. As a result, he set promptly to work on Humble
Inquiry so that his position might be clearly and
fairly represented. Edwards reports that "the
Fermentation was much quell'd,"[21] though only
temporarily, by the publication of the treatise in the
following August. It was little read. Only twenty
copies of the book were distributed in the town; and it
was even banned from some households.[22] So in October
of 1749, Edwards again petitioned the church committee
for the right to deliver a series of public lectures in
explanation of the policy defended in his treatise. "I
desire that the brethren would manifest their consent,
that I should declare the reasons of my opinion,
relating to full communion in the church, in lectures

appointed for that end: . . . for peace sake and to prevent occasion for strife."[23]

In April of 1749, Edwards offered to resign if the church committee so desired, but only on the condition that they read *Humble Inquiry* and sought the advice of a duly appointed council of churches. The committee did agree to convene an ecclesiastical council to adjudicate the issue between themselves and Edwards, for they saw in this an opportunity to be rid of him. However, the process itself of choosing the council proved arduous and contentious. The committee was determined to pack the council with church representatives who were on its side in the issue, and Edwards objected. As he related in a letter of December 1749,

> The People have a Resolution to get me out of Town speedily, that disdains all Controul and Check. . . . they would have a Council all on their own side in the controversy; and are contriving & struggling to their utmost to cut me off from liberty of chusing any Part of the council of such as are of my opinion. . . . They seem to be determined that the arguments for my opinion shall never be publickly heard, if it be possible to prevent it.[24]

An agreed-upon ecclesiastical council did finally sit, and permitted Edwards to give a series of public lectures in his defense. In February and March of 1750, five lectures were delivered by Edwards, but were virtually boycotted by his congregation. It seemed that, in Edwards' words, "nothing would quiet 'em till they could see the Town clear of Root and Branch, Name and Remnant"[25] of him.

Finally, on June 22, 1750, after three days of deliberation, the church council voted ten to nine that

Edwards relinquish his post. "Jonathan Edwards received
ye Shock unshaken."[26] Ten days later, on July 2, he
preached his valedictory *Farewel-Sermon*. Thus ended the
twenty-three years of Edwards' ministry in Northampton.
At the time he was forty-six years old, with a
"numerous and chargeable family."[27] For Miller and
others, the story of Edwards' dismissal is much more
than an unfortunate episode in history; it is classic
tragedy with symbolic import.[28]

Exposition

The doctrine Edwards raises from his text (2 Cor.
1:14) and expounds in the expository part of the sermon
is that *"Ministers, and the people that are under their
care, must meet one another before Christ's tribunal at
the day of judgment."*[29] Edwards' exposition is divided
into three sections: the first section concerns the
manner in which ministers and their people will meet at
the Last Judgment, the second the immediate purposes of
their meeting, and the third section the ultimate
reasons for their so meeting. Since the second section
concerns us most, we shall now turn to it.

According to Edwards, a minister and his
congregation will meet at the Judgment for three
purposes. One purpose is "to give an account, before
the great Judge, of their behavior one to another in
the relation they stood in to each other in this
world."[30] A second is to have any disputes between them
finally and impartially adjudicated. Edwards laments,
as he so often does, the too frequent hostility between
a minister and his flock. "Though they are under the
greatest obligations to live in peace," Edwards reminds

his own congregation, and although "dissensions between persons so related are the most unhappy and terrible in their consequences," he continues, "yet how frequent have such contentions been!"[31] Some contentions are not resolved in this world according to truth, and others are not resolved at all, "but at the day of judgment there will be a full, perfect and everlasting decision of them." And the third purpose of their meeting on this day is "to receive an eternal sentence and retribution from the judge, in the presence of each other, according to their behavior, in the relation they stood in one to another in the present state."[32] Moreover, they will not only "receive justice to themselves, but see justice done to the other party."[33]

In the "Application" of *A Farewel-Sermon*, Edwards moves from the general to the particular case of his meeting with his own congregation at the Last Judgment. He begins by admonishing them that they too are destined to meet with him hereafter for the same purposes. "For then both you and I must appear together," he warns, "and we both must give an account, in order to an infallible, righteous and eternal sentence to be passed upon us."[34] Then too "our late grand controversy" over the qualifications for Communion will be settled once and for all. Who was right in this matter will finally come to light, and both parties will be impartially judged as to their conduct in this affair.[35]

Edwards next "applies" the sermon's doctrine to the different kinds of persons in his congregation whom he distinguishes according to their spiritual condition and age. Thus, he properly warns "professors of godliness" against an insincere profession or possible

delusion over their spiritual estate,[36] and entreats
them to look into their own faith for the "signs" of
authenticity as described in Religious Affections. In
particular, he invokes the twelfth sign by telling
professors of faith that they will be judged largely by
their conduct, the fruit and consummate sign of true
religion. "Whatever your pretences to experiences,
discoveries, comforts and joys have been, at that day
every one will be judged according to his works."[37]
Addressing those in a "graceless condition," Edwards
appropriately declares that his is "a melancholy
parting" from them liable as they are to divine wrath,
but hopes that in the future they will be susceptible
to the influences of saving grace. And he cautions
those "under some awakenings" lest their spiritual
stirrings come to naught, and urges them "to hold on
and hold out to the end."[38]

Edwards then applies himself to the youth and
children, for whose spiritual nurture he confesses a
"peculiar concern." He reminds them that the young have
opportunities unavailable to the old, and that the
elect are usually brought to God in their early years.
He points out that if the youth had a "precious
opportunity for their souls' good," then children had a
"peculiarly precious opportunity."[39] He takes his leave
of them with the grim reminder that "multitudes die
before they grow up," and of those that do
"comparatively few ever give good evidence of saving
conversion to God."[40]

Edwards concludes the "Application" with advice
to families and the congregation as a whole. He
conceives of the family as the church in microcosm and
so an instrument of salvation:

> Every Christian family ought to be as it were
> a little church, consecrated to Christ, and
> wholly influenced and governed by his rules.
> And family education and order are some of
> the chief of the means of grace. If these
> fail, all other means are like to prove
> ineffectual. If these are duly maintained,
> all the means of grace will be like to
> prosper and be successful.[41]

To that end, he advises parents to educate their
children early on and diligently in morality and
religion, and to maintain "government" over them "as a
guard to the religion and morals of the family and the
support of its good order." On the other hand, he urges
the children to "obey their parents, and yield to their
instructions" for "nothing has a greater tendency to
bring a curse on persons in this world, and on all
their temporal concerns, than undutiful, unsubmissive,
disorderly behavior in children towards their
parents."[42]

Then addressing the whole congregation, Edwards
stresses the "vast importance" of avoiding contention
if they would be prosperous and happy. "The contentions
which have been among you," he complains, "have been
one of the greatest burdens I have labored under in the
course of my ministry." He explains that
contentiousness contravenes "the spirit of
Christianity" and tends "to drive away God's Spirit
from a people and to render all means of grace
ineffectual, as well as to destroy a people's outward
comfort and welfare."[43] Edwards entreats his people to
make their latest and greatest controversy, the one
with him over qualifications for Communion, the last.
In the interest of conciliation, he cautions his
friends in that affair, as the aggrieved party, to

"indulge no revengeful spirit" but rather to "seek the prosperity of the town." He reminds them, "never think you behave yourselves as becomes Christians, but when you sincerely, sensibly and fervently love all men, of whatever party or opinion, and whether friendly or unkind, just or injurious, to you or your friends, or to the cause and kingdom of Christ."[44]

To complete our exposition of *Farewel-Sermon*, and to deepen our understanding of that text, we need to locate its argument in the larger context of Edwards' doctrine of the Last Judgment. That context is provided by the fourth chapter, entitled "The Propriety of a General Judgment, and a Future State" (hereinafter cited as "General Judgment"), of his *Miscellaneous Observations on Important Theological Subjects, Original and Collected*.

In *Farewel-Sermon*, Edwards argues that clergy and their congregations will meet at the Last Judgment to be requited according to their behavior towards one another in the special moral relationship in which they stood, and to have their disputes finally and impartially arbitrated. In a "General Judgment," however, he makes clear that the meeting then between clergy and congregations for these purposes will only be part of a vastly larger meeting in which "all mankind shall stand together before the judgment-seat of the supreme Lawgiver and Judge, to have all things *visibly* set to rights--and justice made *visibly* to take place with respect to all the persons, actions, and affairs of the moral world."[45] (Italics mine.) Note Edwards' emphasis on the visibleness or publicness of the justice to be enacted at the Judgment: "each individual will not be judged so, that the transaction

with respect to him will be out of the sight and
knowledge of all others."[46] Indeed, claims Edwards,
"The end of the divine judgment is the manifestation of
the divine justice."[47]

Edwards' emphasis on the visibility of God's
justice at the Judgment follows from his supposition of
there being a divinely sanctioned moral order in the
world. In his view, a moral order requires not only
moral rules with their enforcement through a system of
rewards and punishments, but also the visibility of
them and their enforcements to the moral agents they
bind: "God's moral government not only requires, that
there should be divine laws, and an execution of them
in rewards and punishments; but also, that both should
be made *visible*." Thus, moral agents need to know
(have visible to them), and understand the rationale
behind, the moral rules binding them in order to meet
the obligations they impose; furthermore, they need to
know the obligations of others: "It is requisite, that
the subject should have proper means of knowing what
the laws are, by which he is obligated, and the grounds
of the obligation; and that others who are his fellow-
subjects should also know his obligations." In fact,
the very existence of society depends on its members'
knowledge of one another's moral obligations, and their
ability to morally evaluate each other's conduct: "As
men are made to dwell in society, this cannot well be,
without knowing each other's obligations, and being
able to judge of the good or evil of each other's
actions." Moreover, moral agents need to understand the
rationale behind the rewards and punishments to which
they are subject and, when it occurs, what they are
being requited for:

> It is likewise requisite, that the subject of
> the laws, should have proper means of knowing
> the grounds of the rewards or punishments of
> which he is the subject, in the execution of
> the laws; and that it should be made
> manifest, to the conscience of him who is
> rewarded or punished, what he is rewarded or
> punished for, and the ground on which the
> Judge assigns such a retribution.[48]

Finally, it is appropriate that moral agents see the
enforcement of moral rules because the rules themselves
are publicly known, as often is their infraction which
frequently involves others as either victims or
accomplices.

Edwards' argument for the propriety and necessity
of the visibility of justice is as follows: (1) **Man** is
uniquely endowed with a capacity for appreciating the
beauty, both natural and moral, of the world and God:

> Reasonable creatures are the eye of the
> world; they are capable of beholding the
> beauty and excellency of the Creator's
> workmanship, . . . therefore it is requisite,
> that the beauty and excellency of the world,
> ...should not be hid or kept secret.

(2) The beauty of the world belongs principally to
persons: "But the beauty of God's constitution of the
world, consists mainly, without doubt, in the
intelligent part of the world, which is the head and
end of all the rest, *et instar omnium*." (3) And the
beauty of persons belongs principally to God's moral
government of them: "The beauty and order of God's
constitution of this, consists chiefly in his moral
regulation of it." (4) Now since the secondary beauty
of the natural world is in fact visible to mankind, it
is even more fitting that the vastly superior, primary
beauty of God's moral government, e.g. the
ministrations of divine justice, should be so:

> Since God has made the beauty and regularity
> of the natural world so publicly visible to
> all; it is much more requisite, that the
> moral beauty and regularity of his disposals
> in the intelligent world, should be publicly
> visible. For the beauty of God's works
> consists a thousand times more in this, than
> in the other.[49]

(5) Since the moral evil (deformity) in the world is so
glaringly visible down the ages, it is proper that its
rectification (beauty) be just as visible: "The moral
deformity and confusion of the world, is most public;
. . . . It is therefore fit, that the rectifying of
this deformity and disorder,...should also be
made publicly visible."[50] (6) Finally, those animated
by a principle of true virtue desire seeing the beauty
of justice:

> God has given man a nature, which, if it be
> under the influence of true virtue, desires
> above all things to behold this kind of order
> and beauty. When man sees a great and horrid
> crime committed, . . . the nature of the
> reasonable creature has something in it,
> which desires and makes it requisite, that he
> should see justice done, and right take
> place, with respect to such an act.[51]

The visibility of justice at the Last Judgment
requires that all parties in any way morally involved
on earth (not just clergy and laity) stand together
before God's tribunal when "the whole world will be
then present, all mankind of all generations gathered
in one vast assembly."[52] This, according to Edwards, is
compatible with the biological unity of mankind, and
their moral unity under the divine law. "The whole
world is one commonwealth and kingdom, all made of one
blood, all under one moral head, one law, and one
government," declares Edwards in a passage reminiscent

of *Humble Attempt*. Furthermore, many of the moral
transactions to be adjudicated are "of the most public
nature," implicating as they do many people, such as
those "between princes and heads of great kingdoms and
monarchies, and their people." As an example of civil
leaders standing in a moral relationship to their
people Edwards cites the case of the Roman emperors:

> The Roman emperors had to do with other
> nations that were without the limits of the
> empire, to the utmost ends of the earth;...
> So that it is requisite, when they appear
> to be judged, that not only the people of the
> Roman empire should appear with them, but
> also those other nations.

And then there are the moral transactions "between one
nation and another," and still others "wherein the
greater part of the world is concerned."[53] And even if
mankind at large are not a party concerned in some
moral transaction, they are often witnesses, and so it
is appropriate that they witness its adjudication
hereafter:

> And many of the good and evil acts that are
> done, though the world is not properly
> concerned in them as a party interested, yet
> are public through the world. They are done
> in the sight of the world, and greatly draw
> the attention of mankind. It is fit,
> therefore, that they should be as publicly
> judged.[54]

We shall now consider more closely what Edwards says
about the moral relationships among nations and among
generations.

Each nation stands in a moral relation, either
directly or indirectly, with every other:

> And as all nations of the world are morally
> concerned one with another, though not so as
> each one immediately concerned with every
> other nation; yet all are mutually concerned

> by concatenation.--One nation is concerned
> with the next, and that with the next, and so
> on: So that there is need that all should
> appear together to be judged.[55]

"All the nations of Europe," observes Edwards, "have dealings one with another continually; and these European nations have some dealings with almost all other nations upon earth, in Asia, Africa, and America."[56] Moreover, since the longer that nations coexist the more closely knit they become through communication, then at the end of time the nations still extant will be virtually as one, and will appear as such at the Judgment Seat. Each human generation stands in a moral relation, either directly or indirectly, with every other:

> All generations of men, from the beginning to
> the end of the world, are morally concerned
> one with another. The first generation is
> concerned with the next, and that with the
> next, and so on to the end of the world.
> Therefore, it is requisite, that all should
> appear together to be judged.

Generations might stand in the relation of perpetrator and victim of injustice, as in the case where "parents may injure their children" or children their parents. Alternatively, they might stand in the relation of accomplices in vice or of confederates in virtue, as in the case where "a younger generation and an older, may be accessary to each other's crimes, or united in each other's virtuous deeds"; indeed, "the present generation may become accessary to an injury committed by their ancestors ages ago" inasmuch as "they stand in the stead of those ancestors, and act for them, and have power to continue the injury, or to remove it":[57]

> And some particular persons . . . may injure
> and undo all future generations of many

> individuals, families, or larger communities.
> So that men who live now, may have an action
> against those who lived a thousand years ago:
> or there may be a cause which needs to be
> decided by the Judge of the world, between
> some of the present generation, and some who
> lived a thousand years ago.[58]

Furthermore, the moral actions of earlier generations
or some members thereof can be known to later
generations through history and tradition, thereby
necessitating God's judging the earlier ones in the
presence of the later:

> Many of the moral acts, . . . are made public
> to all following generations, by tradition
> and history. And if the actions of one
> generation be not visible to all, yet the
> actions of one generation are very visible to
> the generation immediately following, and
> theirs to the next; and so all, in this
> sense, are very visible one to another.[59]

Edwards also notes that even certain individuals
can vastly affect, beneficially or banefully, future
generations. Some might wreak havoc, not only on
multitudes of their contemporaries, but also on
posterity; hence, future generations may have a
grievance against an individual member of a previous
generation. The havoc in question might be *material*
(economic, political or social) or *moral*. Thus, of
those who wreak material havoc on future generations,
Edwards cites, "Princes who, by rapine and cruelty,
ruin nations, are answerable for the poverty, slavery,
and misery of the posterity of those nations." And of
those who wreak moral havoc, he cites such as
"Mahomet," whose ideas "tend to the overthrow of
virtue, and propagation of vice, and are contrary to
the common rights and privileges of mankind"; or
"whoever they were, who first drew away men from the

true religion, and introduced and established
idolatry." On the other hand, Edwards cites others,
like the apostle Paul, who "by their virtue, may be
great benefactors to mankind, through all succeeding
generations."[60]

Evaluations & Interpretations

Traditionally, and most often, *A Farewel-Sermon*
has been cited more often for its oratorical virtues
and its disclosures of Edwards' character, and less so
for its ideas. On the few occasions when the latter
have been appreciated, which has been only recently, it
has been so more for their bearing on Edwards'
eschatology rather than on his social philosophy.

Of the four texts we are considering, *A Farewel-
Sermon* is the most neglected, though not the least
admired. Probably the lowest estimate of it comes from
Winslow, who merely remarks, "It is not even a great
sermon, but it is a biographical document of
importance."[61] The highest estimates come from Miller,
who considers it Edwards' "greatest oration"[62]--though
without explanation; from Edward H. Davidson, who
places it "among his most distinguished utterances";[63]
and from Sereno Edwards Dwight who reports, "Few indeed
are the compositions, which furnish so many, or so
unequivocal, marks of uncommon excellence in their
author; and very few are so well adapted to be
practically useful to churches and congregations."
Further testimony to its merit is that it was "the
source, from which subsequent discourses, on occasions
and in circumstances generally similar, have, to a
great extent, been substantially derived."[64]

Others have commented and agreed upon what *A Farewel-Sermon* reveals about the vast magnanimity of Edwards' character. Thus, according to Hopkins, who knew Edwards personally, this sermon is a "remarkably solemn and affecting discourse"[65] which, for Dwight, "could not have discoverd less of passion or of irritation, or have breathed a more calm and excellent spirit."[66] And for Samuel Miller,

> The deep, unaffected solemnity of this discourse; the elevation and fidelity of its sentiments; the pious solicitude which it manifests for the best interest of the people of his late charge, and its freedom from any thing like acerbity of language or spirit, place it in the very first rank of farewell sermons.[67]

For Henry T. Rose, "his [Edwards'] last word is a message marvelous for self-control, full of peace, counsel, conciliation, so admirable in its spirit, Christlike, tender, that it is in our hearts as we read to revere and love the man."[68] While Allen is struck by the emotional vibrancy of the sermon with its graphic disclosure of a man steeped in moral indignation, though not lacking in compassion, and able to see a parochial situation *sub specie aeternitatis*:

> The discourse is still tremulous with the intense feeling of the hour. The whole man stands forth in it, with his moral indignation at a great wrong; with the solemnity of accusation in which he had no equal; with the tender pathos in which he takes his leave of the dear children whom God had given him, warning them all of the final meeting at the judgment day, when the case should be reheard before the tribunal of Heaven.[69]

284

William J. Scheick is one of the few who have
commented on any of the ideas in *A Farewel-Sermon*.
According to him, it "expressed a plea for 'the
maintaining of family order.'"[70] Scheick notes Edwards'
characterization of the family as a microcosm of the
church and as the indispensable means to Christian
nurture. He observes that, in Edwards' sociology, the
family is the building-block of the larger
ecclesiastical and civil societies whose order depends
on the integrity of the family: "When Edwards discusses
the need for order in the actual families of
Northampton, he also has in mind the more extensive
rings of familial relations--especially the church and
the state, both of which are superstructures founded on
individual family units."[71]

Although James P. Martin does not mention *A
Farewel-Sermon* by name, his interpretation of Edwards'
doctrine of the Last Judgment bears on the
interpretation of this text, thereby raising its stock
as a document in Edwards' eschatology. According to
Martin, "Edwards' use of the Last Judgment or eternal
destiny was . . . the product of profound reflection on
the cosmos and man's place in it."[72] Fundamental among
these reflections is that the chief end of God's work
of creation and redemption is the divine glory, which
is manifested and realized through the Last Judgment.
"In this light," remarks Martin, "man cannot be
regarded as an autonomous being but as one whose entire
life is a life of responsibility to God."[73] And, we
might add from our reading of *A Farewel-Sermon*, that a
man's life is equally one of responsibility to other
men, even his ancestors and posterity.

Heimert, in passing, imputes an assumption to *A Farewel-Sermon* regarding the temporal restrictions on God's work of redemption: "Generally the Calvinist sermon in the decades after the Awakening assumed--as did Edwards' Farewell Sermon--that those people of the colonies unconverted in the 1740's were beyond redemption."[74] However, Bryant replies that "Heimert's claim cannot be sustained textually." Bryant's point is that Edwards, through the symbolism of the Last Judgment, asserts that the correct moral interpretation of temporal events is possible only in the eschaton: "By invoking the image of the Last Judgment, Edwards postpones final judgment of historical events to a posthistorical realm."[75] In other words, "the eschatological imagery is invoked . . . to relativize all historical judgments."[76] Bryant demonstrates his point by citing Edwards' comment that "we live in a world of change, where nothing is certain or stable."[77] Such a world, according to Bryant, is "one where *all* judgments are provisional."[78] Furthermore, notes Bryant, Edwards states that "now ministers and their people may disagree in their judgments concerning some matters of religion," and it is only "before the tribunal of the great Judge" that "the evidence of the truth shall appear beyond all dispute, and all controversies shall be finally and forever decided."[79] Presently, no one--neither ministers nor laymen--can know apodictically the true spiritual estate of himself or another:

> Ministers have no infallible discerning of the state of the souls of their own people; . . . Nor are the people able certainly to know the state of their minister, or one another's state; . . . And nothing is more

common than for men to be mistaken concerning
their own state.[80]

But on the Day of Judgment, everyone will know this
infallibly: "Then none shall be deceived concerning his
own state, . . .   And then shall all know the state of
one another's souls."[81]

     In addition, observes Bryant, the looming image of
judgment informing *A Farewel-Sermon* casts a shadow over
the "optimistic view of history" attributed to Edwards
by such as Heimert and Nisbet. This text is also
significant, in Bryant's view, because it indicates
that "the movement of Edwards' thought is away from
millennial symbols and towards the symbol of the Last
Judgment as the horizon that hangs over the historical
drama."[82] Bryant thus cites Edwards' parting advice to
his congregation: "let us all remember and never forget
our future solemn meeting on that great day of the
Lord; the day of infallible decision and of the
everlasting & unalterable sentence."[83]

     Scheick, Martin and Bryant, however, do hint at
the social thought implicit in *A Farewel-Sermon*. Thus,
Scheick, by observing that "the church and the state,"
for Edwards "are superstructures founded on individual
family units," suggests that Edwards had a conception
of how society is constituted, i.e. through the
building blocks of families. Martin, by interpreting
Edwards' doctrine of the Last Judgment as meaning that
"man cannot be regarded as an autonomous being,"
indicates that Edwards has the idea that human
existence is ineluctably social. And Bryant, by saying
that "the movement of Edwards' thought is away from
millennial symbols and towards the symbol of the Last
Judgment as the horizon that hangs over the historical

drama," is saying that for Edwards the hope of the
millennial utopia has become tempered by the
inevitability of justice.

Implications for Social & Political Philosophy

We shall now show that *A Farewel-Sermon*, when read
in light of *True Virtue* and "Of a General Judgment," is
significant from the standpoints of philosophical
sociology and social ethics in disclosing that Edwards
has a radically holistic ethics, a theory of social
structure, an acute sense of the terrible social
ramifications of moral evil, and a suggestive theory of
justice big with social implications. We shall now
establish each of these points in turn, beginning with
the first.

Moral Holism

A Farewel-Sermon brings home Edwards'
understanding that persons are ineluctably bound up
with one another in a web of ever-widening moral
relationships. Thus, a minister and his congregation
are locked in a moral relationship. Two purposes of a
minister and his congregation meeting at the Judgment
are "to give an account,...of their behavior one
to another *in the relation they stood in to each other*
in this world"; and "to receive an eternal sentence,...
according to their behavior, *in the relation they
stood in one to another* in the present state " [italics
mine]. Others likewise morally related who are
mentioned in the sermon are "rulers and subjects,
earthly judges and those whom they have judged,

neighbors who have had mutual converse, dealings and contests, heads of families and their children and servants." And in "Of a General Judgment," Edwards states that it is not only individual persons who are morally related, but indeed whole groups of them as well such as nations and generations. Thus, "all nations of the world are morally concerned one with another," and "all generations of men,...are morally concerned one with another." In the same work, Edwards affirms the radical solidarity of the human race, whose members have commerce with one another in the same place under the moral authority of God:

> The whole world is one commonwealth and kingdom, all made of one blood, all under one moral head, one law, and one government; and all parts of it are joined in communication one with another. . . . All dwell in one habitation, viz. this earth, under the same roof of the visible heavens, having the same sun to enlighten them, &c.[84]

Undergirding Edwards' moral holism is his conception of the metaphysical and moral union of mankind in Adam. Adam and his posterity, as it were, constitute a single corporate "person." Since it is revealed in Genesis that God's covenant with Adam included his descendants, then God regarded them all as one thereby constituting their unity as one person. God dealt with Adam as if "Adam and all his posterity had *coexisted*, and that his posterity had been,... *united* to him, something as the branches of a tree are united to the root, or the members of the body to the head; so as to constitute as it were *one* complex person, or *one* moral whole."[85]

Edwards' moral holism and social organicism as evinced in A *Farewel-Sermon* and "Of a General Judgment"

contravene the presuppositions--atomism and
mechanicism--of the eighteenth-century theory of the
social contract as classically formulated by Hobbes in
the previous century. Hobbes denies the reality of
universals, regarding them simply as bundles of
particulars. This means that social wholes in and of
themselves have no substantial reality. Societies are,
in Hobbes' words, "artificial bodies" or "mechanisms to
serve individuals, in whom reality ultimately
dwells."[86] There are, for Hobbes, no sui generis
"social facts" in Durkheim's sense; all social phenomena
are ultimately reducible without residue to human
individuals. Society cannot exist outside the
conventions of contract and representation, invented
and adhered to by otherwise autonomous individuals.
Hobbes denies that individuals adhere together as any
kind of metaphysical unity: "A multitude of men are
made one person, when they are by one man, or one
person, represented;...and unity, cannot
otherwise be understood in multitude."[87] Within the
social contract theory, human individuals are conceived
of analogously with the atoms of seventeenth-century
physics, and postulated as existing primordially as
discrete and autonomous entities. Nisbet writes:

> In the social thought of the seventeenth
> century all relationships were suspect. Man
> was the whole fact; all else was ephemeral.
> ... Relationships of tradition and inherited
> morality were either expelled from theory or
> were rationalized into relationships
> proceeding ineluctably from man's pre-social
> nature.[88]

And the synthesis of isolated human "atoms" into the
social "molecule" is understood as a process of simple
accretion. This mechanistic conception of society is

latent in Hobbes' arithmetical conception of reason:

> When a man *reasoneth*, he does nothing else
> but conceive a sum total, from *addition* of
> parcels; or conceive a remainder, from
> *subtraction* of one sum from another; . . .
> These operations are not incident to numbers
> only, but to all manner of things that can be
> added together, and taken one out of
> another.[89]

Hobbes includes human individuals among the "things
that can be added together," through contract, to form
a society. Thus, Hobbes' theory of ratiocination,
comments Melvin Rader, "implies that a whole made up
of parts is not an organic unity but an aggregate of
discrete elements which can be freely added and
substracted. It was a short step from this reasoning to
the conception of society as merely an aggregate of
egoistic individuals."[90]

In contrast to the atomism of social contract
theorists like Hobbes, Edwards claims that it is not
men individually but man corporately that is
primordial. The society of all men in Adam subsisted
before the existence of any individual men; the social
group is logically prior to the individual. For Hobbes,
any human association is artificial and contingent upon
human decision and convention. For Edwards, the
fundamental association of all men is real, and
grounded in the will of God. And in contrast to the
mechanicism of the social contract theorists, Edwards
conceives of the primordial unity of the race
organically. Thus he states that men are united to Adam
"as the branches of a tree are united to the root, or
the members of the body to the head."

A Social Morphology

Edwards' moral holism and social organicism
suggest, as one might expect, a theory of social
structure, which can be inferred from *A Farewel-Sermon*
and collateral texts. Edwards has an articulate, if
rudimentary, conception of the structure of society.
Specifically, it is a conception of social structure as
an organism, an hierarchy and a typology.

The Organic Structure of Society

Edwards likens society to a living organism. He
so likens civil society in a revival sermon where he
explains how the moral and religious decay in England
threatened the spiritual health of her colonies:

> This country [America] is but a member of the
> body of which they [England] are the head,
> and when the head is so sick, the members, it
> is to be feared, will not long be in health.
> We are a branch of which they are the stock,
> and shall naturally derive, be assimilated,
> and likened to them.[91]

And he likens pious society to the human body in the
sermon-series *Christian Love*, where he enjoins
Christians to appropriate each other's best interests,
and the Church's, as their own, in view of their
organic union in Christ:

> Christ, and all Christians, are so united
> together that they all make but one body; and
> of this body, Christ is the head, and
> Christians are the members. . . . In the
> natural body, the hand is ready to serve the
> head, and all the members are ready to serve
> one another. . . . So it should be with the
> Christian body. All its members should be

helpers, and comforts to each other, and thus
promote their mutual welfare and happiness,
and the glory of Christ, the head.[92]

Significantly, Edwards' social organicism
prefigures nineteenth-century sociology as represented
by Comte and Herbert Spencer. Both of them conceive of
human societies as organisms. Comte, for example,
writes, "If we take the best ascertained points in
Biology, we may decompose structure anatomically into
elements, tissues, and *organs*. We have the same things
in the Social Organism; and may even use the same
names."[93] Thus, the analogous components of society,
according to Comte, are families, classes, and cities.
And Spencer asserts that "a social organism and an
individual organism are entirely alike"; in
particular, "the permanent relations among the parts of
a society, are analogous to the permanent relations
among the parts of a living body."[94]

The Hierarchical Structure of Society

Edwards' hierarchical conception of social
structure is evident in *A Farewel-Sermon* from what he
says about the family and the analogy he draws between
it and both the church and state. His conception of
domestic society as an hierarchy is evident from his
injunction, "let children obey their parents, and yield
to their instructions, and submit to their orders."[95]
His similar conception of ecclesial society, on analogy
with domestic society, is evident from his description
of it as a spiritual family in which the pastor is a
"spiritual father" and his flock are "spiritual
children" who have duties towards him:

> As the relation of a natural parent brings
> great obligations on children in the sight of
> God; so much more, in many respects, does the
> relation of a spiritual father bring great
> obligations on such whose conversation [*sic*
> read "conversion"] and eternal salvation they
> suppose God has made them the instrument
> of.[96]

And Edwards conception of civil society as an
hierarchy, again on analogy with domestic society, is
evident from his description of it in *God's Awful
Judgment*:

> We may see the need of government in
> societies by what is visible in families,
> those lesser societies, of which all public
> societies are constituted. How miserable
> would these little societies be, if all were
> left to themselves, without any authority or
> *superiority in one above another*, or any head
> of union and influence among them?[97] (Italics
> mine.)

The Typological Structure of Society

Edwards' typological conception of social
structure, his conception of a social order arranged
according to socio-psychological types, is evident from
his using in *A Farewel-Sermon* the rhetorical device of
classifying the members of his congregation into groups
and addressing them accordingly. He had used a more
elaborate form of this device on an earlier occasion in
a sermon preached during the Awakening of 1740. There
Edwards classifies his congregation by age-group, viz.
childhood, youth, middle-aged, and old-aged; by gender;
by socio-economic class; and by moral condition, viz.
sinners, hypocrites, backsliders, seekers of the faith,
the newly "awakened."

However, commentators disagree as to the
significance of Edwards' typological scheme. Miller
sees sociological significance in it which, he says,
"corresponds to Edwards' conception of the structure of
society." In Miller's view, the sermon from 1740
becomes in effect a "sociological analysis of
Northampton," and "shows a highly developed sense of
the groups and types that make up the community."
Miller infers from this that Edwards assumes "that the
social pattern is status, in which all persons are
types determined by their position in the community."[98]
On the other hand, Alexis sees only rhetorical
significance in Edwards' classifying and addressing his
congregation according to social type, objecting that
Edwards' typological scheme is too obvious and trivial
to be of any sociological consequence.[99] However, it
cannot be inconsequential that Edwards uses a similar,
though simpler, scheme in A Farewel-Sermon, one of his
most important addresses. The significant thing, it
seems, is not that Edwards classifies people according
to socio-psychological type, or the subtlety and
sophistication (or lack thereof) of his social
taxonomy, but that a pattern of socio-psychological
types informs his thinking, and that he was
sufficiently impressed by it to make it the basis of a
homiletic strategy.

A Sociology of the Family

As we noted earlier, Scheick was struck by
Edwards' urgent plea in A Farewel-Sermon for good
domestic order since good social order depends upon it.
And this is so, according to Scheick, because for

Edwards the family is the building-block of society and
the most important school of moral and religious
education. Edwards, it seems, has a nascent sociology
of the family. By conceiving of families as "those
lesser societies, of which all public societies are
constituted," Edwards recognizes their sociological
significance both as microcosms and the basic building-
blocks of society, and as the most important schools of
moral and religious education. Consequently, a break-
down of domestic order can have a deleterious effect on
the larger social order. Thus does Edwards roundly
decry "the lamentable consequences of the want of a
proper exercise of authority and maintenance of
government in families,"[100] and further observes "that
nothing has a greater tendency to bring a curse on
persons in this world, and on all their temporal
concerns, than an undutiful, unsubmissive, disorderly
behavior in children towards their parents." The
maintenance of domestic order, moreover, is crucial not
just for the spiritual welfare of children, but for the
general welfare of society as well. "One thing that
greatly concerns you, as you would be a happy people,"
Edwards advises his congregation, "is the maintaining
of family order."[101]

Edwards recognizes the importance of the family as
the place of spiritual and moral nurture. He urges the
parents in his congregation "to great painfulness in
teaching, warning, and directing their children;
bringing them up in the nurture and admonition of the
Lord; *beginning early, where there is yet opportunity*"
[italics mine].[102] Edwards thereby evinces a
remarkable appreciation of childhood and

adolescence as being the formative stages in the
processes of moral, religious, and social development.

Incidentally, it is worth noting that Edwards even
gives an inkling in this pastoral advice to parents of
having a developmental view of human psychology, as he
does also in *A Farewel-Sermon* and the revival sermon
cited above when tailoring the application of his
doctrine to the different stages of psychological
development represented by the various groups in his
congregation. He understands that persons in childhood
and adolescence are more susceptible to spiritual
nurture. Thus, in *A Farewel-Sermon*, Edwards begins his
address to the children by saying, "I have been
sensible that if those that were young had a precious
opportunity for their souls' good, you who are very
young had, in many respects, a peculiarly precious
opportunity."[103] This opportunity, though, is lost in
maturity, and in the 1740 sermon cited by Miller, he
warns the middle-aged in his congregation, "The
hardness of persons' hearts grows as fast as their
age."[104]

Now perhaps the real sociological significance of
Edwards' conception of the family as the indivisible
unit of society lies is his implication that the
individual person does not exist except in relation to
others. For Edwards, it is not the individual, but the
group that is irreducible and primordial. Here,
remarkably, Edwards anticipates August Comte. Comte
understands the family, not the individual, to be the
irreducible atom of the social molecule: "A *society*...
can no more be decomposed into *individuals*, than a
geometric surface can be resolved into lines, or a line
into points. The simplest association, that is the

family, . . . , constitutes the true unit of
society."[105] Comte's conception of families as the
fundamental constituents of society seems to be
implicit in Edwards' conception of families as "lesser
societies, of which all public societies are
constituted." And, like Edwards, Comte regards the
family "as the spontaneous source of our moral
education, and as the natural basis of all political
organisation."[106] For Comte, the family is the chief
vehicle of sociality: "The moral value of the Domestic
Life consists in its being the only natural medium,
through which mere Personal life is gradually enlarged
into a truly Social life."[107]

The Social Ramifications of Sin

A *Farewel-Sermon* together with its collateral
texts makes plain that the sins to be redressed at the
Last Judgment are not so much personal as social in
nature. Now for Edwards, as we have seen, all sin is
inescapably social in character, even if only
implicitly. However, his eschatological texts lay
stress on the more explicitly social sins which loom
large among his moral concerns. These sins are social
insofar as they are concerned with the betrayal of
responsibility on the part of either the individual to
the larger social group, the individual to the group,
or even the group as a whole to other groups. Thus, at
the Judgment, Edwards himself, along with other
pastors, will have to answer for his treatment of the
congregation and the congregation for its treatment of
him. More broadly, individual leaders who have exerted
great influence over the lives of others will have to

answer to that; nations will have to answer for their
treatment of other nations to which they stand related;
and generations must answer to their treatment of each
other. It should be clear from this that, contrary to
some scholarly opinions, Edwards was not a quietist
preoccupied with private religion at the expense of
public, or a theological individualist concerned only
with personal salvation, but rather one who had a fine
sense of the ineluctable interrelatedness of persons
and of the preeminence of the social group.

A Theory of Justice

Edwards' speculations on the Last Judgment in *A
Farewel-Sermon* and "Of a General Judgment" constitute
an allegory of justice the significance of which lies
in its emphasizing the eschatological reality of
justice; disclosing the broader dimensions of the realm
of justice, and hence of beauty, in the world; and
establishing that justice is the normative form of
society, an effect of which is the reconciliation of
persons, both individually and corporately, thereby
making for greater social accord. We shall now consider
each of these points in turn.

Justice is an objectively real relation which will
ultimately obtain in (but only in) the eschaton. For at
the Day of Judgment, Edwards admonishes, "all mankind
shall stand together before the judgment-seat of the
supreme Lawgiver and Judge, to have all things visibly
set to rights--and justice made visibly to take place
with respect to all the persons, actions, and affairs
of the moral world." However, the obtaining of perfect
justice must await the Judgment when there will be the

requisite perspective and enlightenment,
characteristics of the end-time, for it to be
understood and rejoiced in by its subjects. The Day of
Judgment, according to Edwards, will mark the
fulfillment of the process of universal enlightenment
that will have steadily gathered momentum during the
millennium. Then, "all shall know the truth with the
greatest certainty"[108] and "none shall be deceived
concerning his own state, and then shall all know the
state of one another's souls." Thus, all will know
with certainty the truth about erstwhile long-standing,
unresolved disputes, about which disputants were in the
right and how the controversies should be resolved,
acquiescing joyfully in their resolution: "the evidence
of the truth shall appear beyond all dispute, and all
controversies shall be finally and forever decided."
Moreover, the disputants' real motives will then be
disclosed and evaluated: "the principles and aims that
every one has acted from shall be certainly known."[109]

Edwards discloses in "Of a General Judgment" the
broader dimensions of the realm of justice. He does
this by revealing the wide range of social
relationships that need be just. Five kinds of such
relationships can be identified in these texts, viz.
interpersonal, domestic, legal, civil, ecclesial and
social. Interpersonal justice is represented by the
rectification of moral relations between "neighbors who
have had mutual converse, dealings, and contests";
domestic justice by that between "heads of families and
their children"; legal justice by that between "earthly
judges and those whom they have judged"; civil justice
by that between "rulers and subjects"; ecclesial
justice by that between "ministers, and the people that

are under their care"; and social justice by that
between large social groups such as entire nations and
generations. Particularly noteworthy is Edwards'
inclusion of the relationships among large social
groups, such as nations and generations, under the rule
of justice. Hence, apropos Martin, one's life is one of
moral responsibility to numberless others, including
even his ancestry and posterity. Furthermore, entire
societies are morally responsible towards other
societies to which they are related, and entire
generations are so towards past and future ones.

Moreover, by disclosing the broader dimensions of
justice, Edwards thereby discloses the broader
dimensions of beauty in the world since he assimilates
justice to secondary and primary beauty. He does this
by conceiving of justice, as did Aristotle, as
fundamentally a relation of proportionality between the
emotions and actions of one person as directed to
another, or what "consists in one being expressing such
affections, and using such a conduct towards another,
as hath a natural agreement and proportion to what is
in them, and what we receive from them."[110] Thus
defined, justice is a form of secondary beauty: "There
is a beauty in the virtue called justice, which
consists in the agreement of different things, that
have relation to one another, in nature, manner, and
measure."[111] And this is consistent with his statement
in "Of a General Judgment," that justice is an aspect
of "the moral beauty and regularity of his [God's]
disposals in the intelligent world." However, justice
also specifies the very nature of primary beauty or
benevolence which is proportionality between love and
the dignity of the beloved: "He who loves being, simply

considered, will naturally, other things being equal,...
love beings *in proportion* [italics mine] to their
dignity." Indeed, this proportionality is the very
paradigm and source of justice: "Respect to being, in
this proportion, is the first and most general kind of
justice which will produce all the subordinate
kinds."[112] Therefore, "just affections and acts have a
beauty in them, distinct from and superior to the
uniformity and equality there is in them [i.e. their
secondary beauty]."[113] So, in the numberless manifold
acts of remedial and reciprocal justice occurring
between individuals, between individuals and groups,
and between groups, as described in Edwards' depictions
of the Last Judgment, beauty is manifest on an ever
expanding scale which will ravish those who behold it.

These eschatological texts establish that for
Edwards justice is the normative form of society, and
the principle of reconciliation and social harmony. It
is the highest social value. All, and the most
extensive, moral relationships among individuals and
groups come under the rule of justice in accordance
with which they must be regulated. Edwards' vision of
the Last Judgment is preeminently social. It is a
vision not only of the perfectly just and well-ordered
society wherein all the moral relationships among
persons, and groups thereof, are fully rectified, but
also of social accord where parties in conflict are
reconciled. Thus, on the Day of Judgment "all
controversies shall be finally and forever decided,"
and not just those between pastors and their flocks,
but even the great "causes between princes and heads of
great kingdoms and monarchies, and their people; and
causes between one nation and another." For Edwards,

then, justice ultimately means social harmony; it is
the beauty of the social order perfected. The
intellectual illumination culminating at the Judgment
will set in motion a process of reconciliation which
will pervade and harmonize the entire social order
thereby making for complete social accord.

CHAPTER VI

NOTES

[1]Tracy, *Jonathan Edwards*, p. clvi.

[2]Sereno E. Dwight, "Memoirs of Jonathan Edwards, A.M.," in *The Works of President Edwards*, ed. by E. Hickman, I (London, 1834), clvi.

[3]Ibid., p. clvii.

[4] Ola Elizabeth,Winslow, ed., "Foreword," *Jonathan Edwards: Basic Writings* (New York, 1966), p. xxiii.

[5]Tracy, Jonathan Edwards, p. 162.

[6]Winslow, "Foreword," p. xxiii.

[7]Ibid., p. xxii.

[8]Letter, Jonathan Edwards to the First Precinct, Nov., 1744, printed in Tracy, *Jonathan Edwards*, p. 158.

[9]Hopkins, *Life of Edwards*, p. 56.

[10]Letter, Jonathan Edwards to Joseph Hawley, Nov. 18, 1754, printed in Faust and Johnson, *Jonathan Edwards*, p. 394.

[11]Dwight, "Memoirs," p. clxxv.

[12]Griffin, *Jonathan Edwards*, p. 11.

[13]Tracy, *Jonathan Edwards*, p. 178.

[14]Miller, *Jonathan Edwards*, p. 210.

[15]Edwards, *Misrepresentations Corrected*, p. 488.

[16]Miller, *Jonathan Edwards*, p. 210.

[17]Harriet Beecher Stowe, *Oldtown Folks*, ed. by Henry F. May (Cambridge, Massachusetts, 1966), p. 401.

[18]Miller, *Jonathan Edwards*, p. 219.

[19]Ibid., p. 326.

[20]Angoff, ed., *Jonathan Edwards*, p. 59.

[21]Winslow, *Jonathan Edwards*, p. 246.

[22]Ibid., p. 247.

[23]Dwight, "Memoirs," p. clviii.

[24]Letter, Jonathan Edwards to Joseph Bellamy, Dec. 6, 1749, printed in Faust and Johnson, *Jonathan Edwards,* p. 388.

[25]Letter, Edwards to Hawley, p. 395.

[26]Winslow, "Foreword," p. xxiv.

[27]Hopkins, *Life of Edwards*, p. 63.

[28]See Miller, *Jonathan Edwards*, pp. 201-229.

[29]Jonathan Edwards, *A Farewel-Sermon Preached at the First Precinct in Northampton, after the People's Publick Rejection of Their Minister*, in *Selected Sermons of Jonathan Edwards*, ed. by H. Norman Gardiner (New York, 1904), p. 119.

[30]Ibid., p. 128.

[31]Ibid., p. 129.

[32]Ibid., p. 130.

[33]Ibid., p. 131.

[34]Ibid., pp. 136-137.

[35]Ibid., p. 137.

[36]Ibid., p. 139.

[37]Ibid., p. 140.

[38]Ibid., pp. 143-144.

[39]Ibid., p. 146.

[40]Ibid., p. 147.

[41]Ibid., p. 147.

[42]Ibid., p. 148.

[43]Ibid., pp. 148-149.

[44]Ibid., p. 149.

45Jonathan Edwards, "The Propriety of a General Judgment, and a Future State," *Miscellaneous Observations on Important Theological Subjects, Original and Collected*, in *The Works of President Edwards*, Burt Franklin: Research and Source Work Series, No. 271, ed. by E. Williams and E. Parsons, VIII (London, 1817), p. 167.

46Ibid., p. 168.

47Ibid., p. 171.

48Ibid., p. 167.

49Ibid., p. 168.

50Ibid., pp. 168-169.

51Ibid., p. 169.

52Edwards, *A Farewel-Sermon*, pp. 120-121.

53Edwards, "The Propriety of a General Judgment," p. 169.

54Ibid., pp. 169-170.

55Ibid., p. 170.

56Ibid., p. 169.

57Ibid., p. 170.

58Ibid., p. 171.

59Ibid., p. 170.

60Ibid., p. 171.

61Winslow, *Jonathan Edwards*, p. 257.

62Miller, *Jonathan Edwards*, p. 225.

63Davidson, *Jonathan Edwards*, p. 128.

64Dwight, *Life of Edwards*, p. 404.

65Hopkins, *Life of Edwards*, p. 61.

66Dwight, "Memoirs," p. clix.

67Samuel Miller, *Jonathan Edwards*, p. 116.

[68]Henry T. Rose, "Edwards in Northampton," in *Jonathan Edwards: A Retrospect*, ed. by Harry Norman Gardiner (Boston, 1901), p. 109.

[69]Allen, *Jonathan Edwards*, p. 262.

[70]William J. Scheick, *The Writings of Jonathan Edwards: Theme, Motif, and Style* (College Station, Texas, 1975), p. 114.

[71]Ibid., p. 115.

[72]James P. Martin, *The Last Judgment in Protestant Theology from Orthodoxy to Ritschl* (Grand Rapids, Michigan, 1963), p. 76.

[73]Ibid., p. 68.

[74]Heimert, *American Mind*, p. 135.

[75]Bryant, "History and Eschatology," p. 129.

[76]Ibid., p. 130.

[77]Edwards, *A Farewel-Sermon*, p. 119, quoted in Bryant, "History and Eschatology," p. 129.

[78]Bryant, "History and Eschatology," p. 130.

[79]Edwards, *A Farewel-Sermon*, p. 124, quoted in Bryant, "History and Eschatology," p. 130.

[80]Jonathan Edwards, *A Farewel-Sermon*, p. 125.

[81]Ibid., p. 126.

[82]Bryant, "History and Eschatology," p. 131.

[83]Edwards, *A Farewel-Sermon*, p. 153, quoted in Bryant, "History and Eschatology," pp. 132-133.

[84]Edwards, "The Propriety of a General Judgment," p. 169.

[85]Jonathan Edwards, *The Great Christian Doctrine of Original Sin, Defended*, in *The Works of Jonathan Edwards*, ed. by Clyde A. Holbrook, III (New Haven, 1970), p. 391.

[86]Rader, *Ethics*, p. 283.

[87]Thomas Hobbes, *Leviathan, or the Matter, Form, and Power of a Commonwealth, Ecclesiastical and Civil*, in *The English Works of Thomas Hobbes of Malmesbury*, ed. by Sir William Molesworth, III (London, 1839),p. 151.

[88]Robert A. Nisbet, *The Quest for Community* (London, 1953), p. 131.

[89]Hobbes, *Leviathan*, p. 29.

[90]Rader, *Ethics*, p. 283.

[91]Miller, "Edwards' Sociology," p. 55.

[92]Edwards, *Christian Love*, pp. 263-264.

[93]Auguste Comte, *System of Positive Polity*, trans. by Frederic Harrison, Burt Franklin: Research and Source Work Series, No. 125; Philosophy Monographs Series, No. 4, II (New York, 1875),p. 240.

[94]Herbert Spencer, "The Nature of Society," in *Theories of Society: Foundations of Modern Sociological Theory*, ed. by Talcott Parsons (New York, 1961), p. 140.

[95]Edwards, *A Farewel-Sermon*, p. 148.

[96]Ibid., p. 141.

[97]Edwards, *God's Awful Judgment*, p. 88.

[98]Miller, "Edwards' Sociology," p. 54.

[99]Alexis, "Theocratic Ideal," p. 332.

[100]Edwards, *God's Awful Judgment*, p. 88.

[101]Edwards, *A Farewel-Sermon*, p. 147.

[102]Ibid., p. 148.

[103]Ibid., p. 146.

[104]Miller, "Edwards' Sociology," p. 64.

[105]Comte, *Positive Polity*, p. 153.

[106]Ibid., p. 154.

[107]Ibid., p. 155.

[108]Edwards, *A Farewel-Sermon*, p. 124.

[109]Ibid., p. 127.

[110]Edwards, *True Virtue*, p. 37.

[111]Ibid., p. 36.

[112]Ibid., p. 38.

[113]Ibid. p. 39.

CHAPTER VII

SUMMARY AND CONCLUSION

Our study was prompted by a continuing
disagreement among scholars over the socio-theoretic
import of Edwards' thought, which can be epitomized as
follows: The traditional opinion has been that, in
Perry Miller's words, "social theory is conspicuous by
its absence" in Edwards' thinking; whereas the
revisionist opinion is that there is, in Heimert's
words, "the primacy of a social vision in his
thinking." This conflict is apparent in the opposed
positions taken by commentators on certain topics vis-
a-vis Edwards. Thus, the traditionalists cite in their
favor Edwards' alleged abandonment of theocracy or the
covenant-scheme, two mainstays of Puritan social
thought, or his supposed quietism; whereas the
revisionists cite one or another of the following:
Edwards' social conception of redemption, the socio-
political resonances of his metaphysical category of
consent, his sociological insight and social criticism,
or the social activism purportedly implied by his
theory of piety. We have demonstrated that implicit in
Edwards' thought, beyond even its "imposing social
vision," there are at least the rudiments of both a
social and political philosophy, and a "philosophical
sociology." And we have shown that these can be best
made explicit through an explication of Edwards' four
neglected texts from the last three years of his
Northampton pastorate. Our study, then, really does
nothing more than substantiate, amplify, and in places
qualify, the revisionist argument, thereby resolving

the conflict by establishing once and for all that
Edwards' thought indeed has considerable socio-
theoretic merit.

We shall now take stock of our various and
disparate findings from the four neglected texts. We
shall summarize and systematize Edwards' socio-
political theory by pulling together the sundry threads
of Edwards' social and political thought surfacing in
our interpretation of these texts. Edwards' random
speculations on the nature and function of society can
be considered under the distinct rubrics of
philosophical sociology and social philosophy.
Finally, we shall specify the role of the neglected
texts in the explication of Edwards' social and
political thought.

Edwards' Philosophical Sociology

The focus of Edwards' philosophical sociology is a
descriptive theory of society: its elements are a
conception of the social bond, a social typology, and a
social morphology.

The Social Bond

A conception of social bonding, i.e. an
explanation of how human individuals coalesce into
groups, can be identified in Edwards' category of
consent. Hence, Edwards' category of consent is an
implicitly sociological one. Consent is either cordial
or natural; and if cordial, it is either love or
choice. Cordial consent is a volition--it is an
inclination towards or an approval of either someone or

something. If of someone, it is love, and thus an
affection; but if of something, it is choice. Natural
consent, on the other hand, is not a volition; it is
simply any kind of agreement or harmony within or among
things, which involves no exercise of the will.
According to Edwards, cordial consent is the archetypal
form of consent and natural consent is its typical
form.

Edwards' anatomy of consent suggests distinct
modes of bonding. Cordial consent *qua* love bonds
persons through their mutual empathy or fellow-feeling
whereby each has the other's best interest as his own.
This is the deepest and most vital kind of bond between
persons because it is affective and engages them in
their wholeness. Cordial consent *qua* choice (e.g.
political consent) bonds persons through contract or
rational agreement for purposes of mutual gain. This
kind of social bond is more superficial than the bond
of love: it is merely volitional, not affective; it
engages persons only segmentally, or solely with
respect to their reason. Moreover, choice has as its
objects impersonal things; therefore, it represents a
relationship, not between persons, but between persons
and abstractions like means and ends. Consent *qua*
choice is consent, not to persons, but *through* them to
particular things. Finally, natural consent bonds
persons through their social roles or functions, for in
these various capacities they complement one another
and cooperate to expedite common, prudential ends.

A conception of symbolic interaction, i.e. an
explanation of how human individuals express and
maintain their sociality, can be identified in Edwards'
concept of *conversation*. Conversation is the medium of

consent. It is the vehicle through which the social
bond is articulated and maintained. Edward conceives of
conversation (symbols) as mediating not only the socio-
political order, but the whole of the moral order
(human culture) as well.

Social Typology

Edwards' distinctions between the modes of consent
or social bonding correspond to and lay the foundation
for his distinction between the two fundamental types
of society, viz. pious and civil society. The "pious"
social bond, according to Edwards, is disinterested
love or benevolence. The members of a pious (sacred)
society are cordially united inasmuch as each has
appropriated as his own the greatest possible public
good, which is the good of being in general. A pious
society, therefore, is a visibly virtuous community. It
is a social union cemented by benevolent affection
wherein persons have primacy as ends in themselves.
Edwards conceives of pious society as the archetypal
society, universal in extent and eschatological in
orientation. Its typical activities are prayer,
communion with God, and witnessing to the Last Things.
It is preeminently a redemptive and redeemed society
whose aim is the enfranchisement of all persons as
friends in Christ.

By contrast, the "civil" social bond, according to
Edwards, is contract. The members of a civil
(utilitarian) society are cordially united inasmuch as
they, in their diverse but complementary roles,
cooperate to promote the good of their particular
society. A civil society is a rational society whose

norms are efficiency and expediency, good order and
utility. It is a social union cemented by volition,
rather than affection, wherein roles, not persons, have
primacy as the means to ends. Edwards conceives of
civil society as the type of pious society: the civil
bonds of contract (cordial consent *qua* choice) and of
order and utility (natural consent) are but pale copies
of the pious bond of benevolence. A civil society is
finite, and entirely historical in orientation. Its
typical activities are politics, law and commerce. It
is preeminently an administrative society whose aim is
the preservation of the political order.

Social Morphology

Edwards understands the structure of society,
whether civil or pious, in the following ways: (1) as
an *hierarchy*--in which persons, in civil society, are
ranked according to social role or function; but, in
pious society, according to mental capacity and
virtue; (2) as a *patriarchy*, where authority is
ultimately vested in a parent, pastor, governor, or
God; (3) as a *macrocosm* of the domestic order, with
family-units being the irreducible atoms from which the
social molecule is formed; (4) and, as an *organism*
whose parts are conceived of as being interrelated
analogously to the branches of a tree or the organs of
an animal body.

Edwards' Social and Political Philosophy

There are both theoretical and practical sides to
Edwards' socio-political philosophy. On the theoretical

side, the following elements can be differentiated: a philosophy of society; normative theories of society and of citizenship; a social ethics; and a principle of social and political criticism. On the practical side, there is a strategy for implementing the social ideal.

Philosophy of Society

The idea of society holds enormous significance for Edwards and figures prominently in his thought. It is significant ontologically, axiologically, theologically, and socio-psychologically. Society is ontologically significant as the primordial and irreducible human reality. It is primordial, for Edwards posits the metaphysical unity of mankind in Adam--a primeval social union preceding and determining the emergence of human individuals--and the biological unity of humankind as a species. It is fundamentally irreducible, for Edwards conceives of society as decomposing ultimately into families, or domestic societies, not isolated individuals.

Society is axiologically significant as that which has supreme value, both intrinsic and extrinsic. Its intrinsic value is either aesthetic or moral. Society's aesthetic value (secondary beauty) consists in its good order and utility, and its moral value (primary beauty) consists in its justice and benevolence. Society's extrinsic value, on the other hand, consists in its enabling man to realize his social nature--especially his capacity for friendship--and in facilitating his survival.

Society (pious) is theologically significant as the means and end of redemption. Edwards thus extolls

the society of prayer as a necessary means to
precipitating the millennium, the penultimate goal of
the history of redemption. And he conceives of
beatitude as a consummately benevolent community, such
as the societies of the millennium and heaven.

Society is socio-psychologically significant
inasmuch as it yields psychological and sociological
benefits. Thus a "pious union" in prayer, according to
Edwards, benefits the individual uniters by
strengthening their motives for praying, heightening
their public mindedness, fostering their sense of
belonging, and deepening the mutuality among them. And
such a union benefits the group as a whole by effecting
the conciliation and integration of its members.

A Normative Theory of Society

Edwards has a conception of the ideal society. His
social ideal is pious society, or the *community* of
virtue, whose members are benevolently united through
appropriating as their own the highest good of being in
general. Edwards' paradigms of such authentic community
are the societies of heaven and the millenium; its
historical form is the church. That pious society is
Edwards' social ideal is evident from his exalting it
as the goal of redemption and his esteeming it as
exemplifying a superior kind of beauty to that of civil
society.

A Normative Theory of Citizenship

Complementing Edwards' conception of the ideal
society is a conception of the ideal citizen. Edwards

conceives of "true" citizenship as consisting
essentially in a radical public mindedness, made
manifest in the specific virtues of absolute loyalty to
God and man, personal rectitude, social decorum, and
social beneficence directed to both the material and
the spiritual well-being of others.

A Social Ethics

Edwards' ethics is essentially a social ethics.
This is evident from his ethical imperative of absolute
loyalty to the largest "society" of sentient beings,
i.e. benevolence to being in general; from his ideal
that the moral order presupposes the social order; and
from his theory of justice as the normative form of
society.

Social Criticism

Edwards' social ideal of the pious society, and
his idea of justice as the normative form of society,
together yield a principle of social criticism. His
many strictures on the factiousness and schisms of
Northampton society can be understood in light of his
vision of the benevolent, just, and harmonious society
of the millennium. Yet Edwards' social philosophy did
not lack its practical side. His restrictive policy on
Communion represents a strategy for implementing his
ideal of the pious society.

Edwards' social thought is determinate and
differentiated enough to admit comparison not only with
the dominant social thinking of his own century but
with that of the subsequent one as well. Thus, Edwards'

social typology, i.e. his distinction between pious and civil society, prefigures Weber's, i.e. the latter's distinction between sacred and utilitarian society. Edwards' conception of social bonding, i.e. consent, parallels Tönnies': his cordial consent *qua* love is analogous to Tönnies' "natural" or "essential" will; and his cordial consent *qua* choice is analogous to Tönnies' "rational" or "selective" will. Edwards' conception of symbolic interaction, i.e. conversation, and his insight that human culture depends on and is articulated through symbols, anticipate the insights of George Herbert Mead. Finally, Edwards' social morphology, i.e. his social holism and organicism, though at odds with the social atomism and mechanicism of Hobbes and his followers, has much in common with the similar views of Comte and Spencer. Indeed, the whole tenor of Edwards' social theory runs counter to the social contract theory, and his social philosophy represents an implicit critique of the eighteenth-century principles of individualism and enlightened self-interest.

The value of the four Northampton texts focused in this study consists in their providing a way into Edwards' social thought and resolving the issues pertinent to Edwards' significance as a social and political thinker. These texts furnish clues to the latency of a philosophical sociology and a socio-political philosophy in Edwards' thinking.

Thus, his distinction in *Humble Attempt* between pious and civil society suggests a social typology. His conception there of society as a form of beauty implies a conception of the social bond as consent. And Edwards' esteeming pious society as a form of beauty

superior to that of civil society indicates a
differentiation between two kinds of consent or social
bond. Furthermore, his ranking pious society above
civil society, and his elevating millennial society as
a goal of redemption, point to a normative theory of
society.

Edwards' description in the *Life of Brainerd* of
Brainerd's piety as benevolence is a clue that the
pious bond is benevolence. Since benevolence means that
the public and private good coincide, it suggests that
Edwards' social ideal is authentic community.
Furthermore, the conception here of piety, or virtue,
as a radical public mindedness suggests a normative
theory of citizenship.

Edwards' conception of the church in *Humble
Inquiry* as a pious society, and the policy defended in
this text of restricting church membership in complete
standing to the visibly pious, are clues that he hoped
to implement his social ideal. His attempt to make his
local congregation an exclusive society suggests a
strategy for facilitating the emergence of a truly
virtuous community.

Finally, the sense pervading *A Farewel-Sermon* of
the vast network of relationships in which persons are
inescapably bound suggests that the group--not the
individual--is primordial, and organic in structure.
Furthermore, Edwards' conceptions in this text of the
place and role of the family in society, and of
patriarchal authority, suggest an hierarchical
conception of the social order. And the depictions in
this sermon and elsewhere of the true extent and the
various dimensions of the order of justice, and of

justice as the normative form of society, are clues
that Edwards' ethics is fundamentally social.

The four Northampton texts enable us to resolve
the following issues broached in the first chapter
relating to Edwards' status as a social and political
thinker.

Edwards and Theocracy

Both *Humble Attempt* and *Humble Inquiry* demonstrate
that Edwards was not a theocrat. His clear distinction
between a civil and pious union is fundamentally
incompatible with the monolithic social conception of
theocracy. And Edwards' exclusion of all but the
visibly pious from Communion undermines the
inclusiveness essential to theocracy.

Edwards and the Covenant

Humble Inquiry demonstrates that Edwards did not
abandon the covenant-scheme but instead made it the
cornerstone of his theology. Thus, Edwards identifies
the act of convenanting with piety: "To own this
covenant, is to profess the consent of our *hearts* to
it, and that is the sum and substance of true piety."
He equates the owning of the covenant with the
profession of faith, thereby instituting the covenant
as the foundation for the constitution of the church:
"For a person explicitly or professedly to enter into
the union or relation of the covenant of grace with
Christ, is the same as professing to do that which on
our part is the uniting act and that is the act of
faith." Furthermore, Edwards identifies the covenant of

grace as what is renewed and ratified by the Lord's
supper: "thus the Lord's supper is plainly a *mutual*
renovation, confirmation, and seal of the covenant of
grace." Edwards, then, certainly did not envision, in
Heimert's words, "a union of Americans freed from the
covenant relationships of the parochial past." What he
did envision, in *Humble Attempt*, and strove to
implement through *Humble Inquiry*, was a *pious* union--
not a civil or national one--undergirded by the
covenant relationship, not freed from it.

Edwards and Revivalism

Edwards' chief socio-political relevance has been
located in his indirect influence, through his
promulgation of the Great Awakening and his revival
writings, on the American Revolution and the social
reform movements of the nineteenth century. Edwards has
been depicted as one who, however unwittingly, helped
enervate traditional civil and ecclesiastical
authority; and as the prophet, however unconsciously,
of socio-political revolution in the direction of
egalitarianism, libertarianism, and American
nationalism. However, three of Edwards' Northampton
texts provide a corrective to this portrayal of Edwards
as a social and political revolutionary. These texts
reveal Edwards as a conservative in his social and
political thinking as shown in the following: his
predilection for duly constituted authority, whether
civil or ecclesiastical; his emphasis on the
maintaining of good order in both civil and ecclesial
society; his abhorrence of the religious individualism

of sectarianism and antinomianism; and his profound sense of historical continuity.

Thus, in *A Farewel-Sermon*, Edwards affirms patriarchal authority: that of the parent in the family, the pastor in the church, and the governor in the state. He admonishes parents to govern their children steadfastly and resolutely "as a guard to the religion and morals of the family; and the support of its good order." Moreover, he cautions children to "obey their parents, and yield to their instruction," since "nothing has a greater tendency to bring a curse on persons, . . . than an undutiful, unsubmissive, disorderly behaviour in children towards their parents." Edwards clearly conceived of society as a richly differentiated hierarchy of social types and functions, with its secondary or aesthetic beauty largely consisting in order and specializations "as, when the different members of society have all their appointed office, place and station, according to their several capacities and talents, and every one keeps his place, and continues in his proper business." Edwards' social conservatism is also manifest in his affirmation of institutional religion and his condemnation of the unbridled religious individualism of extreme sectarianism and antinomianism. In the preface to *Humble Inquiry*, Edwards roundly condemns "that wild enthusiastical sort of people," e.g. religious separatists and fanatics, who arrogate to themselves ministerial authority, and defy the legitimate authority or established churches and ministers by accusing them of apostasy, and setting up their own churches and ordaining their own ministers:

> I have no better opinion of their notion of a
> *pure church* by means of a *spirit of*
> *discerning*, their *censorious outcries* against
> the standing ministers and churches in
> general, their *lay-ordinations*, their *lay-*
> *preaching*, & *public-exhortings*, and
> administering *sacraments*; their assuming,
> self-confident, contentious, uncharitable
> *separating spirit*; their going about the
> country, as *sent by the lord*, to make
> proselytes; with their many other extravagant
> and wicked ways.[1]

Finally, Edwards' social conservatism is further
evident in his understanding of society, revealed in
our discussion of *A Farewel-Sermon*, as an historical
continuum in which "all generations of men,...are
morally concerned one with another." This conception of
a vast moral community extending over time and in which
all generations of mankind are ineluctably bound
plainly runs counter to revolutionary ideology
sanctioning a complete break with the past, as occurred
in the revolutions of France, Russia, and China.

Edwards as Sociologist

Our explication of *A Farewel-Sermon* adds stronger
color to Miller's portrait of Edwards as an eighteenth-
century sociologist. This sermon too, like the one
cited by Miller, evinces "in the organization of the
remarks, a sense of a pattern of human relations" which
Miller interprets as "status, in which all persons are
types determined by their position in the community."

Edwards as Social Critic

Both *Humble Attempt* and *A Farewel-Sermon* enable us
to enhance our appreciation of Edwards as a social
critic. His distinction in the former text between
pious and civil society is the foundation of a
"theological critique of culture." A pious or virtuous
society, which is a society constituted by benevolence
or public mindedness (primary beauty), is Edwards'
social ideal. It is the standard of judgment for civil
or secular society, which is a society constituted by
complacence or private mindedness (secondary beauty),
and thereby exposes and furnishes a corrective to the
idolatry to which the temporal social order is prone.
Specifically, it was Edwards' interest in pious society
that Conkin has in mind in remarking that "his unending
interest in the corporate whole, was diametrically
opposed to the rampant individualism, in politics and
economics that was developing in his lifetime." *Humble
Attempt* focuses Edwards' "image of the good society,"
which is the society of the millennium. *Humble Inquiry*
supplies a blueprint for the local implementation of
the good society. And *A Farewel-Sermon* specifies that
the normative form of pious society, and thus of civil
society, is justice.

Edwards' Social Conception of Redemption

"The theme (both implicit and explicit) of all
Edwards' thinking, writes Nagy, "is the theological
message that redemption is social, and that society is
the instrument as well as the end of salvation." The
full meaning of this statement is made clear in both

324

Humble Attempt and *A Farewel-Sermon*. According to
Humble Attempt, "redemption is social" inasmuch as its
means and end is a type of society. The type of society
is pious society; specifically the "redemptive" society
is the church and the concert for prayer, whereas the
"redeemed" society is millennial society. Now a society
is redemptive insofar as it cordially unites persons in
benevolence; and a society is redeemed insofar as it is
cordially united in benevolence. And according to *A
Farewel-Sermon*, social redemption involves rectifying
and harmonizing all human relationships, personal and
corporate.

Edwards' Conception of Piety

From our reading of the Northampton texts, we
might characterize Edwards' conception of true piety as
pietism embodied in a social gospel. For Edwards,
neither personal sanctification nor the performance of
good works, as in acts of public charity and the
promotion of social justice, is alone a sufficient
condition for true piety, but both are necessary for
it. Edwards conceives of the relationship between them
in this way: Sanctification is necessarily expressed in
good works; and good works, though neither the essence
nor end of piety, are the validation of a peron's
sanctification. Thus, in the *Life of Brainerd*, we read
that Brainerd was sanctified, for according to Edwards,
"the change that was wrought in him at his conversion,
was . . . a change of nature, a change of the abiding
habit and temper of his mind." Such a transformation,
in Edwards' view, could be effected but by "those
influences and operations on the heart, which are

spiritual, supernatural and divine."[2] Under the first
sign in Religious Affections, Edwards stipulates that
personal sanctification is the necessary condition for
piety. Yet we also read in the Life of Brainerd that
Brainerd was diligent in the performance of good works,
or Christian practice: "All his inward illuminations,
affections, and comforts seemed to have direct tendency
to practice, and to issue in it; . . . a practice
positively holy and Christian."[3] Under the twelfth sign
in Religious Affections, Edwards states that the
performance of good works in the public sphere is a
necessary condition for piety: "Christian practice is
the most proper evidence of the gracious sincerity of
professors, to themselves and others; and the chief of
all the marks of grace, the sign of signs, and evidence
of evidences, that which seals and crowns all the
signs."

In Humble Inquiry we again find described a
socially significant piety in which personal holiness
has public consequences. Edwards thus requires visible
sanctification for church membership in complete
standing: "none ought to be admitted as members of the
visible church of Christ but visible and professing
saints"; and "the thing which must be visible and
probable, in order to visible saintship, must be
saintship itself, or real grace and true holiness." Yet
by requiring that personal piety or holiness be visible
as the necessary qualification for full Communion,
Edwards ensures that it is both socially and socio-
theoretically significant. Personal piety, insofar as
it is made visible, is socially significant in three
ways: First, since one way personal sanctification is

326

"outward behaviour," it is made manifest in social actions. As Smith remarks concerning Edwards' conception of piety, "If it is true that a man must be in right relations with God, but also show this through an outward and visible form of life, then the entire social order must ultimately be affected." In his depiction of the social ideal, or millennial society, in *Humble Attempt*, Edwards states that piety, far from being just a private and subjective affair, will be fully public and objective, permeating the very fabric of society: "holiness should be as it were *inscribed on every thing*, on all men's common business and employments, and the common utensils of life, and all shall be dedicated to God, and improved to holy purposes"; and "vital piety shall take possession of thrones and palaces, and those that are in most exalted stations shall be eminent in holiness." Second, personal piety, insofar as it is visible, is the necessary condition for full membership in ecclesial society. Third, personal piety, in being visible, takes a social form as pious society. In Edwards' conception of it, piety can be made visible not only in the individual through his behavior, but also in society through its mode of social bonding. Thus a pious society, which is constituted by the love of benevolence, manifests piety as much as a pious individual who performs good works.

Personal piety is socio-theoretically significant in two ways. First, as benevolent love or cordial consent to being, it is socio-theoretically significant as the mode of social bonding in pious society. Second, personal piety, as the necessary qualification for full Communion in the church, is socio-theoretically

significant as a principle of exclusion whereby the
emergence of a distinctly pious or virtuous community
is facilitated.

Edwards' Concept of Consent

Both Nagy and Delattre have appreciated the socio-
political implications of Edwards' category of consent,
which is fundamental to his theories of being and
value. Thus for Nagy, Edwards notion of consent is "a
standpoint for achieving reconciliation when the
reconcilers are isolated." And for Delattre, "consent
is a political as well as an aesthetic concept." Now
our explication of *Humble Attempt* has enabled us to see
that consent functions in Edwards' thought not only as
an explicitly ontological and axiological category, but
also as an implicitly sociological category. As we have
seen, "consent" is Edwards' term for the social bond, a
concept of modern social science, and refers to the
interaction among persons that makes for human society.
And it is Edwards' distinctions between the two kinds
of consent, viz. cordial and natural, and the two kinds
of cordial consent, viz. love and choice, that
illuminate his distinction in *Humble Attempt* between
pious and civil social union--a key and sociologically
significant distinction between sacred (religious) and
utilitarian (civil) society.

In conclusion: We have shown that there is a
socio-political dimension to Edwards' thought. We have
identified both a philosophical sociology and a social
and political philosophy in his thinking. The focus of
Edwards' philosophical sociology is a descriptive

Edwards' philosophical sociology is a descriptive
theory of society which comprises a conception of the
social bond, a social typology, and a social
morphology. The key to Edwards' social theory is his
implicitly sociological categories of consent and
conversation. "Consent," his term for the social bond,
identifies a principle of social aggregation; and
"conversation," Edwards' term for symbolic interaction,
identifies a principle whereby the social bond is
articulated and maintained. Furthermore, Edwards'
distinctions between cordial and natural consent, and
between cordial consent qua love and cordial consent
qua choice, explain his typological distinction between
religious and secular society--a distinction between an
eschatologically oriented society whose essential bond
is benevolence, whose business is communion with God,
and whose end is friendship; and an historically
oriented society whose essential bond is contract,
whose business is politics, and whose end is the
preservation of the civil order. Complementing a
conception of the social bond and a social typology,
Edwards' philosophical sociology also includes a social
morphology. Edwards conceives of the structure of
society as a patriarchal, hierarchal, and organic
system whose basic building-block is the family-unit.
    The focus of Edwards' socio-political philosophy
is a normative theory of society which comprises (on
its theoretical side) a philosophy of society, a
conception of the ideal society and of its citizen, a
social ethics, a principle of social criticism, and (on
the practical side) a strategy for implementing the
social ideal. Thus for Edwards, society is significant
in the following three ways: ontologically as the

as a supreme form of intrinsic and extrinsic value, and theologically as the means and end of redemption. Edwards' social ideal is benevolent society, represented paradigmatically by millennial society and historically by ecclesial society. His ideal of citizenship is a radically public mindedness whose exemplar is David Brainerd. Edwards' ethics is *social* insofar as he considers true virtue as loyalty or cordial union with the totality of uncreated and created persons, society as the foundation of morality, and justice as the normative form of society. And Edwards' resultant principle of social criticism is that the ultimate moral norm for any historical society is eschatological society. Finally, Edwards' strategy for implementing his social ideal was the expedient of making his congregation into an exclusive society of the visibly benevolent.

In a way, social theory is latent in Edwards' thought from the start. For in his early essay, "The Mind," Edwards introduces his implicitly sociological category of consent while developing a pluralistic, or "social," metaphysics. However, he never formally worked out the socio-theoretic implications of his relational theories of being and value. Edwards' social thought is most explicit in the four neglected texts from his last years in Northampton, for only in them does the social group, viz. the concert of prayer, millennial society, the church, and the congregation, receive his sustained and theoretical attention. Consequently, we have explicated these Northampton texts so as to make Edwards' social and political thinking explicit. Thus, we have exposed the social theory undergirding Edwards' vision of the Christian

utopia in *Humble Attempt*, the implications for good
citizenship of the piety documented in the *Life of
Brainerd*, the strategy for implementing his social
ideal implicit in the restrictive policy on church
admission defended in *Humble Inquiry*, and the
conception of social structure and justice informing *A
Farewel-Sermon*. It is hoped, moreover, that the
retrieval of these neglected texts as significant
documents in Edwards' socio-political thought will help
restore them to a central place in the Edwards' corpus.

It should be clear that our aims have not only
determined the overall structure of our study, but also
set certain necessary limits on it. Thus we have argued
only *that* Edwards has a social and political philosophy
as disclosed in a group of his neglected texts. We have
not attempted an exposition of the full range of
Edwards' social and political thought as might be
disclosed from an examination of all his writings. Nor
did we look in detail at the philosophical and
theological background to Edwards' social thinking or
develop all of its implications. These things fall
outside the scope of our present project. For what is
presently at issue in Edwards' scholarship is neither
the nature, the provenance, nor the implications of
Edwards' social thought--but merely its existence. "A
major study of the social philosophy of Jonathan
Edwards has yet to be written,"[4] writes Nagy. It is
hoped that our own study, at least, has proved the
feasibility of such a project, and might even provide
an impetus to its undertaking.

CHAPTER VII

NOTES

[1]Edwards, Humble Inquiry, p. 432.

[2]Edwards, Religious Affections, p. 197.

[3]Edwards, Life of Brainerd, p. 661.

[4]Nagy, "Beloved Community," p. 93.

BIBLIOGRAPHY

Primary Sources: Jonathan Edwards and his Contemporaries

Dwight, Sereno E. "Memoirs of Jonathan Edwards, A. M."
   The Works of President Edwards. Edited by E.
   Hickman. Vol. I. London, 1839.

Edwards, Jonathan. *An Account of the Life of the Rev.
   David Brainerd. The Works of President Edwards*.
   8th Edition. Vol. I. New York, 1851.

   *The Life of David Brainerd. The Works of Jonathan
   Edwards*. Edited by Norman Pettit. Vol. VII. New
   Haven, 1985.

   "Beauty of the World." *The Works of Jonathan
   Edwards*. Edited by Wallace Earl Anderson. Vol. VI.
   New Haven, 1980.

   *Christian Love, as Manifested in the Heart and
   Life*. Edited by Tryon Edwards. 6th American
   Edition. Philadelphia, 1874.

   *A Dissertation concerning the End for Which God
   Created the World. The Works of President Edwards*.
   Edited by E. Williams and E. Parsons. Burt
   Franklin: Research and Source Work Series, No.
   271. Vol. I. London, 1817.

334

A Farewel-Sermon Preached at the First Precinct in Northampton, after the People's Publick Rejection of Their Minister. Selected Sermons of Jonathan Edwards. Edited by Harry Norman Gardiner. New York, 1904.

God's Awful Judgment in the Breaking and Winthering of the Strong Rods of a Community. The Works of President Edwards. Edited by E. Williams and E. Parsons. Burt Franklin: Research Source Work Series, No. 271. Vol. VIII. London, 1817.

The Great Christian Doctrine of Original Sin, Defended. The Works of Jonathan Edwards. Edited by Clyde A. Holbrook. Vol. III. New Haven, 1970.

A History of the Work of Redemption, containing the Outlines of a Body of Divinity, including a View of Church History, in a Method Entirely New. The Works of President Edwards. Edited by E. Williams and E. Parsons. Burt Franklin: Research and Source Work Series, No. 271. Vol. V. London, 1817.

An Humble Attempt to Promote Explicit Agreement and Visible Union of God's People in Extraordinary Prayer for the Revival of Religion and the Advancement of Christ's Kingdom on Earth, Pursuant to Scripture-Promises and Prophecies concerning the Last Time. The Works of Jonathan Edwards. Edited by Stephen J. Stein. Vol. V. New Haven, 1977.

An Humble Inquiry into the Rules of the Word of God, concerning the Qualifications Requisite to a Compleat Standing and Full Communion in the Visible Christian Church. The Works of President Edwards. Edited by E. Hickman. Vol. I. London, 1834.

The Life and Diary of the Rev. David Brainerd: with Notes and Reflections. The Works of President Edwards. Edited by E. Williams and E. Parsons. Burt Franklin: Research and Source Work Series, No. 271. Vol. III. London, 1817.

"The Mind." *The Works of Jonathan Edwards.* Edited by Wallace Earl Anderson. Vol. VI. New Haven, 1980.

Miscellaneous Observations. The Works of President Edwards. Edited by E. Hickman. Vol. II. London, 1834.

Miscellaneous Observations on Important Theological Subjects, Original and Collected. The Works of President Edwards. Edited by E. Hickman. Vol. II. London, 1834.

Miscellanies. The Philosophy of Jonathan Edwards from His Private Notebooks. Edited by Harvey Gates Townsend. Eugene, Oregon, 1955.

Misrepresentations Corrected, and Truth Vindicated, in a Reply to the Rev. Mr. Solomon Williams's Book. The Works of President Edwards. Edited by E. Hickman. Vol. I. London, 1839.

The Nature of True Virtue. Edited by William K. Frankena. Ann Arbor, Michigan, 1960.

Personal Narrative. Jonathan Edwards: Representative Selections, with Introduction, Bibliography, and Notes. Edited by Clarence H. Faust and Thomas H. Johnson. American Writers Series. New York, 1935.

The Portion of the Righteous. The Works of President Edwards. Edited by E. Hickman. Vol. II. London, 1834.

Remarks on Important Theological Controversies. The Works of President Edwards. Edited by E. Hickman. Vol. II. London, 1834.

Some Thoughts concerning the Revival. The Works of Jonathan Edwards. Edited by C. C. Goen. Vol. IV. New Haven, 1972.

A Treatise concerning Religious Affections. The Works of Jonathan Edwards. Edited by John E. Smith. Vol. II. New Haven, 1959.

Treatise on Grace and other Posthumously Published Writings. Edited by Paul Helm. Cambridge, England, 1971.

The True Christian's Life, a Journey towards Heaven. The Works of President Edwards. Vol. IV. Eighth edition. New York, 1851.

True Saints, When Absent from the Body, are Present with the Lord. The Works of President Edwards. Edited by E. Hickman. Vol. II. London, 1834.

Faust, Clarence H., and Johnson, Thomas H., eds. *Jonathan Edwards: Representative Selections, with Introduction, Bibliography, and Notes.* American Writers Series. New York, 1935.

Hopkins, Samuel. *The Life and Character of the Late Reverend Mr. Jonathan Edwards.* Boston, 1765. Reprinted in *Jonathan Edwards: A Profile.* Edited by David Levin. American Profiles. New York, 1969.

Stoddard, Solomon. *An Appeal to the Learned, being a Vindication of the Rights of Visible Saints to the Lord's Supper, though They be Destitute of a Saving Work of God's Spirit on Their Hearts: Against the Exceptions of Mr. Increase Mather.* Boston, 1709.

The Doctrine of the Instituted Churches. London, 1700.

338

Secondary Sources

Aldridge, A. Owen. "Edwards and Hutcheson." *Harvard Theological Review*, XLIV, No. 1 (1951), pp. 35-53.

Jonathan Edwards. New York, 1964.

Alexis, Gerhard T. "Jonathan Edwards and the Theocratic Ideal." *Church History*, XXXV, No. 1 (1966), pp. 328-343.

Allen, Alexander V. G. *Jonathan Edwards*. American Religious Leaders. Boston, 1896.

Angoff, Charles, ed. *Jonathan Edwards: His Life and Influence*. The Leverton Lecture Series. Rutherford, New Jersey, 1975.

Bates, Ernest Sutherland. *American Faith: Its Religious, Political, and Economic Foundations*. New York, 1940.

Bercovitch, Sacvan. *The American Jeremiad*. Madison, Wisconsin, 1978.

Bogue, Carl W. *Jonathan Edwards and the Covenant of Grace*. Cherry Hill, New Jersey, 1975.

Bryant, Marcus Darrol. "American as God's Kingdom." *Religion and Political Society*. Edited and translated in the Institute of Christian Thought. New York, 1974.

"History and Eschatology in Jonathan Edwards: A
Critique of the Heimert Thesis." Unpublished Ph.D.
dissertation, Institute of Christian Thought,
University of St. Michael's College, 1976. In
Dissertation Abstracts International, 38 (1978),
6180A.

Carse, James Pearce. *Jonathan Edwards and the
Visibility of God*. New York, 1967.

Cherry, Charles Conrad. *The Theology of Jonathan
Edwards: A Reappraisal*. Garden City, New York,
1966.

Comte, Auguste. *System of Positive Polity*. Translated
by Frederic Harrison. Burt Franklin: Research and
Source Work Series, No. 125; Philosophy Monographs
Series, No. 4. Vol. II. New York, 1875.

Conkin, Paul K. *Puritans and Pragmatists: Eight Eminent
American Thinkers*. New York, 1968.

Davidson, Edward Hutchins. *Jonathan Edwards; the
Narrative of a Puritan Mind*. Cambridge, Mass.,
1968.

Deininger, Whitaker Thompson. *Problems in Social and
Political Thought, a Philosophical Introduction*.
London, 1969.

DeJong, Peter Y. *The Covenant Idea in New England
Theology, 1620-1847*. Grand Rapids, Michigan, 1945.

340

Delattre, Roland André. "Beauty and Politics: A
    Problematic Legacy of Jonathan Edwards." *American*
    Philosophy From Edwards to Quine. Edited by Robert
    W. Shahan and Kenneth R. Merrill. Norman,
    Oklahoma, 1977.

    "Beauty and Politics: Towards a Theological
    Anthropology." *Union Seminary Quarterly Review*,
    XXV, No. 4 (1970), pp. 401-419.

    "Beauty and Sensibility in the Thought of Jonathan
    Edwards: An Essay in Aesthetics and Ethics." Ph.D.
    dissertation, Yale University, 1966.

Disraeli, Benjamin, Earl of Beaconsfield. *Sybil, or the*
    Two Nations. Novels and Tales by the Earl of
    Beaconsfield with Portrait and Sketch of His Life.
    Hughenden Edition. Vol. VIII. London, 1881.

Durkheim, Emile. *The Elementary Forms of the Religious*
    Life. Translated by Joseph Ward Swain.   London,
    1915.

Dwight, Sereno Edwards. *The Life of President Edwards*.
    New York, 1830.

Emerson, Everett H. "Jonathan Edwards." In *Fifteen*
    American Authors before 1900: Bibliographical
    Essays on Research and Criticism, ed. Robert A.
    Rees and Earl N. Harbert. Madison, Wisconsin,
    1971, pp. 169-184.

Fawcett, Arthur. *The Cambuslang Revival: The Scottish Evangelical Revival of the Eighteenth Century.* London, 1971.

Fiering, Norman. *Jonathan Edwards's Moral Thought and Its British Context.* The Institute of Early American History and Culture. Chapel Hill, North Carolina, 1981.

Gaustad, Edwin Scott. *The Great Awakening in New England.* New York, 1957.

Goen, C. C. "Editor's Introduction." *The Great Awakening. The Works of Jonathan Edwards.* Vol. IV. New Haven, 1972.

"Jonathan Edwards: A New Departure in Eschatology." *Church History,* XXVIII, No. 1 (1959), pp. 25-40.

Griffin, Edward M. *Jonathan Edwards.* University of Minnesota Pamphlets on American Writers, No. 97. Minneapolis, 1971.

Gutkind, Erwin Anton. *Community and Environment: A Discourse on Social Ecology.* London, 1953.

Haroutunian, Joseph G. *Piety versus Moralism: The Passing of the New England Theology.* Hamden, Connecticut, 1932.

Heimert, Alan. *Religion and the American Mind: From the Great Awakening to the Revolution.* Cambridge, Mass., 1966.

Heimert, Alan, and Miller, Perry, eds. *The Great Awakening: Documents Illustrating the Crisis and Its Consequences.* The American Heritage Series, No. 34. Indianapolis, 1967.

Hobbes, Thomas. *Leviathan, or the Matter, Form, and Power of a Commonwealth, Ecclesiastical and Civil. The English Works of Thomas Hobbes of Malmesbury.* Edited by Sir William Molesworth. Vol. III. London, 1839.

Loomis, Charles P. "Tonnies, Ferdinand." *The Encyclopedia of Philosophy.* Edited by Paul Edwards. Vol. III. New York, 1967.

Manspeaker, Nancy. "Did Jonathan Edwards' Thought Develop? A Comparison of the Doctrine of Love Expressed in his First and Last Writings." Unpublished Ph.D. dissertation, Institute of Christian Thought, University of St. Michael's College, 1983.

_____. *Jonathan Edwards: A Bibliographical Synopses.* New York, 1981.

Martin, James P. *The Last Judgment in Protestant Theology from Orthodoxy to Ritschl.* Grand Rapids, Michigan, 1963.

McGiffert, Arthur Cushman. *Jonathan Edwards*. New York, 1932.

Mead, Sidney E. *The Old Religion in the Brave New World: Reflections on the Relation between Christendom and the Republic*. The Jefferson Memorial Lectures. Berkeley, 1977.

Miller, Perry. *Errand into the Wilderness*. Cambridge, Mass., 1956.

    Jonathan Edwards. The American Men of Letters Series. New York, 1949.

    "Jonathan Edwards and the Great Awakening." *The Great Awakening: Event and Exegesis*. Edited by Darrett Bruce Rutman. Huntington, New York, 1977.

    "Jonathan Edwards' Sociology of the Great Awakening." *The New England Quarterly*, XXI, No. 1 (1948), pp. 50-77.

    Nature's Nation. Cambridge, Mass., 1967.

Miller, Samuel. *The Life of Jonathan Edwards, President of the College of New Jersey*. In *Library of American Biography*, ed. Jared Sparks. New York, 1837. Vol. VIII, pp. 1-256.

Morgan, Edmund S. "The Great Awakener." Review of *Jonathan Edwards, Pastor*, by Patricia Tracy. *The New York Times Book Review*, July 13, 1980, pp. 13, 38.

344

Nagy, Paul J. "The Beloved Community of Jonathan
Edwards." *Transactions of The Charles S. Peirce
Society*, VII, No. 2 (1971), pp. 93-104.

Nicoll, William Robertson. *The Seen and the Unseen*.
London, n.d.

Niebuhr, H. Richard. *The Kingdom of God in America*.
Chicago, 1937.

Nisbet, Robert, A. *History of the Idea of Progress*. New
York, 1980.

*The Quest for Community: A Study in the Ethics of
Order and Freedom*. New York, 1953.

*The Social Bond: An Introduction to the Study of
Society*. New York, 1970.

Parkes, Henry Bamford. *Jonathan Edwards: The Fiery
Puritan*. New York, 1930.

Parson, Talcott. "An Outline of the Social System."
*Theories of Society: Foundations of Modern
Sociological Theory*. New York, 1961.

Perry, Ralph Barton. *Puritanism and Democracy*. New
York, 1944.

Pfisterer, Karl Dietrich. *The Prism of Scripture: Studies on History and Historicity in the Work of Jonathan Edwards.* Anglo-American Forum, Vol. I. Bern, 1975.

Plant, Raymond. *Community and Idealogy: An Essay in Applied Social Philosophy.* London, 1974.

Rader, Melvin. *Ethics and the Human Community.* New York, 1964.

Rose, Henry T. "Edwards in Northampton." *Jonathan Edwards: A Retrospect.* Edited by Harry Norman Gardiner. Boston, 1901.

Scheick, William J. *The Writings of Jonathan Edwards: Theme, Motif, and Style.* College Station, Texas, 1975.

Schneider, Herbert Wallace. *The Puritan Mind.* New York, 1930.

Simmel, Georg. "Secrecy and Group Communication." *Theories of Society: Foundations of Modern Sociological Theory.* Edited by Talcott Parsons. New York, 1961.

Smith, John E. "Editor's Introduction." *Religious Affections. The Works of Jonathan Edwards.* Vol. II. New Haven, 1959.

"Jonathan Edwards as Philosophical Theologian."
The Review of Metaphysics, XXX, No. 2 (1976),
pp. 306-324.

"Jonathan Edwards: Piety and Practice in the
American Character." *The Journal of Religion*, LIV,
No. 2. (1974), pp. 166-180.

The Spirit of American Philosophy. New York, 1963.

Söderblom, Nathan, Late Archbishop of Upsala. *The
Living God: Basal Forms of Personal Religion*. The
Gifford Lectures of 1931. London, 1933.

Spencer, Herbert. "The Nature of Society." *Theories of
Society: Foundations of Modern Sociological
Theory*. Edited by Talcott Parsons. New York, 1961.

Spurgeon, Charles Haddon. *Lectures to my Students: A
Selection from Addresses delivered to the Students
of the Pastors' College, Metropolitan Tabernacle*.
First Series. London, 1875.

Stokes, Anson Phelps. *Church and State in the United
States*. Vol. I. New York, 1950.

Stowe, Harriet Beecher. *Oldtown Folks*. Edited by Henry
F. May. Cambridge, Massachusetts, 1966.

Tönnies, Ferdinand. *Community and Society (Gemeinschaft
and Gesellschaft)*. Edited and translated by
Charles P. Loomis. East Lansing, Michigan, 1957.

Tracy, Patricia, J. *Jonathan Edwards, Pastor: Religion and Society in Eighteenth-Century Northampton*. American Century Series. New York, 1980.

Walker, Williston. *The Creeds and Platforms of Congregationalism*. New York, 1893.

Weber, Max. *The Theory of Social and Economic Organization*. Translated by A. M. Henderson and Talcott Parsons. New York, 1947.

Westbrook, Robert B. "Social Criticism and the Heavenly City of Jonathan Edwards." *Soundings*, LIX, No. 4 (1976), pp. 396-412.

Winslow, Ola Elizabeth. *Jonathan Edwards, 1703-1758: A Biography*. New York, 1940.

Jonathan Edwards: Basic Writings. New York, 1966.

Wolff, Kurt H., ed. *The Sociology of Georg Simmel*. London, 1950.

INDEX

354

STUDIES IN AMERICAN RELIGION

22. Stafford Poole and Douglas J. Slawson, **Church And Slave in Perry County, Missouri, 1818-1865**

23. Rebecca Moore, **The Jonestown Letters: Correspondence of the Moore Family 1970-1985**

24. Lawrence H. Williams, **Black Higher Education in Kentucky 1879-1930: The History of Simmons University**

25. Erling Jorstad, **The New Christian Right, 1981- 1988: Prospects for the Post-Reagan Decade**

26. Joseph H. Hall, **Presbyterian Conflict and Resolution on the Missouri Frontier**

27. Jonathan Wells, **Charles Hodges' Critique of Darwinism: An Historical-Critical Analysis of Concepts Basic to the 19th Century Debate**

28. Donald R. Tuck, **Buddhist Churches of America: Jodo Shinshu**

29. Suzanne Geissler, **Lutheranism and Anglicanism in Colonial New Jersey: An Early Ecumenical Experiment in New Sweden**

30. David Hein, **A Student's View of The College of St. James on the Eve of the Civil War: The Letters of W. Wilkins Davis (1842-1866)**

31. Char Miller, **Selected Writings of Hiram Bingham (1814-1869), Missionary To The Hawaiian Islands: To Raise the Lord's Banner**

32. Rebecca Moore, **In Defense of Peoples Temple-And Other Essays**

33. Donald L. Huber, **Educating Lutheran Pastors in Ohio, 1830-1980: A History of Trinity Lutheran Seminary and its Predecessors**

34. Hugh Spurgin, **Roger Williams and Puritan Radicalism in the English Separatist Tradition**

35. Michael Meiers, **Was Jonestown A CIA Medical Experiment?: A Review of the Evidence**

36. L. Raymond Camp, **Roger Williams, God's Apostle of Advocacy: Biography and Rhetoric**

37. Rebecca Moore & Fielding M. McGehee III (eds.), **New Religious Movements, Mass Suicide, and Peoples Temple: Scholarly Perspectives on a Tragedy**

38. Annabelle S. Wenzke, **Timothy Dwight (1752-1817)**

39. Joseph R. Washington, Jr., **Race and Religion in Early Nineteenth Century America 1800-1850: Constitution, Conscience, and Calvinist Compromise** (2 vols.)

40. Joseph R. Washington, Jr., **Race and Religion in Mid-Nineteenth Century America 1850-1877: Protestant Parochial Philanthropists** (2 vols.)

41. Rebecca Moore & Fielding M. McGehee III (eds.), **The Need for a Second Look at Jonestown**

42. Joel Fetzer, **Selective Prosecution of Religiously Motivated Offenders in America: Scrutinizing The Myth of Neutrality**

43. Charles H. Lippy, **The Christadelphians in North America**